POLITICS, IDEOLOGY AND THE LAW
IN EARLY MODERN EUROPE

Essays in honor of J. H. M. Salmon

POLITICS, IDEOLOGY AND THE LAW IN EARLY MODERN EUROPE

Essays in honor of J. H. M. Salmon

EDITED BY Adrianna E. Bakos

UNIVERSITY OF ROCHESTER PRESS

First published 1994

University of Rochester Press
34–36 Administration Building, University of Rochester
Rochester, New York 14627, USA
and at PO Box 9, Woodbridge, Suffolk IP12 3DF, UK

ISBN 1 878822 39 X

Library of Congress Cataloging-in-Publication Data
Politics, ideology, and the law in early modern Europe : essays in
honor of J.H.M. Salmon / edited by Adrianna E. Bakos.
    p.   cm.
  Includes bibliographical references.
  ISBN 1–878822–38–X (hardback : alk. paper)
  1. Ideology – Europe – History. 2. Political science – Europe –
History. 3. Law – Europe – History. I. Bakos, Adrianna E.
II. Salmon, J. H. M. (John Hearsey McMillan), 1925– .
JA84.E9P63   1994
320.94′09′03–dc20   94–20552

British Library Cataloguing-in Publication Data
Politics, Ideology and the Law in Early
Modern Europe : Essays in Honour of
J.H.M.Salmon
  I. Bakos, Adrianna E.
  940.2
  ISBN 1–878822–39–X

This publication is printed on acid-free paper

Printed in the United States of America

Contents

Editor's Acknowledgements

In the course of preparing this volume in honour of J. H. M. Salmon, I have incurred a debt of gratitude to all of those who helped bring this worthwhile project to fruition. My thanks to Janet Oppenheim, with whom I had numerous conversations; suggestions and encouragement whispered over the telephone in the hopes of keeping John in the dark about our progress. At the outset, the advice of Donald Kelley was invaluable in drawing together such a fine list of contributors. Perez Zagorin kindly offered useful editorial suggestions. My colleague Linda Levy Peck also provided helpful editorial advice as well as encouragement over the last eighteen months, both of which were much appreciated.

Patricia Neill, editorial assistant in the English department graciously employed her desk-top publishing skills to produce a lovely brochure advertising the book. Evelyn Walker of the Rare Books Room kindly assisted in finding appropriate graphic images to grace both the publicity brochure and the book's dust jacket. Robert Easton, Managing Editor of the University of Rochester Press, made himself available to answer my questions, however trivial; the efforts of both he and the staff at the press are appreciated.

My greatest debt is owed to the scholars whose work appears in this book. My thanks to Sir Geoffrey Elton for writing a preface which makes clear both his warm personal regard for John Salmon and his view of John's contribution to the field of early modern European history. On a practical level, all the contributors responded to my anxious requests for papers with wonderful dispatch and unfailing good humour. Their enthusiasm for the project testifies to the universally high regard in which John is held by his colleagues. Collectively, the essays blend the best in more traditional approaches to the history of ideas with an awareness and appreciation of newer methodologies, reflecting the vibrant state of early modern studies. While possessing thematic unity, they present the reader with a diversity of topics and methods which parallels the breadth both of John's interests and of his expertise.

Preface

SIR GEOFFREY ELTON

I first met John Salmon in 1953 when, twenty-seven years old, he came to Cambridge from New Zealand as a graduate student. He made an immediate and lasting impression, both as a scholar and as a friend. The memory of those days, forty years ago, remains significantly strong. John now tells us that he was then somewhat brash and somewhat contemptuous of the dry and conventional sobriety that he first expected to encounter, but that he soon discovered the flexibility, variety and enterprise of the kind of history that was then coming to the fore at Cambridge. I have to say that he did not strike me as in any way brash but always seemed willing both to learn from and to contribute to the ardent fervour which was so manifestly spreading among the generation that took over after the Second World War. In retrospect, we can see how that generation set about the task of making the old University into the centre and breeding ground of future strength more especially in historical studies. With Oxford still dominated by conventional undergraduate labours, and with the London Institute of Historical Research distinctly staid and even ordinary after the departure from it of V. H. Galbraith, Cambridge in the 1950s represented the vigorous spearhead of scholarly advance. The young New Zealander manifestly both fitted into all this and soon showed that he had a line of his own to strike out along. It was at that time that he made himself into a leading interpreter of early modern European thought on the state and politics. He took off from France but from the first spread out to other parts of the West, a fruitful manner of operating that he always maintained thereafter. It was then also that he laid the foundations of his major work on the interaction of ideology, political unrest and the settlement of affairs which he has continued to explore in a massive accumulation of books and articles. He took his learning and the stimulus of his teaching to a succession of universities in Australia and New Zealand, before in 1969 settling in Bryn Mawr in Pennsylvania, an institution which when he joined it was mainly a distinguished liberal arts college but which he was instrumental in helping to develop into a research university.

As a working scholar, John Salmon claims special attention because he faced and solved some highly complex problems of method.[1] By starting work on

[1] See the introduction to his *Renaissance and Revolt: Essays in the Intellectual and Social History of Early Modern France* (Cambridge, 1987).

French political writings in the much disturbed era of the sixteenth and seventeenth centuries, he quickly became involved in two of the most virulent historiographical debates of recent times. Both of them originated in France and became very influential elsewhere, especially in the United States. The first of them—much the most important—concerned the critique of the so-called *annalistes*, so named after the journal in which they developed and presented their case. Founded by Marc Bloch and Lucien Fevre—scholars both formidable and genuinely impressive—they next produced two very powerful propagandists in Fernand Braudel and Emmanuel Le Roy Ladurie who (as is the habit in such cases) promoted the sensible critique established by the originators into sometimes wildly excessive prescriptions.[2] The *Annales* school reacted against the very dry and narrowly empiricist practices preached in the nineteenth century which, they argued with some justice, resulted in limited and unreal historical analyses of a mechanical kind. They called for a history in the round, incorporating social and ideological investigations, heeding the work of the social scientists, and fully aware of the great variety of human experience beyond the traditional themes of power politics or international relations. Braudel added an attack on the mere event and sang the praises of the long-term and enduring structure, while Le Roy Ladurie called for the analysis of conditions (states of existence) consequent upon such circumstantial influences as myths or epidemics. At their most influential, the *annalistes* decried attention to individuals, played around with entities (often called crises) lasting centuries, and in effect rendered narrative history unacceptable. They therefore altogether dismantled the traditional history of ideas which tended to confine itself to the writings of allegedly great thinkers, attended to the exercise of philosophical arguments with only occasional reference to the circumstances that called them into existence, and tended to stand on the edge of an abyss of abstraction. Their prophetic demands thus cast aside the inheritances of the history of political thought which dominated English-speaking manifestations of it—the work of such old heroes as J. N. Figgis, C. H. McIlwain, or J. W. Allen. When John Salmon formed his approach to the historical problems he wished to understand, the theories of placing ideas into context later developed by Quentin Skinner and John Pocock had not yet been put forward, but in many ways Salmon led the way towards them. He listened to the *annalistes* but retained his independence; he broadened the reach of intellectual history but

---

2 I have never really got over discovering that Braudel's famous treatise on the Mediterranean World opens with some fifty pages of an incredibly commonplace setting out of his favourite "structure." Did anyone have to be told that mountains are higher than seashores or that fisherman are found only in the latter? As for Le Roy Ladurie, see my review of some of his collected papers in my *Studies in Tudor Politics and Government*, vol. 4 (Cambridge, 1992), pp. 286–92.

retained the virtues of precision and of a proper recognition of the availability of evidence that he found in the older tradition.

The other French attack coming to the fore in the second half of our century was potentially more damaging to the writing of history. It sprang from studies which reduced all the work done to the use of language and denied any existence or reality to the subjects supposedly expressed in words. This curious refusal to allow real existence only to the person reading writings now to be called "texts" could be particularly dangerous to the history of ideas because it proclaimed that one cannot ever discover what people long dead thought they were saying: at all points, the mind and preconceptions of the historian deconstructing the "text" were supposed to form the only content of the account he rendered. Salmon firmly resisted this nihilist nonsense, put out in the main by linguists and philosophers who had never tried to do any real history on the real sources. He says now that he certainly found past literature useful in illuminating the past but he rightly did so because in it he discovered and worked out what the past (and its writers) had intended. That is to say, he enlarged the catchment area of the evidence brought into play by the historian of ideas but controlled the additional material by the correct historical method which endeavors to grasp those products of an age gone by through the minds and events of that age, not of ours. Nor could he accept the notion that language tells only of language, or that the only person who matters is the self-satisifed decoder of other people's speech. That is to say, he saw through historically invalid philosophies of Roland Barthes, Michel Foucault and Jacques Derrida. To him, the teaching of the *Annales* school offered assistance in that they called for the expansion of both the questions asked and the evidence studied beyond the narrow confines of traditional "political thought", but he always remained a historian so that linguistic aberrations could make no impression. Salmon set about integrating intellectual and social history and thus produced a splendidly penetrating account—three-dimensional—of the social and political upheavals, the quarrels and the writings, and indeed the personalities of the age and country that he had made his stamping ground.

A third dispute over method also crossed his path but proved much less troublesome. This one sprang from the Marxist approach to unrest and rebellion, here exemplified in Boris Porschnev's analysis of the seventeenth-century Fronde as a class struggle. As usual at the time, this schematic simplification was treated with respect until thoroughly demolished by Roland Mousnier, French historian of office-holding and venality, who demonstrated that the social structure of seventeenth-century France had nothing to do with classes of the Marxist conviction but represented a pyramidal system of orders, generally found in early modern Europe. Furthermore the factions engaged in unrest and strife contained people of the same social standing, though divided by allegiances political and religious, and reacting variously to the centralising policies of the monarchy (as they did in seventeenth-century England also). Here Salmon found no problems to accommodate in his interpretation of the age: all his work supported the anti-Marxist position. However, he did sterling service by reviewing the debate and underwriting Mousnier for an English-speaking readership.

Thus Salmon arrived at a penetrating and fascinating understanding of the political and religious writings (mostly but not solely French) of that much disturbed period, an understanding augmented by the absorption of new approaches but always firmly based on what may still be called the traditional method—on a wise respect for the past, its inhabitants, and the material evidence they left behind. He then carried out the other chief duty of the historian, a duty too often neglected by too many of the tribe: he communicated his understanding frequently, at length and in excellent prose. Salmon believes in direct speech, in lucidity even when the subject matter is complex, and in maintaining the reader's interest, without in any way departing from accuracy and an embracing thoroughness. Reading Salmon is a real pleasure because he never evades the problems arising but also never hides behind jargon. All of us who have battled for this know how difficult the undertaking can be, especially if the subject matter consists of the interaction of ideas and conditions, working themselves out in political and social action. This was the task that Salmon expressly set for himself and (what is more) turned into reality.

He demonstrated his purpose in various ways but never, perhaps, more successfully than in the series of articles he published in the early issues of *History Today*, a journal founded to bring new learning to a wider audience. Unlike too many, somewhat arrogant, younger historians of those days, Salmon realised the virtue of ambition and method and ignored a degree of comtempt oozing from more conventional pores. His formation in New Zealand probably helped, as did the fact that when he came to England he did not opt for starchy Oxford (as most visitors from overseas then did) but discovered foundations and purpose in Cambridge. His work of dissemination involved not only fine books like the remarkable history of sixteenth-century France, but also frequent travels: he participated in various European conferences, and I myself am especially grateful for his willingness to revisit England regularly. Working outwards from a solid and ever increasing base in the United States, John Salmon became a figure of widely recognized eminence, a scholar of fame and a teacher of true excellence. The profession contains quite a few good men, but very few who better deserve the sort of recognition represented by this volume than does John Hearsey McMillan Salmon. It is hard to believe that time has caught up even with him, but retirement is after all only a new beginning.

PART ONE

Culture and Ideology

1

Neostoicism and Absolutism in Late Elizabethan England

LISA FERRARO PARMELEE

A key intellectual development of the late sixteenth century in Europe was the Neostoic movement, which arose as a direct response to decades of religious conflict and civil war throughout the continent. Its origins were rooted in longstanding humanist efforts to reconcile the moral philosophies of the ancients with the tenets of Christianity. The strict morality of the Stoic path to virtue appealed to some Renaissance scholars, but most found its standards of behavior impossibly high, its view of life stern and cold. Moreover, while Stoicism was seen as compatible in most respects with Christianity, the condemnation of emotions such as pity and fear ran counter to Christian belief, as did Stoic ideas regarding fate and the Stoic practice of regarding all sins or vices as equivalent to one another.[1] The descent of the Netherlands and France into civil war, however, caused many scholars and philosophers to look at Stoicism in a different light. Even in an age accustomed to violence and aggression, the extraordinary upheaval and destruction of these unrelenting conflicts came as a frightening revelation. The benefits of a philosophy that called for suppressing emotion while emphasizing reason became more evident: for the nation it would mean a cooling of dangerous passions; to the individual it offered a way of enduring the hardships of the times.[2]

The initiator and main proponent of the Neostoic movement was Justus Lipsius. A classical scholar among whose many editions of classical works those of Tacitus and Seneca were best known, Lipsius set forth in his 1584 book *De Constantia* to reconcile the pagan philosophy of Stoicism with the moral

---

[1] Jill Kraye, "Moral Philosophy," in *The Cambridge History of Renaissance Philosophy*, ed. Charles B. Schmitt, Quentin Skinner, Eckhard Kessler, and Jill Kraye (Cambridge: Cambridge University Press, 1988), pp. 360–368; Justus Lipsius, *Two Bookes Of Constancie*, trans. John Stradling, 1604, ed. Rudolf Kirk (New Brunswick, NJ: Rutgers University Press, 1939) p. 35.

[2] Kraye, "Moral Philosophy," p. 370.

teachings of the Christian church. Emerging most forcibly from the exigencies of civil war was the theme of the title: that of constancy. Constancy, said Lipsius, was "a right and immoveable strength of the minde, neither lifted up, nor pressed downe with externall or casuall accidentes." It was "a stedfastnesse not from opinion, but from judgement and sound reason."[3] This idea of constancy, which could also be expressed as great patience or endurance, lent to the philosophy a far more positive emphasis than the mere apathy prescribed by the classical Stoics. While Lipsius still regarded emotions as "a disease of the mind" which must be cured,[4] he offered an appealing preoccupation to take their place: the cultivation of constancy. To stand, as the Stoics put it, like an oak tree in the wind was a most attractive image to those on the continent being endlessly buffeted by civil war—and to those in England assailed by the fear of it.[5]

Lipsius, whose philosophical works were the product both of the author's extensive knowledge of classical literature and of domestic strife in his own land, was first embraced by French thinkers seeking a philosophical ground upon which they could take a stand for the duration of their country's turmoil. His influence could also be seen in the works of French writers of political propaganda, specifically among those who wrote in opposition to the Catholic League between 1584 and 1595. In their support of Henri of Navarre's claim to the French throne, many of these propagandists began to combine Bodin's theory of absolute legislative sovereignty with the Protestant belief that the monarch's power is directly ordained by God.[6] A considerable number of these increasingly absolutist tracts were translated into English and printed in England during this period.

These works were only a few among many translated documents that were available to the English reading public in those years and in the decade to follow, and they held great appeal for English readers. Neostoic-inspired tracts arrived in England alongside tales of military exploits which offered highly heroic portrayals of Henri IV being supported by English soldiers; riveting stories of ambition and betrayal, featuring the villainous Guises, the hated Jesuits, the Pope, and, always looming in the background, the Spanish threat; flattery of the English and their queen; and efforts to convince them that they were occupying the same leaking boat as the French. To paraphrase Matthias A. Shaaber, the hopes of the English readers were flattered, their prejudices

---

3 Lipsius, *Of Constancie*, p. 79.
4 Ibid., p. 74.
5 Kraye, "Moral Philosophy," pp. 370–371; Peter Burke, "Tacitism, Scepticism and Reason of State," in *The Cambridge History of Political Thought, 1450–1700*, ed. J. H. Burns (Cambridge: Cambridge University Press, 1991), p. 491.
6 Quentin Skinner, *The Foundations of Modern Political Thought. Vol. II: The Age of the Reformation* (Cambridge: Cambridge University Press, 1972), p. 301; William Farr Church, *Constitutional Thought in Sixteenth Century France: A Study in the Evolution of Ideas* (NY: Octagon Books, 1969), pp. 243–244.

encouraged, their notions confirmed.[7] Such a constant flow of information congenial to the minds of the English public would have opened those minds and made them receptive to ideas some of the information carried with it—including Neostoic ideas.

The works of the classical Stoics had been appearing in translation in England in the early modern period since 1481, when Caxton printed English versions of Cicero's *De Amicitia* and *De Senectute*. Not until the end of the sixteenth century, however, did English scholars undertake the task of interpreting the thought of the pagan philosophers. As on the continent, this task was shaped by the atmosphere of continuing religious conflict, and focused largely upon the reconciliation of Stoicism with Christianity.[8] Thus the Neostoic movement arrived in England, interpolated through the works of Lipsius and his French followers and imitators, whose ideas were, in turn, rendered in the crucible of civil war.

Neostoic precepts cannot be tied definitively to any single political ideology. Peter Burke shows how Stoic values could be associated with republicanism, yet, in another sense, be in harmony with reason of state.[9] J.H.M. Salmon refers to the competing forces within Neostoicism that would emerge in the Jacobean period and notes how conflict in the royal court was spurred by those who attempted to adapt its message for their own respective political purposes.[10] Through examining the works of Lipsius and the French Neostoics and by following the passage of their ideas into Elizabethan works, it can be seen that a number of Stoic themes consistently emerge that tend to support a strong royalist position. These themes pertain to constancy and innovation.

Lipsius and the French writers

Justus Lipsius' *De Constantia* was published in English as *Two Bookes of Constancie* in 1604. In this work were laid out the fundamental precepts of Neostoicism, and the philosophic interpretation of constancy from a Christian viewpoint. It was in the *Politicorum sive civilis doctrinae libri sex*, however, that Neostoic philosophy met real life. Although published in the Netherlands four to five years after *De Constantia*, it appeared in England a full decade prior to the translation of the earlier work, under the title of *Six Bookes of Politickes or Civil Doctrine*, and it offered applications of Neostoic ideas in terms certain to galvanize the attention of an English readership worried about religious division and fearful of the prospect of civil war in their own country.

For Lipsius, constancy forms the basis for order, and is best manifested by an

---

[7] Matthias A. Shaaber, *Some Forerunners of the Newspaper in England, 1476–1622* (Philadelphia: University of Pennsylvania Press, 1929), p. 7.

[8] Lipsius, *Of Constancie*, pp. 20, 23, 33.

[9] Burke, "Tacitism," pp. 491–492.

[10] J. H. M. Salmon, "Seneca and Tacitus in Jacobean England," in *The Mental World of the Jacobean Court*, ed. Linda Levy Peck (Cambridge: Cambridge University Press, 1991), p. 202.

adherence to tradition and a faithfulness to established institutions, whatever their weaknesses. The best kind of government, says Lipsius, is that principality which is imposed according to customs and laws; and the gravest danger to any country is dissent from customs and laws, in matters of either religion or government, for the purpose of innovation. The greatest assurance of stability in any commonwealth is a constant form of government. Things changed could be made worse; therefore, it is incumbent upon the prince to avoid innovation and remove the authors of innovation, and it is incumbent upon the people to endure things as they are with Stoic constancy.[11] These Lipsian themes— endurance and restraint of innovation—will be found to resonate again and again through the writings of the French Neostoics, quoted here in translation, as the English readers of the time would have seen them.

The question as to whether or not Michel de Montaigne was a Stoic has been a matter of longstanding dispute among historians. The question remains open, but on two points there can be no doubt: Montaigne was a great admirer of Lipsius, and, whether he was himself a Stoic at some stage or not, his *Essays* are permeated by several Neostoic themes which strongly color the author's perspectives on war, government and religious toleration.

Montaigne lived the majority of his life literally surrounded by civil war. As well might be expected of an observant and sensitive man struggling to main- tain a "sanctuarie" through decades of turmoil, he places the highest premium on public order. Time and again throughout his *Essays*, he addresses the prob- lems of conflict and instability within a society, and his prescription for avoid- ing both is always the same: one must endure whatever comes of the status quo, and reject innovation.

For Montaigne, custom and tradition are very powerful things. Nature deter- mines the place of each individual in society, but "It is by the [mediation] of customs that every man is contented with the place where nature hath setled him."[12] The ancient traditions behind laws and governments lend them their legitimacy. When custom and tradition are undermined by change, the inevi- table result is disorder. While Montaigne expresses understanding of, if not sympathy for, the motivations of both sides in France's troubles, he is far less concerned with who is right and who is wrong than he is with the damaging effects of the upheaval itself, and he blames the upheaval on innovation:

> I am distasted with noveltie, what countenance soever it shew: and I have reason so to be, for I have seene very hurtfull effects follow the same. That which so many yeares since doth so presse us, hath not yet exploited all. But some may alleage with apparence, that by accident, it hath produced and

---

[11] S.T.C., 15701, Justus Lipsius, *Sixe bookes of politickes or ciuil doctrine*, trans. W. Jones (London: R. Johnes, 1594), pp. Dii, Liii + 3.

[12] Michel de Montaigne, *Montaigne's Essays*, trans. John Florio, 3 vols. (London: J.M. Dent & Sons Ltd., 1965) 1:115.

engendred all, yea both the mischiefes and ruines, that since are committed without and against it: it is that a man should blame and finde fault with.[13]

Innovation of any kind, says Montaigne, carries with it a profound risk, and no matter how bad things are, meddling can only make them worse.

But if innovation is forbidden, what, according to Montaigne, can one do in the face of conditions that are unjust or oppressive? One can adopt a Stoic solution, and endure. What is just is not necessarily what is best for the stability of the society, and often an individual must endure undeserved hardship or punishment in the interest of keeping the peace:

> Publike societie hath nought to do with our thoughts; but for other things, as our actions, our travel, our fortune, and our life, that must be accommodated and left to it's service and common opinions: as that good and great *Socrates*, who refused to save his life by disobeying the magistrate, yea a magistrate most wicked and unjust. For that is the rule of rules, and generall law of lawes, for every man to observe those of the place wherein he liveth.[14]

As the passage indicates, the touchstones for Montaigne are, once again, tradition and custom. That which profits the community is that which has the *imprimatur* of ancient lineage. His professed loyalty to the royal government is based on his veneration for what has been long established, whatever its flaws may be:

> . . . in publike affaires, there is no course so bad [provided it be ancient and has been constant] that is not better than change and alteration. . . . *It is an easie matter to accuse a state of imperfection, since all mortall things are full of it.* As easie is it to beget in a people a contempt of his ancient observances: No man ever undertooke it, but came to an end: But to establish a better state in place of that which is condemned and raced out, divers who have attempted it, have shronk under the burthen. . . . Oh happy people, that doth what is commanded, better than they which command, without vexing themselves about causes; which suffer themselves gently to be rowled on, according to the heavens rowling.[15]

Ultimately, it is perfect non-resistance of the established government that Montaigne's Stoic stance of patience and constancy entails. The Christian religion nowhere shows its utility and justice more clearly, he says, than in its "exact commendation" to yield absolute obedience to the civil magistrates, and to maintain and defend the existing laws, whatever their nature:[16]

> . . . the most excellent and best policie, for any nation to observe, is that under which it hath maintained it selfe. It's forme and essentiall commoditie

---

13 Ibid., vol. 1, pp. 118–119.
14 Ibid., vol. 1, p. 118.

15 Ibid., vol. 2, pp. 382–383.
16 Ibid., vol. 1, p. 120.

doth much depend of customs. We are easily displeased with the present condition: yet doe I hold that to wish the government of few, in a popular estate: or in a Monarchie, another kinde of policie, it is a manifest vice and meere follie.[17]

Constancy under the established regime and avoidance of change, no matter what its apparent merits, means, in France, full acquiescence to the king:

Wee owe . . . obedience and subjection to all Kings; for it respects their office. . . . If they be unworthy, wee are to endure them patiently, to conceale their vices, and to aid their indifferent actions with our commendations, as long as their authoritie hath need of our assistance, and that ought to be ascribed unto politike order.[18]

While Montaigne is clearly impressed by Lipsius and expresses strains of Neostoic thought throughout his *Essays*, Guillaume du Vair is an outright imitator of Lipsius who attempts to present Neostoicism as a systematic philosophy. Where Lipsius wrote his scholarly exposition of Neostoicism for the scholarly world, however, du Vair addresses the ordinary reader who might adopt the philosophy as the basis for a Christian life.

Du Vair's work, *La Philosophie Morale des Stoiques*, was first published in France around 1585 and appeared in English translation in 1598 as *The Moral Philosophie of the Stoicks*. Here are explicated the fundamental Stoic themes of virtue through reason and order, endurance and fate. Du Vair advocates the banishment of any disturbing influences such as love, ambition, honor and fear; above all, he counsels *acceptance* of things as they are:

Truly there is no greater wisdome, nor more profitable in this world, then patience in enduring the follie of other men. For otherwise it so falleth out divers times, that because wee cannot suffer their foolishnes, wee make it become ours, and so receive much harme thereby. . . .[19]

. . . [S]eeke not to avoyd the evill which is falling upon you by turning it upon her head.[20]

As in Montaigne, the exhortation to avoid innovation and maintain constancy for the sake of order is clear. The message is even more explicit in *A Buckler Against Adversitie: or A Treatise of Constancie*, the 1594 work in which du Vair's philosophy is confronted by reality in the form of the siege of Paris. In the face of such tragedy, du Vair finds he must moderate somewhat his Stoic strictures on emotion; there is a place for grief after all, provided it is kept within

[17] Ibid., vol. 3, p. 197.
[18] Ibid., vol. 1, p. 26.
[19] Guillaume du Vair, *The Moral Philosophie of the Stoicks*, ed. Rudolf Kirk (New Brunswick, NJ: Rutgers University Press, 1951), pp. 147–148 [This is also S.T.C., 7374].
[20] Ibid., p. 168.

bounds.[21] But in his insistence on acceptance of that which is set by tradition and custom, du Vair is unwavering:

> Doe wee come into [the world] to command, or to serve, or to give the Law, or to receive it? I thinke you will answer me in a word that we come into it, to obey, and follow what we finde alreadie established. We must accommodate our selves . . .[22]

Such accommodation means endurance. For their own quietness of mind and for the good of the country, individuals ought to be able to bear whatever hardship is imposed by God or through the desires of the king:

> . . . Shall we not in the presence of Men, Angels, Nature, and of God him-selfe, endure somewhat that we may shew we can accommodate our selves unto the Lawes of the World, and to the Will of our Soveraigne?[23]

And if in the end the only reward for endurance is destruction, why be "vexed at it"? All kingdoms, states and towns must age and die; it is a part of nature.[24] This is all the more reason "to beare more patiently, and with more resolution, the fall of [the] state."[25] Du Vair does not equate forbearance with passivity, however. In accordance with the Stoic belief in a cosmic order which assigns every individual a role to play even when the results of human efforts are beyond human control, the writer, a political activist, will play his role to the end; he concludes his piece with a quintessentially Stoic call for constancy: "[L]et them overwhelme you with the Rudder in your hand still."[26]

Of Wisdome, the English translation of Pierre Charron's book Traicte de Sagesse, was not published in London until after the death of Queen Elizabeth. (The exact year is unknown; it was sometime between 1603 and 1612.) However, the original French version appeared in 1601 and would certainly have been known to some late Elizabethan readers. Charron defines human reason as "a beautifull and noble composition of the entire man," comprised of self-knowledge, freedom of spirit, harmony with nature, and true contentment.[27] The attainment of wisdom lies in a constant questioning of the world in order to know the self. "The true office of man," Charron says, "his most proper and naturall exercise, his worthiest profession is to judge."[28] His judging may well

---

21 S.T.C., 7373, Guillaume du Vair, A buckler against adversitie: or a treatise of constancie, trans. A. Court (London: B. Alsop, 1622), p. 6.

22 Ibid., pp. 42–43.

23 Ibid., p. 32.

24 Ibid., pp. 40–41.

25 Ibid., p. 47.

26 Ibid., p. 162.

27 S.T.C., 5051, Pierre Charron, Of wisdome, trans. S. Lennard (London: Eliot's Court Press, 1608[?]), pp. A2, A2 + 1.

28 Ibid., p. 232.

lead him to question whether the laws, customs and opinions of his country are, indeed, truer and more reasonable than those of all others. Unlike Montaigne, Charron does not offer refuge in the legitimizing stamp of tradition, except in matters of church law, which must be accepted without question. One who seeks wisdom may very well find that he is surrounded by a world where nearly all things, no matter how venerable, are flawed and mistaken.

But where Charron does not revere tradition, he recognizes the utility of it, and to resolve the conflict between the knowledge wisdom brings and the need to preserve order he recommends prudence, "the first vertue . . ., which consisteth in three things . . .; to consult and deliberate well, to judge and resolve well, to conduct and execute well."[29] Prudence dictates that one draw a distinction between the pursuit of internal wisdom and the way in which one acts in the external world. "A wise man," he says, must often "carie himselfe outwardlie after one maner, and judge inwardlie after another . . . to preserve equitie and justice in all."[30]

In this way, the effective import of Charron's argument becomes identical to that of Montaigne and du Vair. For all practical purposes, it makes no difference what opinions wisdom engenders within an individual if the prudent prescription for behavior remains strict conformity to the status quo. One who would be accorded wise "must do, and carie himselfe outwardly, for publike reverence, and so as he offend no man, according to the law, customs, and ceremonie of the countrey. . . ."[31] This means, as it does for Montaigne and du Vair, that one must maintain constancy to that which is established, no matter what hardships might be incurred in the process. The "rule of rules" is unswerving, unquestioning obedience. Furthermore, in a passage strongly reminiscent of Montaigne, Charron says there must be no attempt at innovation:

> All change and alteration of lawes, beleefes, customes and observances is very dangerous, and yeeldeth alwaies more evill than good; it bringeth with it certaine and present evils for a good that is uncertaine and to come. Innovatours have alwaies glorious and plausible titles, but they are but the most suspected, and they cannot escape the note of ambitious presumption, in that they thinke to see more cleerely than others, and that to establish their opinions, the state, policie, peace and publike quiet must be turned topsy turvy.[32]

In *Of Wisdome*, the conclusion that the principle of constancy mandates support for absolute monarchy is not merely implied; it is clearly stated. "Wee must absolutely obey" all commandments of superiors, without regard to their [the superiors'] "worth and merit," Charron writes.[33] Even in the case of a tyrant, endurance must be maintained, for rebellion, sedition and civil war will

29 Ibid., p. 350.
30 Ibid., p. 233.
31 Ibid., p. 234.

32 Ibid., pp. 313–314.
33 Ibid., p. 314.

only incite a wicked prince to be more cruel.[34] A sovereign ought to obey the laws of God and nature, keep his promises to the people and do them justice; but he is above all civil and human law. While Charron urges resistance to a tyrant who has attained his position by usurpation, in no other case will he permit it. Even if obedience is out of the question, as when a king is commanding subjects to violate the laws of God and nature, the subjects have no recourse but to flee—or to adopt a Stoic solution and patiently suffer the consequences of their disobedience.

Montaigne, du Vair and Charron all, to varying degrees, propound Neostoic ideas as an important part of their philosophical systems. This is not the case with most of the propaganda documents produced by anti-Leaguers in the period between 1584 and 1595. Still, behind many of the arguments advancing support for royal absolutism can be discerned the influence of these ideas. The anonymous author of *An answere to the last tempest and villanie of the League* (1593) offers the same Stoic choice as does Charron in the face of persecution from a prince who would command subjects to do something that goes against the service of God: to flee or to endure.[35] Michel Hurault (1589) gives Old Testament examples of rulers who were endured no matter how idolatrous or tyrannical they were, and, to illustrate the importance of upholding tradition and public order even at the expense of justice, offers the supreme example of Christ, who acknowledged Tiberius as emperor: "Are we greater and more honorable than Jesus Christ, that we should pervert th'order of successions, the lawes & estate of the Realme to chuse us a king?"[36]

As this passage suggests, it may be objected that non-resistance has a stronger base in Christianity than in Stoicism. It is the joining of the two, however, that serves to make the non-resistance argument all the more potent. Philippe du Plessis-Mornay, for instance, presents a lengthy exposition on Providence in *A woorke concerning the trewnesse of the christian religion* (1587) which would lead him to a royalist position in other, more openly political works (a position he assumed when the succession of protestant Henri of Navarre became imminent). That same tract also contains Neostoic overtones in its admonitions to readers not only to understand that both good and evil in the world are equally expressions of God's purpose, but to endure adverse occurrences as an acceptance of God's justice. Mornay faults those who are not content to wait for God's punishment of tyrants, saying that God has his own inscrutable ways of administering retribution and must not be questioned. Wickedness, he says, "is a

---

[34] Ibid., p. 414.

[35] S.T.C., 662, *An answere to the last tempest and villanie of the League*, trans. T. H. [T. Scarlet] (London: C. Burby, 1593), p. 22.

[36] S.T.C., 11289, M. Hurault[?], *The restorer of the French estate* . . ., (London: R. Field, 1589), p. 55.

punishment to it selfe. Seneca in his Thebais [writes] Feare not: for he shalbe punished, & that right sore."[37]

Other political writers who apply Neostoic values to the question of resistance to tyranny are Antoine Arnauld, who cites the word of God, "who enjoyneth us with patience to tolerate evil Princes";[38] and Etienne Pasquier, who, in his attack on the Jesuits (1602), assails them for even proposing that a distinction can be made between a king and a tyrant. No subject has a right to form such a judgement, he says, and to do so would pose a threat to public order. Once again, it is preferable to remain constant and endure what is required by established authority rather than invite upheaval:

> . . . we are to blindfold our eyes under their obedience, otherwise we shroud a rebellion of subjects against their Prince; Rebellion which produceth much more evell than the tyrannie whereunto we were subject.[39]

Thus the tenets of Neostoicism and related ideas bolstered the position of non-resistance to established authority, and to kings, in these and other French works (of which limited space does not permit discussion) that would have been familiar to English readers, even to the extent of explicitly supporting absolutist rule. In the view of Gerhard Oestreich, Lipsian Neostoicism helped lay the foundations for the development of absolutist theories on the continent. Virtue, for the Neostoics, lay in patient endurance of the established regime; the political application of Neostoicism "entailed rationalization of the state and its apparatus of government, autocratic rule by the prince, the imposition of discipline on his subjects, and strong military defence."[40] While the political stance of absolutism would not be openly reflected in the works of most English writers in the last decade of Elizabeth, the philosophical underpinnings for it would, in the form of Neostoicism.

The English writers

The rise of the Neostoic movement in England can best be represented as a confluence of tributaries whose tumbling waters forced together, confused and ultimately changed the direction of the philosophy from that taken by the main stream as it flowed from the continent. In France, Neostoicism was to provide a firm foundation for reason of state and the building of royal absolutism. In

---

37 S.T.C., 18149, Philippe du Plessis-Mornay, *A woorke concerning the trewnesse of the christian religion*, trans. Sir Philip Sidney and A. Golding (London: G. Robinson, 1587), p. 201 margin note.

38 S.T.C., 780, Antoine Arnauld, *Le franc discours. A discourse, presented of late to the French king*, trans. W. Watson (London: J. Roberts, 1602), p. 26.

39 S.T.C., 19449, Etienne Pasquier, *The jesuites catechisme. Or examination of their doctrine*, trans. W. Watson (London: J. Roberts, 1602), pp. 158^R–158^V.

40 Gerhard Oestreich, *Neostoicism and the Modern State*, ed. Brigitta Oestreich and H. G. Koenigsberger, trans. David McLintock (Cambridge: Cambridge University Press, 1982), p. 30.

England, its influence was less clear, and manifested itself in more than one form.

The works of Lipsius and other Neostoic writers were well received in England in the 1580s, making their way into English intellectual circles largely through courtier and poet Sir Philip Sidney and his followers. "With Lipsius," writes Salmon, "the way lay open for rational statecraft and the prudential participation of the subject as the servant of the absolutist state."[41] But upon Sidney's death at the Battle of Zutphen in 1586, the mantle of his intellectual pursuits passed to Robert Devereux, Earl of Essex; and it was with Essex's revolt and execution in 1601 that the Neostoic movement was to veer sharply from the path it had taken in the rest of Europe and eventually become a refuge for malcontents and cynics in the Jacobean court, and a target of suspicion for budding English absolutists rather than a basis for their monarchist political theory. This strain of Neostoicism was more Tacitean in nature, making more of the corruption of the tyrants of Roman history than of their established right to rule, and being more apt to be associated with the sanctioning of sedition.[42]

But while this turn toward a more Tacitean Neostoicism was to be the dominant characteristic of the cult in the Jacobean court and would, eventually, raise the ire of King James I, who found its ideas antithetical to his belief in the divine right of kings, it did not wipe away the more positive aspects of Neostoicism that had been carried into English thought in the pre-Essex years of Elizabeth. Anxiety over the unsettled succession and fears of an uncertain future spurred English writers, particularly the writers of civil war literature, to be drawn by the same aspects of Neostoicism that had attracted their war-tossed counterparts on the continent. Tacitean accounts of Roman tyranny and cynicism toward the corruptions and deceits of rulers were overshadowed for these writers by Senecan values that seemed to promise stability and security through constancy, respect for established tradition, and restraint of innovation.

An historicall collection of the continuall factions, of the Romans and Italians, by jurist William Fulbecke (1601), is a narrative account of Republican Rome up to the accession of Augustus. This long cataloguing of bloodshed, ambition, assassination, suicide, cruelty, treachery, destruction, torture and massacre depicts civil war as wasteful, futile, and something to be avoided at all costs. Fulbecke's proposal for averting such mayhem is for all to take a Stoic approach. The "mischiefes of discord and civill discention" can be remedied, he says, "by contenting our selves with our lot, and not contending to our losse: by hoping without aspiring, and by suffering without conspiring."[43]

Thomas Lodge, who would later translate the works of Seneca, published his play, *The Wounds of Civil War*, in 1594. The play begins in 88 B.C., when a

---

41 Salmon, "Seneca and Tacitus," pp. 187–188.

42 Ibid., pp. 172–173, 187–188.

43 S.T.C., 11412, William Fulbecke, *An historicall collection of the continuall factions, of the Romans and Italians* (London: W.Ponsonby, 1600), p. A2.

quarrel between Marius and Sulla over the generalship of a military campaign sparks many long years of battle. Lodge's emphasis on the great destruction of civil war is tied securely to the Stoic theme of avoiding innovation. A climactic moment occurs in the fifth act with Sulla's return to Rome after the death of Marius. He surveys the evidence of carnage all around him, and pins the blame squarely on those who were not content to bear with the status quo:

> The reasons of this ruthful wrack
> Are your seditious innovations,
> Your fickle minds inclin'd to foolish change.[44]

A far better model for behavior in adverse circumstances than that of the factious Roman people is provided by the noble Cornelia and Fulvia, wife and daughter of Sulla, who, earlier in the play, were captured by Marius. Displaying a Stoic acceptance of their fate, they resolve to be the agents of their own deaths rather than to allow Marius to kill them:

> [Fulvia:] For full confirm'd that we shall surely die,
> We wait our ends with Roman constancy.[45]

For these women, maintaining constancy by submitting bravely to the inevitable rather than railing against it is seen as a way of dealing with a tyrant—or even vanquishing him—without posing a threat to order. As Fulvia declares:

> Marius, I doubt not but our constant ends
> Shall make thee wail thy tyrant's government.[46]

Samuel Daniel, author of *The Civil Wars*, was a poet who was very much a part of the English Neostoic movement. He was a client of Mary Herbert, Countess of Pembroke, sister of Sir Philip Sidney. His later patrons included Fulke Greville and Charles Blount, Baron Mountjoy, both friends of Essex. His works included a tragedy of *Cleopatra*, modelled after Seneca, and during his career he maintained clear connections with French literary currents. In 1586 he may have been a servant to Sir Edward Stafford, an English ambassador to France who was instrumental in sending French works to England for translation and publication there, and in 1603 he contributed a poem to Florio's translation of Montaigne.

The Civil Wars was entered into the Stationers' Register in October 1594. Its first four books were published in 1595, a fifth book was added to the 1599 edition, and Book VI first appeared in 1601. This epic poem recounts the

---

44 Thomas Lodge, *The Wounds of Civil War*, ed. Joseph W. Houppert (London: Edward Arnold, 1970), Vi, Lines 1–10.
45 Ibid., IV, Lines 334–335.
46 Ibid., IV, Lines 375–376.

history of the deposition of Richard II and the subsequent elevation of Henry Bolingbroke to the throne of England as Henry IV. In it, Daniel displays a decidedly ambivalent attitude toward this historical event. On the one hand, he plainly despises the king, who "Riots in pleasure and neglects the law: / . . . [and] thinkes his Crowne is licenst to do ill."[47] On the other, he forbears from expressing any real support for the usurper Bolingbroke's course of action. Those in the epic who urge on Bolingbroke constitute a faceless and emotional "multitude," a "many-headed monster" and a "vulgar body," but those who think otherwise are depicted as a wiser, "graver sort," able to foresee the outcome of Bolingbroke's resistance.[48] They are not blind to the faults of their king, but, like Montaigne and Charron, they fear the bad bargain that would be struck by trading, through innovation, an unpleasant situation for one that might be far worse:

> They saw likewise, that Princes oft are faine
> To buy their quiet, with the price of wrong:
> And better 'twere that now a few complaine,
> Then all should mourne, aswell the weake as strong:
> Seeing still how little, Realme by chaunge do gaine;
> And therefore learned by observing long,
> T'admire times past, follow the present will,
> Wish for good Princes, but t'indure the ill.[49]

Here once again can be seen, in the exhortation "T'admire times past," an invoking of tradition, and a Stoic call "t'indure the ill" for the sake of what has always been. Richard himself, watching the people flock to Bolingbroke, asks why they "Run headlong to that change that nothing gaines / But gaine of sorrow, onely change of wo?" instead of remaining faithful to their lawful sovereign.[50] And in the pivotal verses describing the actual deposition, Daniel presents the scene in parliament as a mockery of the tradition for which he has expressed such reverence. The members of parliament themselves recognize the importance of draping their actions in the cloak of tradition to restore order, but their efforts are rooted in falsehood and represent no more than a perversion of a sacred heritage:

> A Parlement is foorthwith summoned
> In *Richards* name; whereby they might pretend
> A forme, to grace disorder, and a showe
> Of holy right, the right to overthrowe.

---

47 Samuel Daniel, *The Civil Wars*, ed. Laurence Michel (New Haven, CT: Yale University Press, 1958), Book I, Stanza 57, p. 86.

48 Ibid., Book I, Stanza 71, p. 89; Book II, Stanza 12, p. 104.

49 Ibid., Book I, Stanza 72, p. 89.

50 Ibid., Book II, Stanza 13, p. 104.

> Order, how much predominant art thou!
> That if but onely thou pretended art;
> How soone, deceiv'd mortalitie doth bow
> To follow thine, as still the better part!
> Tis thought, that reverent forme will not allow
> Iniquitie, or sacred right parvart,
> Within our soules, since then thou dwell'st so strong;
> How ill do they, that use thee, to do wrong![51]

Daniel reserves his praise for Richard's few remaining supporters, lauding them for their "so memorable constancy";[52] and when all is over, the final assessment is left to "The better fewe, whom passion made not blinde." They still think the safest course would have been to endure things as they were, "Saying, better yeeres might worke a better care, / And time might well have cur'd what was amisse."[53]

In addition to finding their way into English awareness through the civil war literature, Neostoic ideas conducive to the future development of royalist political theory also were expressed in the work of essayist Sir William Cornwallis. A student of moral philosophy, Cornwallis was acquainted with the works of Plutarch, Seneca and Diogenes Laertius and was a great admirer of Montaigne, whose *Essays* he read, in part, in translation.[54] In his own *Essayes*, published in two parts in 1600 and 1601 respectively, Cornwallis extolls Montaigne as an author who "speakes nobly, honestly, and wisely, with little method but with much judgement."[55] He writes that "*Seneca* of moralitie is the best," and of Tacitus that "never was there so wise an author so ill handled by commenters."[56] He also cites Lipsius.

In his essay "Of Keeping State," he stresses the importance to the public order of individuals maintaining the social rank they have been assigned in "times past." Tradition means order, and order means obedience:

> Wee have then from our auncestors differences, which tradition is not so tyrannicall as not to satisfie us with any other reason but customs. For shee tells us that obedience makes way for Wisedome which otherwise, whatsoever it could doe, should doe nothing for the clamor and noyse of communitie. . . .

---

51 Ibid., Book II, Stanzas 94–95, pp. 123–124.
52 Ibid., Book II, Stanza 26, p. 107.
53 Ibid., Book II, Stanzas 102–103, p. 125.
54 Roger E. Bennett, "Sir William Cornwallis's Use of Montaigne," *Publications of the Modern Language Association* 48 (1933): 1080–1085. Florio's translation of Montaigne was not published until 1603, two to three years after Cornwallis's *Essayes* appeared in print. Bennett speculates that Cornwallis either saw an early, unpublished version of Florio's translation, or else read another translation that is no longer extant.
55 William Cornwallis, *Essayes by Sir William Cornwallis, the Younger*, ed. Don Cameron Allen (Baltimore: Johns Hopkins Press, 1946), p. 42. Also see S.T.C., 5775.
56 Ibid., pp. 201, 112.

[Without obedience there would be] Many determinations, no resolutions; clamours, not counsels; confusion, not government; for government's supporters are commaund and obedience, the foundation and chiefe causes upholding States.[57]

Chaos, says Cornwallis, is avoided by everyone following the "rules and orders" of his or her sex or calling. Any deviation is an innovation and, as such, pernicious,

As greatnesse attyred in a servile forme or a servile in greatnesse is an innovation and no lesse dangerous particularity then innovations more generall to the body of a State.[58]

In "Of Nature's Policie," Cornwallis says that just as it is vital for individuals to keep to their positions in society, so, too, must commonwealths keep to the "states" they have been assigned. He calls practitioners of innovations "the monsters of states," which ought "to bee with all diligence suppressed. . . ."[59]

On June 22, 1601, Cornwallis entered into the Stationers' Register his *Discourses Upon Seneca the Tragedian*, the first English book devoted entirely to Seneca. In this book, which consists of commentaries on eleven sentences taken from Seneca's plays, Cornwallis not only further elaborates on the Stoic themes he had expressed in his *Essayes*, but also applies them more directly to questions of polity.

The greatest plague inflicted on humanity, Cornwallis writes in *Discourses*, is a wicked governor, for his subjects cannot prosper. Since princes are above the law, there is little subjects can do about such a situation.[60] This creates a terrible dilemma:

. . . there is no safetie under such Magistrates, since refusing or obeying, ruines one of the two best parts of man. The good obey the ill; it is worth the observation, how the eternall wisdome applies and suffers: ill is here made the touch-stone of good, and good obeyes ill, to trie goodnesse constancie. . . .[61]

Thus the evil magistrate sets good and evil in a contest with each other, to see if evil can alter good or good overcome evil. Trapped in the arena of this contest, the hapless subject may conspire to overthrow the prince only if the latter seized power unlawfully; otherwise, says Cornwallis, "there is hardly any

[57] Ibid., pp. 85–86.
[58] Ibid., p. 88.
[59] Ibid., p. 152.
[60] S.T.C., 5774, William Cornwallis, *Discourses upon Seneca the tragedian* (London: E. Mattes, 1601), pp. A4 + 1, B4 + 4.
[61] Ibid., p. B4 + 4.

counsell to be given." Both law and a Stoic stance of constancy indicate that "hee must be suffered."[62]

Stoic-inspired ideas of royal absolutism did not find open expression in specific matters of political debate between English thinkers during the Elizabethan years; however, through French influence the ground was made fertile for them to be sown. A final literary work demonstrating the interaction of the Neostoic movement with political thought in England in a particularly telling way is Ben Jonson's play *Sejanus His Fall*. The playwright draws heavily on Suetonius, Pliny, Juvenal, Seneca and, especially, Tacitus' *Annals* and Dio Cassius' *History of the Romans* in relating the story of Tiberius' unscrupulous favorite. The tragedy sets up dichotomies of treachery and loyalty, of fortune and constancy. Sejanus and the mob who follow him are slaves of fortune, tying their actions to novelty and the ascending star of the moment. Opposed to them are those who hate and fear Sejanus but refuse to rise against him and the Emperor Tiberius because their anchor is virtuous constancy. The difference between the two is summed up in an exchange between Latiaris, a supporter of Sejanus, and Sabinus, who is loyal to Tiberius:

> [Latiaris:] It is a noble constancy you show
> To this afflicted house: that not like others,
> (The friends of season) [do you] follow fortune,
> And in the winter of their fate forsake
> The place, whose glories warmed you. You are just,
> And worthy such a princely patron's love.[63]
>
> [Sabinus:] They [the gods] must be patient, so must we.[64]

Both men bewail the troubled times, and the extinguishing of "the genius of the Roman race." Latiaris says "active valour" is the only thing that will "redeem/ our loss," but Sabinus disagrees:

> [Sabinus:] 'Twere better stay,
> In lasting darkness, and despair of day.
> No ill should the subject undertake
> Against the sovereign, more than hell should make
> The gods do wrong. A good man should, and must
> Sit rather down with loss, than rise unjust,
> Though, when the Romans first did yield themselves
> To one man's power, they did not mean their lives,
> Their fortunes, and their liberties should be
> His absolute spoil, as purchased by the sword.[65]

---

[62] Ibid., p. B4 + 5.
[63] Ben Jonson, *Sejanus his Fall*, ed. W. F. Bolton (NY: Hill and Wang, 1966), IViii, Lines 115–120.
[64] Ibid., IViii, Line 127.
[65] Ibid., IViii, Lines 162–170.

Thus Sabinus directly links constancy with non-resistance to the sovereign, and prescribes endurance and adherence to established tradition as the only correct response to tyranny, no matter how unjust it might seem. Sejanus, on the other hand, is torn apart by the mob—the embodiment of opinion and innovation.

Sejanus His Fall was first performed in 1603, only months after the death of Queen Elizabeth. Ben Jonson was hauled before the privy council, under suspicion of having written his play as an allegory of the career of the late traitor Essex. Nothing came of the matter, but when in 1605 Jonson published *Sejanus*, he was careful to add the following introductory paragraph:

> This [play] do we advance as a mark of terror to all traitors, and treasons; to show how just the heavens are in pouring and thundering down a weighty vengeance on their unnatural intents, even to the worst princes. . . .[66]

With this sentiment, the duality of *Sejanus*'s theme was extended to the history of the play itself. Resting on the cusp between the Elizabethan and Jacobean reigns, *Sejanus* could be interpreted as containing both ideological strains in English Neostoicism, depending upon the reader's point of view and political agenda. As the Stuart age unfolded, the Neostoic message was pushed by some in a decidedly absolutist direction.

[66] Ibid., Lines 40–45, p. 8.

2

Notions of Social and Religious Pollution in Nicolas Remy's *Demonolatry*

RICHARD M. GOLDEN*

"Dirt is essentially disorder," and "uncleanliness is matter out of place," states the English anthropologist Mary Douglas, who further observes that pollution does not make a neat distinction between sacred and secular. Pollution attacks order, the holiness that unites a society.[1] The social and religious structure of Catholic France in the late sixteenth and early seventeenth centuries faced two great threats of pollution: Protestantism[2] and diabolical witchcraft, which were linked in the minds of many. Satanic witchcraft was doubtless the greatest danger, for it aimed by means of a secret conspiracy to overthrow all of Christendom. It is not surprising that this era of rapid social, economic, and religious change, a period of intermittent civil wars and endemic political intrigue, comprised the golden age of demonology in France. Jean Bodin, Henri Boguet, Pierre de Lancre,[3] and Nicolas Remy were the most noteworthy demonologists. While the latter has received the least attention from scholars, his demonological treatise, *Daemonolatreiae* (*Demonolatry*), expresses clearly the fear of witches' pollution of godly society.[4]

Remy was arguably the most important French-speaking writer and judge of

* I wish to thank Adrianna Bakos, Thomas Kuehn, and David Nicholas for their comments and suggestions.

[1] *Purity and Danger: An Analysis of Concepts of Pollution and Taboo* (London and Henley, 1966), 2, 40.

[2] On Catholic-Protestant fears of pollution, see Natalie Zemon Davis, *Society and Culture in Early Modern France* (Stanford, 1975), 157–60.

[3] On these demonologists, see Sophie Houdard, *Les Sciences du diable. Quatre discours sur la sorcellerie* (Paris, 1992).

[4] Lyon, 1595. The book was an immediate success, subsequent editions appearing the next year (Cologne and Frankfurt), in 1597 (Frankfurt), and a German edition in 1598 (Frankfurt). Two later German translations came out in 1693 and 1698. Lucien Dintzer, *Nicolas Remy et son oeuvre démonologique* (Lyon, 1936), 56–57; Rossell Hope Robbins, *Witchcraft: An Introduction to the Literature of Witchcraft* (Millwood, NY), 34, 102; Henry Charles Lea, *Materials toward a History of Witchcraft*, 3 vols. (Philadelphia, 1939), 2:604.

witchcraft, for he bore responsibility for the burning of more witches in Lorraine than were executed legally in the neighboring kingdom of France. The number of lynchings are not known, but French courts condemned to death only hundreds of witches, despite the notoriety that public displays of demonic possession and trials involving lecherous priests and nubile women gave to the kingdom.[5]

In the duchy of Lorraine, in only two decades, Remy sentenced nearly two thousand witches to death, a remarkable accomplishment considering that Lorraine's population hovered around four hundred thousand, while the population of France in 1600 was perhaps sixteen million. Indeed, Remy had a hand in between 2 and 4 percent of the witches executed throughout Europe, from Iceland to the Urals, during the so-called witch-craze.

Failure to pay close attention to the time gap between Remy's writing of the *Demonolatry* and its date of publication has misled scholars about the numbers of witches Remy sentenced to death. While the title page of Remy's *Demonolatry* states that he drew information "from the capital trials of nine hundred persons, more or less, who within the past fifteen years have in Lorraine paid the penalty of death for the crime of witchcraft," he claimed in the book to have condemned "no less than eight hundred" in sixteen years.[6] The actual number may be well over twelve hundred. Since Remy compiled the *Demonolatry* in July 1592, the eight hundred may represent convictions between 1576 and 1592. But because the treatise was not published until 1595, the nine hundred probably represents the fifteen years prior to 1595. For the entire period, 1576-1595, he averaged fifty to sixty deaths per year, for a total of 950 to 1140 executions.[7]

However, executions were possibly more numerous when Remy was *procureur-général* of Lorraine from 1591 to 1606. In that office, Remy travelled through the duchy and his tours were marked by the burnings of witches. For example, in 1596 he visited all the *baillages* of Nancy, whose villages were

    [5] Alfred Soman's meticulous research has been primarily responsible for appreciating the great gap between the vitriolic writings of the demonologists and the mild sentences handed down by the *Parlement* of Paris. See, for example, "Decriminalizing Witchcraft: Does the French Experience Furnish a European Model?" *Criminal Justice History* X (1989), 5; "La Decriminalisation de la sorcellerie en France," *Histoire, économie, société* 4, 2 (1985), 189; "Trente procès de sorcellerie dans le Perche (1566–1624)," *L'Orne littéraire* 8 (1986), 42. Unfortunately, we do not know exactly the number of accused witches killed throughout France because of ignorance about regional parlements' trials of witchcraft cases and because few records remain of trials in courts of first instance (Robin Briggs, *Communities of Belief: Cultural and Social Tensions in Early Modern France* [Oxford, 1989], 10).

    [6] Remy, *Demonolatry*, trans. by E. A. Ashwin and ed. by Montague Summers (Seacaucus, NJ), 56.

    [7] Lea argues for twelve hundred, but he erred in believing Remy assembled the material for the book in 1591, rather than in 1592, and in dating his witch-hunting from 1595 (*Materials toward a History of Witchcraft*, 2:607).

decimated as a result.[8] If we extend the average of fifty to sixty through 1606, we arrive at a figure of 1500 to 1800, considerably higher than the number of executions many historians have attributed to Remy.[9] We will never know the exact number of those he condemned, for the records have disappeared,[10] possibly because they were burned along with the witches. Approximately three thousand witchcraft trials took place in Lorraine between 1580 and 1630, with a conviction rate of almost 90 percent.[11] Lorraine thus experienced intensive witch-hunting and Remy deserves his infamous reputation as the "scourge of witches" (a term used in his own day) and as the Torquemada of Lorraine.[12]

Lorraine in the sixteenth century was situated precariously between the Holy Roman Empire and France. According to the treaty of Nuremberg in 1542, the Holy Roman Emperor served as protector of the duchy of Lorraine. Yet, culturally and religiously, as well as linguistically, Lorraine looked to France. French political followed cultural hegemony, as the French state annexed Metz, Toul, and Verdun in the mid-sixteenth century. During Remy's lifetime, socioeconomic conditions in Lorraine were as harsh as the climate and were worsening.[13] The population rose dramatically during the first two-thirds of the sixteenth century, putting increased pressure on the land—devoted in Lorraine

---

[8]   So claims Charles Pfister ("Nicolas Remy et la sorcellerie en Lorraine à la fin du XVIe siècle," *Revue historique* 93 [n.3] [1907], 234), who guesses that Remy sent between two and three thousand witches to the stake (239). Other French historians have accepted as well the figure of two or three thousand, and I myself feel comfortable with the lower number. See, for example, Jean Palu, *La Sorcellerie* (Paris, 1957), 64; Robert Mandrou, *Magistrats et sorciers en France aux XVIIe siècle. Une analyse de psychologie historique* (Paris, 1968), 135; Jean Delumeau, *La Peur en Occident XIVe-XVIIIe siècles* (Paris, 1978), 350; Robert Muchembled, *Popular Culture and Elite Culture in France, 1400–1750* (Baton Rouge and London, 1985), 239.

[9]   In writing about the European witch-hunts, historians over time have tended to lower figures of alleged executions, but the number of Remy's victims warrants standing as an exception. Many writers simply cite Remy's claim to have executed nine hundred witches. Some examples include Julio Caro Baroja, *The World of the Witches* (Chicago, 1965), 117; Charles Alva Hoyt, *Witchcraft* (Carbondale and Edwardsville, IL, 1981), 62; Geoffrey Scarre (although he says the nine hundred may have been an exaggerated assertion), *Witchcraft and Magic in 16th and 17th Century Europe* (Atlantic Highlands, NJ, 1987), 20; G. R. Quaiffe, *Godly Zeal and Furious Rage: The Witch in Early Modern Europe* (New York, 1987), 27; Rosemary Ellen Guiley, *The Encyclopedia of Witches and Witchcraft* (New York, 1989), 281. Brian P. Levack accepts 800 as the number of Remy's victims (*The Witch-hunt in Early Modern Europe* [New York, 1987], 51).

[10]   Dintzer, *Nicolas Remy et son oeuvre démonologique*, 32–33.

[11]   Briggs, *Communities of Belief*, 67.

[12]   I disagree with Briggs, who in his excellent study of witchcraft in Lorraine, offers evidence about the strength of witch-hunting and then inexplicably concludes that the evil name of the Lorraine judges, including Remy, is exaggerated (idem).

[13]   For what follows on the demographic, economic, social, and political situation in Lorraine, I rely for the most part on Guy Cabourdin, *Terres et hommes en Lorraine*, 2 vols. (Nancy, 1984). See also Michel Pernot, "Lorraine," in *Dictionnaire du Grand Siècle*, ed. François Bluche (Paris, 1990), 892–94.

to cereal crops and viticulture. Many peasants became indebted and had to sell their holdings. Lorraine was a rural society, where village communities maintained ties to small towns. Both the urban elite and the aristocracy, who dominated the countryside and imposed onerous obligations on the peasants, benefitted from acquisitions of new lands. In late sixteenth-century Lorraine, the wealthy thrived while peasants labored under the weight of demographic potency, taxes, and economic hardship. Overall, peasants were in much worse shape after 1580 than had been their grandparents early in the century. Poverty and begging infused Lorraine. It is no wonder that Remy and the elevated social group he represented feared witchcraft because they believed it to be the weapon of choice of the poor (especially beggars) and powerless against the rich and powerful. During the sixteenth and seventeenth centuries in Europe, there was a positive correlation between economic decline and the increase in poverty, on the one hand, and witch hunts on the other.[14] Lorraine fit this general European pattern.

The despoliations of soldiers constituted a fact of life in Lorraine between 1552 and the onset of the Thirty Years' War. Situated between France and her German Protestant allies, Lorraine fell prey to destruction, confiscations, and murders from French troops and from Spanish soldiers and mercenaries as they traversed the "Spanish Road" between Milan and the Low Countries in order to suppress the Dutch revolt.

Conditions could have been much worse; fortunately, the duchy managed to escape the worst of the French civil and religious wars. Duke Charles III (1545–1608), Remy's patron, avoided involvement in France's domestic turmoil until after 1580, when he helped organize the Holy League. The duke supported his relatives, the Guise family. Charles's championing of extremist Catholicism went hand-in-hand with the Catholic Renaissance then flourishing in Lorraine and with Remy's witch-hunts, which the duke wholeheartedly endorsed.

Thus Remy's period saw the government of Lorraine mostly at peace and so able to concentrate on the domestic disease of witchcraft. Throughout Europe, extensive warfare tended to exhaust governments and populations and leave little energy for witch-hunting. Sporadic warfare, on the other hand, disposed people to look to human causes—witches—of the destruction and accompanying economic hardships. Lorraine in the late sixteenth century experienced an amount of warfare conducive to an outbreak of witch-hunting. The depredations of foreign armies, epidemics, bad harvests, and increased social tension inclined those in power to seek the individuals responsible for natural and supernatural calamities. The primary agent for carrying out the battle against the witches was Nicolas Remy.

Born between 1525 and 1530 in Charmes, not far up the Moselle River from

14 See, for example, Levack, 135.

the episcopal city of Toul, Remy possessed the family connections and education for a career as a judge and eventually advisor to the duke of Lorraine. His
father was a provost, while his maternal uncle was lieutenant-general of the
bailliage of the Vosges, a position to which Remy succeeded in 1570 after
receiving a legal education in Toulouse and teaching there.[15] Remy spent the
next five years at Mirecourt, south of Nancy, discharging administrative and
judicial functions. In 1575, Charles called him to the capital, Nancy, to be his
secrétaire ordinaire, his private secretary. A year later, Duke Charles appointed
Remy to the ducal court (the *échevinat* or *tribunal des échevins*) in Nancy. This
tribunal had both civil and criminal jurisdiction (in seventy-two villages in
Lorraine); there was no appeal from its verdict.[16] Some areas were independent
of the tribunal, but it did enjoy immense power, particularly in cases pertaining
to witchcraft. This was an area of special concern to Duke Charles, who
ordered Remy to cleanse Lorraine of witchcraft.[17] In fact, lower criminal
courts—prevotal, seignorial, and communal—requested advice in capital sentences from the tribunal at Nancy. This consultation soon became obligatory.[18]
Consequently, Remy's nefarious witch-hunting career began. His pursuit of
witches proved to be so successful because Remy enjoyed the support of the
other three members of the tribunal, of the duke, and of the population.[19]

It is impossible to know with any certainty what led Remy to accept the
reality of the demonic presence. His scholastic education in Toulouse opened to
him the world of the Church Fathers (and their bitter misogyny) and of
classical writers who accepted the daily intrusion of the supernatural into the
natural world. He mentions in the *Demonolatry* that, in order to escape the
plague in Toulouse around 1563, he had gone to Auch, where he had an
experience with a "wanton demon" who threw stones at him and a friend.[20]
Sixteenth-century France was agog with accounts of Satanic activity. Forty
witches were burned while Remy was at Toulouse in 1557. In 1566, priests in
Laon, in northern France, exorcised a girl, Nicole Obry (Aubrey), infected by
as many as thirty demons; this case became known throughout France and led
to an outpouring of writings about demonology. Even the king intervened to
order the continuation of Obry's exorcism. This possession—so dramatic, attended by thousands of witnesses—seemed to many Frenchmen to demonstrate

[15] Dintzer (*Nicolas Remy et son oeuvre démonologique*) remains the best source for Remy's
life.

[16] Dintzer, *Nicolas Remy et son oeuvre démonologique*, 23–24.

[17] Allban Fournier, "Une épidémie de sorcellerie en Lorraine," *Annales de l'Est* 5
(1891), 252.

[18] Charles Pfister, "Nicolas Remy et la sorcellerie en Lorraine à la fin du XVIe siècle,"
228–29.

[19] Alban Fournier ("Une épidémie de sorcellerie en Lorraine," 256, 258) pointed this
out over one hundred years ago, but historians who glance at Remy's work and book
neglect to mention the political support he needed.

[20] Remy, *Demonolatry*, 82–3.

the real presence of Satan in the world and to validate the teachings of Catholicism against the Protestant heresy (for Protestants eschewed the ceremony of exorcism, preferring to rely on prayer and fasting to fend off Satan).[21] (If a priest could unerringly make bread the body of Jesus and wine His blood, could not Satan invade the body of a nubile woman in order to make her His?) Remy compared the demonic takeover of Nicole Obry to other examples of Satan's guile. Satan's strategy was to enter Christianity's camp, which he tried to do via Obry and others.[22]

Remy remained on the *tribunal des échevins* for fifteen years, earning a reputation as serious and capable. On 9 August 1583, letters patent granted him nobility. Thus did Remy realize the great ambition of every bourgeois or middling sort, not only in Lorraine, but throughout Europe. The process of wholesale ennoblement came relatively late to Lorraine, but the dukes initiated what one historian has called (with some exaggeration) the "deluge of ambition."[23] Charles III issued over eight ennoblements a year. His motivation was to reduce the influence of the highest aristocrats as well as to reward men who had served the duke well and were devoted to him.[24]

Six years later, Duke Charles rewarded Remy yet again, appointing him to the *conseil privé*, which, among other state functions, heard legal appeals. This gave Remy access to the duke on an almost daily basis; the appointment demonstrated conclusively Charles III's support for Remy's handling of witchcraft cases on the *tribunal des échevins*, where Remy continued to serve for two more years. In 1591, the duke named Remy to the highest judicial post in the duchy, *procureur-général* of Lorraine. As *procureur-général* Remy represented the duke in the Estates-General and his judicial functions took him through the entire duchy—his authority was not attached to one jurisdiction alone, but extended to lower courts and to the *tribunal des échevins*.[25]

While *procureur-général*, Remy served his duke as a diplomat, collaborated in drawing up the customs (the customary laws) of Lorraine, pursued literary studies, wrote a history of Lorraine, and participated in Duke Charles's brilliant court, a gathering place for artists, poets, and scholars. Remy remained *procureur-général* until 1606, when he resigned in favor of his son Claude, who was to follow in his father's footsteps and become a "judicial assassin."[26] When Charles died in 1608, Remy took part in the funeral procession. In April 1612,

---

[21] On the exorcism at Laon, D. P. Walker, *Unclean Spirits: Possession and Exorcism in France and England in the Late Sixteenth and Early Seventeenth Centuries* (Philadelphia, 1981), 21–32; Jonathan L. Pearl, "Demons and Politics in France, 1560–1630," *Historical Reflections/Réflexions historiques*, 12 (1985), 243–44.

[22] Remy, *Demonolatry*, 35.

[23] Cabourdin, *Terres et hommes en Lorraine*, I, 159.

[24] Ibid., I, 160.

[25] Dintzer, *Nicolas Remy et son oeuvre démonologique*, 25–26.

[26] Ibid., 27.

Remy himself passed away, leaving at least seven children and the book that was to ensure his reputation.

For Remy, Satan, his demons, and his witches manifested the pollution of Christendom. Purity comprised a hierarchical social order, where the poor and women showed deference and knew their place, and included a Tridentine religiosity free from popular superstitions and the Satanic cult. Purity was cleanliness and sweetness; impurity was dirt and foulness. Not coincidentally, Remy wrote his *Demonolatry*, his discourse on devilish pollution, when Lorraine experienced rapid social change and religious upheaval. This witch-hunter's concept of pollution reinforced social distinctions and religious orthodoxy, both under attack.[27]

According to the *Demonolatry*, Satan and his minions (the demons and witches) polluted everything: marriage and the family, the human body, social relationships, nature, and the Church. Of course, Satan could do this without help, but the use of human servants added to the evil by making witches accomplices in the crimes committed.[28]

Although witches possessed free will and always served their demon voluntarily[29]—the prime reason why Remy as judge refused to grant clemency to those guilty of witchcraft—the joining of witch to devil was a seduction, at first with promises, but later with threats if necessary.[30] This seduction led to the defilement of body, family, and soul and was sealed by the devil's mark, his personal brand that canceled the priest's baptism. The brand could be virtually anywhere; Remy knew this through empirical evidence, for he supports his assertions in the *Demonolatry* with evidence from specific cases that he himself had tried. A demon branded Quirina Xallaea on the back of the head, Claude Fellét on the back and breast, Dominique Euraea on the hip, and Jacquelina Xalueta on the left shoulder.[31] Because these scars proved insensitive to pain, needles could be thrust into the accused's body in order to determine whether she had indeed been marked. This was common practice in many European courts, for discovery of the devil's mark gave proof of the pact and sufficed as evidence to convict. Furthermore, for Remy the search for the devil's mark led to the imposition of torture, whose efficacy the judge did not doubt. Torture made the witch's body, defiled by a demon, a battleground whereupon Remy fought the devil. This was a formidable struggle, for witches could bear torture, demons comforted the witch in prison, and the devil did all he could to prevent the witch from confessing.[32] The witch had lost her right to her body after

---

[27] According to Douglas (*Purity and Danger*, 139), pollution ideas support social lines that have been crossed. Remy recognized that witches had crossed those fixed boundaries that defined his worldview.

[28] Remy, *Demonolatry*, 120, 181.

[29] Ibid., 187.

[30] Ibid., 1–2.

[31] Ibid., 9.

[32] Ibid., 164–68.

consenting to unite with her demon; now Remy demonstrated that her body could be disfigured by the forces of righteousness in order to extract a confession. As a judge, Remy was immune from the blandishments of the devil, inviolable, secure in a role analogous to that of a priest.[33] There was no escape for the witch; Remy says he had never condemned an innocent and certainly never pardoned the guilty. Witches could expiate their crimes, "so notoriously befouled and polluted," only through burning. God demanded their punishment, which served as an example to others.[34] The fires and witches' deaths purified and reinforced Christian Lorraine. Execution by fire was a ritual killing that effaced the crime and purified a society that needed to appease God's possible wrath.[35]

Central to Satan's pollution of Christian order was his sexual politics, overturning proper husband-wife, parent-child, and human-god relationships. If Christianity had poisoned eros, the devil could do little worse then inflame eros, though in especially sordid ways that would stain Christians irreparably. So demons led witches into adultery or fornication, polluting the marriage bed and the witch's body. Remy agrees with other demonologists that intercourse with the devil was extremely painful, both because demon semen was so cold and because his member was excessively large. Alexée Drigie reported to Remy in 1586 that her demon's penis, even when half erect, was as long as some kitchen utensils.[36] No good, and certainly no pleasure, could result from entering into contact with the devil. The demon was barren, rendering offspring impossible, though a woman could in rare instances give birth to a deformed baby by having looked at a demon.[37]

Adulteresses through their fornication with their demons (their "little masters"), witches further mocked their marriages by deceiving their husbands when the witches left their beds to travel to the sabbat. The witches either charmed their husbands into a deep sleep or they placed some object in the bed to dupe them.[38] Alexée Belheure, trapped in an unhappy marriage, begged her demon to rid her of her husband; the demon subsequently beat the husband to death.[39] Some witches polluted the sacrament of matrimony further by actually marrying their demons. The demon-bridegroom blew on the bride's anus in-

---

[33] Ibid., 4–5. On the sincerity and godly mission of judges, see Etienne Delcombre, "Les procès de sorcellerie en Lorraine. Psychologie des juges," *Tijdschrift voor rechtsgeschiendenis* 21 (1953): 389–419.

[34] Remy, *Demonolatry*, 184, 188.

[35] So argues Richard van Dülmen, *Theatre of Horror: Crime and Punishment in Early Modern Germany* (Cambridge, MA, 1990), 130.

[36] Remy, *Demonolatry*, 12–14.

[37] Ibid., 19–20, 26.

[38] Ibid., 43.

[39] Ibid., 117.

stead of offering her a ring. The couple celebrated their union at a feast where the main entrée was a roasted she-goat.[40]

The repository of pollution, the educational locus of Satan's plans, and the main theatre where the varying elements of pollution were played out was, of course, the sabbat. Here witches contravened a central message of Christianity, embodied in John 13:34, that love of others, love born of faith, is the supreme law of Christ.[41] In Satan's domain, hatred replaced love. The witches, the "scum of humanity," whom Remy, as with other demonologists, found to be primarily female, engaged in one reprehensible act after another. Massive orgies—Catherina Ruffa testified to seeing no less than five hundred witches at her first sabbat[42]—took place, but that was not the greatest of the evils. At the sabbat banquet, witches ate human flesh. This cannibalism associated the witches with personified uncleanliness: stench-filled human corpses, elsewhere a favorite hiding place for demons (in churchyards and in places of execution).[43] Remy knew well the Hebrew Bible and the long Jewish association of death with impurity. He saw too that witches' foul cannibalism mocked both respect for society's relationship with the dead and the purity of Catholic cannibalism, where practitioners ingested their god in the Eucharist. "For there is in demons a deeply implanted and seared hatred of all pure religion and divine worship, and they detest and abhor all sacred rites and ceremonies . . ."[44] The central event in the Mass became the main course at the witches' feast; god became dead human flesh, eaten along with other refuse. No wonder that salt, symbol of purity, was absent from the banquet table, weighted down with dead cats, kids, and dunghill-cocks. Whereas the communion wafer could even suffice as nourishment for holy women,[45] witches, the unholiest of women, received no satisfaction from Satan's communion table.[46]

Dancing that led to fatigue and distress followed sabbat banquets in Lorraine, as elsewhere in Europe. Here joy was absent, just as in the witches' painful copulations with demons, in their feasts that did not satisfy flesh, and in the very failure of all the glorious benefits that demons promised their minions. To Remy all was disorder, discordance, and disobedience to established social harmony and religious purity. The dancing that went on was back-to-back, a "preposterous inversion," that had the dancers in masks, looking at the ground, and gyrating to madness. A madness it was, for their function, according to Remy, was the destruction of the human race. Thus noxious music and

---

[40] Ibid., 93.
[41] Ibid., 46.
[42] Ibid., 56.
[43] Ibid., 88.
[44] Ibid., 57.
[45] See Caroline Walker Bynum, "Fast, Feast, and the Flesh: The Religious Significance of Food to Medieval Women," *Representations* 11 (Summer 1985): 1–25.
[46] Remy, *Demonolatry*, 57–60.

30   RICHARD M. GOLDEN

shouting, yelling, and hissing, helped to whip the witches into the frenzy that would make their destructive vocations easier.[47]

At the sabbat, the devil also ordered his witches to swear fealty to him with the *osculum infame*, the infamous kiss of shame planted on his posterior after he had assumed the form of a goat. Remy explains the devil's fondness for the figure of a goat (noting that devils have changed into other creatures, including dogs, horses, flies, cats, wolves, and bears) because goats stank and were lascivious and belligerent. Their bodies were deformed and their saliva poisonous.[48] Poison was crucial to the devil's plans to destroy humanity and played a large part in the *Demonolatry*. The sabbat with its perversities was no exotic, erotic, and neurotic sideshow for Remy, but dangerous reality that included classes where the devil taught witches how to commit crimes with magic. Impure symbol became daily crime through magic and poison powders.

The most far-reaching of those villainies involved the destruction of nature. Witches sent armies of mice, showers of frogs, wolves, killing breezes, whirlwinds, and hailstorms. Remy notes proudly having sent some two hundred witches to the stake for stirring up water to create clouds that they subsequently directed to rain down hail. Barbeline Rayel swore that witches rolled great jars through clouds until coming to a locality singled out for ruin, where the jars broke up into stones, beating flat everything they fell upon.[49] In sum, witches ravaged individuals' private lives, the family, and society as well with their weather magic. With their demons they possessed the capability of obliterating entire towns or villages through disease, a blight, lightning, or the opening up of the earth.[50]

Nurture as well as nature was a prime target for Satan's destructive plans. Witches led their own children into witchcraft, giving them to demons and/or turning them into murderers. In 1591, a seven-year-old boy witch came before the *tribunal des échevins*. He confessed that his parents had taken him to the sabbat and that his personal demon had given him poison "more than once." The judges debated among themselves whether the child should be executed before finally deciding to banish him to a monastery. Remy apparently did not share the leniency of his colleagues on the bench, because the security of innocent people outweighed the life of a child and because children who committed crimes inevitably pursued crimes more fervently as adults.[51] Leniency was anathema to purity.

If witches' procurement of their own children for the devil were not evil enough, they utilized aborted foetuses for poisons and the skin for parchment. According to Remy, witches disinterred stillbirths from cemeteries and expended them for magic, sometimes cutting off limbs as well. Witches even

[47] Ibid., 60–65.
[48] Ibid., 65–72.
[49] Ibid., 67, 74–75, 135.
[50] Ibid., 125.
[51] Ibid., 92–96.

slashed open wombs and ate the foetuses. Three witches stole Johann Molitor's one-year-old child from the cradle, burned the baby, and used its ashes to destroy vines, crops, and trees.[52] Thus neither Remy nor witches gave consideration to age—the judge did not believe that age freed a child from culpability, while witches did not spare either babies or foetuses.

Is it surprising that the principal components of the sabbat involved debased sexuality? The central place of witches practicing cannibalism signified women devouring their own infants, who had been born through "natural" sexual congress (as opposed to sodomy). To add horror to the unthinkable, they used baby fat, the essence of the most innocent and fertile of human bodies, as the prime ingredient to manufacture evil potions and unspeakable deeds. Following their lascivious nude dancing, the feral witches performed rites/wrongs of incest and bestiality, often copulating in cold, painful frenzy with devils or with Satan Himself. That accused witches in Europe were usually hags, greater than fifty years old,[53] increased the perverse mockery of beautiful, married intercourse, life-affirming, rather than life-denying. Incest revealed the ultimate pollutant of family relations, adding confusion to the perfect household, which contained the husband physically on top of the obedient wife, and hierarchically superior to everyone else (children and servants), who were subordinate to him and who possessed well-defined traditional roles. Incest consequently challenged Christianity's sexual politics and the state's image of the family, where the father played to wife and children the same role the monarch enjoyed vis-à-vis his subjects. Male witches practicing homosexuality did the perverse and unpardonable, denying God's Chain of Being as well as the authority of theologians and magistrates whose duty it was to define and enforce sexual Revelation.

As befitting a zealous Christian, the ultimate pollutant for Remy was sex and the cause of that contamination was women. The *Demonolatry* did not go to the extremes that the *Hammer of Witches* (1486) had done in excoriating females, fragile in everything save their carnality and proclivity for evil. Syncretistic and rich in its pluralism, Christianity has been able to carry under its umbrella many contradictory strands of thought and behavior—extreme asceticism and rank indulgence, a concentration on individual salvation and social reform, mysticism and hierarchy, denominationalism and ecumenicism, persecution and (albeit recently) toleration. But no current has run its course as boldly and consistently as misogyny, from Paul to the present.

Christianity early on cast its lot with virginity as the preferred condition and patriarchy as the godly rule for state and family. Hostility toward women ebbed and flowed, but it was always there, invariably embedded in the perceived necessity of controlling them. During the sixteenth and seventeenth centuries,

---

[52] Ibid., 99–102.
[53] Edward Bever, "Old Age and Witchcraft in Early Modern Europe," in Peter Stearns, ed., *Old Age in Pre-industrial Society* (New York, 1982), 157, 181.

the hatred and fear of women crested, not only in the witch-hunts, but in pursuit of infanticides—always women, the quintessential sex-linked crime—and of homosexuals, who imitated the part of women while performing "unnatural" acts. Christianity has been and remains obsessed with sexuality and its control (it would not be exaggerating to maintain that Christianity is transfixed by the need to control *per se*). Nicolas Remy manifested this rampant fixation with female sexuality/pollution.

While Remy feared the poor, it was women who were predominant among the poor. While Remy dreaded disorder and impurities, it was women who planned mayhem and practiced a sexuality that polluted the world.[54] The destruction of personal, marital, familial, and social relationships began with the practice and use of all that was disgusting to Remy: stench, excrement, semen, foetuses, corpses, dirt.[55] Everything concerning the witches—rape, incest, cannibalism, hyper-charged and perverted sexuality—involved the profanation of the sacred and the creation of chaos with an intention of overturning the Christian world order.[56]

That Christian-cosmic order was to be immutable, for purity was "the enemy of change, of ambiguity, and compromise."[57] Remy did not compromise—his ease of conscience in condemning accused witches and the numbers of executed attest to his steadfastness—and he had no sense of ambiguity, although he maintained a scholastic's fascination with debate. But Remy's defense of religious purity and the status quo actually admitted one indispensable change, the final anomaly that would end all changes. The Bible shows, Remy wrote, that "God has appointed His ministers of vengeance."[58] What demons have done, God permitted. The demons were cunning in their efforts to pollute mankind,[59] but God had made judges immune from their blandishments in order to thwart the establishment of Satan's empire. Remy's God was a terrible one[60] who commanded merciless severity against the disordered witches, whose potent threat signified a real danger in the disordered world of the sixteenth century. God then had ordained the seminal conflict pitting demons and wit-

[54] Nicole Jacques-Chaquin points out that those who ascribed to the idea of a witches' conspiracy saw sexual subversion linked to fears of social and political subversion ("Demoniac Conspiracy," in *Changing Conceptions of Conspiracy*, edited by Carl F. Graumann and Serge Moscovici [New York and Berlin, 1987], 76).

[55] For example, even witches' cures use "filth, sordid matters, excrements, and many other such things than which nothing could be imagined more foreign to that purity. . . ." (Remy, *Demonolatry*, 155).

[56] R. L. Masters emphasizes nicely the preoccupation of all the demonologists with scatology and sexual perversities (*Eros and Evil: The Sexual Psychopathology of Witchcraft* [New York, 1962], especially 93, 147).

[57] Douglas, 162.

[58] Remy, *Demonolatry*, 137.

[59] Ibid., 142.

[60] As Remy indicated in quoting the prophet Jeremiah (ibid., 188).

ches against Remy and other witch-hunters. This battle of evil against good, of pollution versus purity, and of witches facing judges would, Remy was sure, usher in the Second Coming, ultimate changelessness, sacredness, and purity.

> It is, indeed, blasphemy . . . for judges to deal leniently with those who are liable to the just punishment of Heaven. This is to delay the coming of His Kingdom; for nothing can so firmly establish it as the routing, overthrow and destruction of all His enemies, together with Satan, . . .[61]

Citing Saint Ambrose, Remy declares that "When the wicked is slain . . . Christ is received."[62]

Accordingly, Remy's actions as a witch-hunting judge and his explanation and vindication of his severe behavior should be understood with reference to his cosmic dualism—man/woman, judge/witch, God/Satan, pollution/purity— that presaged the Second Coming. His eschatology was hardly extraordinary, for millenarianism, misogyny, and religious purity were fundamental to the religious climate of the sixteenth century. Remy's battle against demons and witches during the age of the witch-hunts was only one among many in Christianity's ongoing drive to usher in the Age of Purity.

[61] Ibid., 188.   [62] Idem.

3

Strengthening the Noble Male Body: Guillaume du Choul on Ancient Bathing and Physical Exercise

OREST RANUM

Noble Guillaume du Choul, royal councilor and bailiff in the Dauphiné mountains, believed that ancient bathing practices and physical exercises could be imitated quite literally in his own sixteenth century. As antiquarian, official, *gentilhomme*, and quiet civic activist not unlike Montaigne and La Noue, du Choul sought to carry out his king's commands.[1] He says in his Dedication to Francis I that his king has asked him to find out what ancient Greek and Roman bathing practices were. Du Choul completed the assignment as best he could by pulling together all the information about the subject that he could find in the writings from Antiquity that were available in recent editions, and archeological evidence. The discourse on bathing follows one on Roman religion, really a careful exploration of Roman coinage, and one on *castrametation*, that is fortification and military discipline in ancient Rome that was coupled and indexed with the *Discourse on Antique Bathing*.[2]

J. H. M. Salmon, in his "Cicero and Tacitus in Sixteenth-Century France," explores the ways in which ancient thought could have an impact on both

---

[1] Apart from old and brief biographical sketches, which no doubt contain errors, little is known about du Choul's life. See Dominique de Colonia, *Histoire Littéraire de la Ville de Lyon* (Lyon, 1728–1730) II, 564.

[2] The *Discours de la Religion des Anciens Romains* was first published in 1547. There was a new edition in 1556. The first edition of the *Discours de la Religion . . .*, the *Discours sur la Castrametation, et Discipline Militaire des Anciens Romains*, and the *Discours des Bains et Antiques Exertations Greques et Romaines* as a single volume occurred in 1555, published by Roville. See J. Baudrier, *Bibliographie Lyonnaise* (Lyon and Paris, 1845–1921) IX, 163, 219–220, 239, 256. There was an Italian translation of the *Discours des Bains* in 1556, a Spanish one in 1579, another French one in Wesel, 1672, a Latin one published in Amsterdam in 1685, and a Dutch one in 1684.

political and philosophical thought in the late sixteenth century.[3] A literalist Humanist endeavor to recover ancient learning and eloquence broke down as a result of an increasingly intense debate over the interpretation of ancient authors, and a disquieting religious, political, and philosophical environment. From this perspective, du Choul seems disengaged, perhaps because much of his research and reflection took place before the great storms of the early 1560s.

Du Choul was noble and a royal official, and if tradition is accurate, he began his study of Antiquity through curiosity about the objects peasants had plowed up in their fields and brought to him, rather than as a result of university studies. These facts may help to explain his passion for archeology, technology, and his imperviousness to controversy.[4] His works are sprinkled with Greek terms, with straight-forward translation presented in a tone that indicates little certainty that he was right. If du Choul had doubts about his translations he does not allude to his reasons for choosing one word over another. Indeed, his aim was to present his research as directly and in as uncluttered a form as possible, and to attract and convince the royal reader–and anyone wise who read the book–of the authoritative truth of his findings. It would not be correct, however, to infer that du Choul lacks a critical perspective toward his subject.

The 1581 edition has a very fine, state-of-the-art woodcut depicting his arms, and the *devize*, HONOR SINE HONORE BEATUS, set in an antique-style architectural frame. His dedication ends with an exhortation to the king to "take care and to protect the *gendarmerie*," that is the loyal noblesse in the provinces. Robert Harding has discerned the social and political importance of the companies of noble gens d'armes in the mid-sixteenth century, as they were torn apart and divided owing to feuds between governors in the client networks that constituted the military and political order in the provinces on the eve of the Wars of Religion.[5] This was du Choul's social environment.

Du Choul's treatise on Roman military organization ends with a summary of the pay scales which the legionnaires received, a not simply scholarly topic. Domitian, du Choul claims, added supplements of three gold *deniers* to the regular *gages* received by each legionnaire; and, du Choul adds: "I weighed these coins, which weigh a quarter of an ounce each, or more . . . today these are worth a double ducat . . ."[6] This is an example of how the research of this noble antiquarian could have a direct bearing on contemporary life. Without any apparent difficulty he makes the "translation" from what in Roman history were the legionnaires to the French *gendarmerie*. Had not the great Budé used

---

[3] *Renaissance and Revolt: Essays in the Intellectual and social history of Early Modern France* (Cambridge, Cambridge University Press, 1987), 27–53.

[4] Bourriot, Félix, "Un Ouvrage lyonnais de la Renaissance . . ." *Revue du Nord* LXVI (1984): 653–675; Richard Cooper, "Collectors of Coins and Numismatic Scholarship in Early Renaissance France," *Warburg Institute Surveys and Texts* XXI, 5–23.

[5] *Anatomy of a Power Elite: the Provincial Governors of Early Modern France* (New Haven, Yale University Press, 1978).

[6] *Discours de la Religion . . .*, 110.

philology to discern the amounts of the pensions that Augustus awarded gens de lettres?

The same noble-interested and civic-minded outlook prevails in his work on baths and exercises. He claims that the king asked him to report everything that was "beautiful for the eye and useful and profitable for the health of the body." Note the ordering here—the emphasis on aesthetics and then on utility—which would pre-determine the arrangement of his observations about architecture and the human body.

Du Choul had recently visited what he refers to as the *maison royale* at Fontainebleau, where he "looked at" and "admired" what Francis I had accomplished in creating architecture that served as a stage for monarchical power.[7] This description of Fontainebleau is interesting because it was drafted by a nobleman with minimal apparent familiarity with the much richer vocabularies of the Pléiade. Indeed, it is du Choul's relatively limited vocabulary for describing architectural spaces and the decorative arts that makes his prose particularly interesting. The limitations serve to convey a literalism and force to his descriptions, largely because he was not literary enough to be very metaphorical. The painting on the walls, the stucco work and the royal orchard, gardens, pond (not the more poetic pool) and ditches are bluntly and undecorously noted in the metaphor of a residence that is so attractive that "the gods will choose it in order to invite nymphs there to hear the music." Du Choul sees the royal décor as inviting and attracting, not as projecting or prestige enhancing for the royal *châtelain*. This compliment is followed by one about the *thermes*, the baths that in his opinion deserve to be compared by those built by "M. Agrippe." The Agrippa in question was Marcus Vipsanius Agrippa, statesman and council to Augustus who built great public baths and gardens in Rome and elsewhere in the Empire. The parallel that du Choul makes between the king and Agrippa is revealing of du Choul's, and perhaps the sixteenth century's casualness about rank. Agrippa was a commoner. Paralleling in a Plutarchian manner someone who was not of royal blood with a royal would become unacceptable in the rarefied classicizing decades after the founding of the French Academy, but not for du Choul. For him the essential feature about the ancient Roman social order was that these were Romans, and, therefore illustrious enough to be compared with a contemporary king.

Lest it be inferred that du Choul was some sort of noble rustic, it must be mentioned that his publisher, Guillaume Roville, and friends, notably Claude and then Jacques d'Urfé, to whom he dedicated his treatise on Roman military arts–placed him in a learned noble literary and antiquarian sub-culture, civic activist and commercial, that was in symbiosis with the outstanding printers and illustrators of Lyon.[8] Du Choul's works were printed on the presses that

---

[7] *Discours des Bains . . .*, "Au Roy" np.

[8] Claude Longeon, *Une Province Française à la Renaissance* (St. Etienne, Centre d'Etudes Foréziennes 1975), chapter X. Longeon's phrase "Ce fut dans ces livres de pierre

were turning out editions in Italian of Petrarch, Boccaccio, Castiglione, and Ariosto. Serlio, Francis I's favorite Italian architect, also had works published by Roville, hence it is entirely accurate to describe du Choul's writings as part of a unique Humanist royally sponsored project for recovering ancient architecture, ways of life, or manners, and culture. The learned, non-university trained French nobles of the sixteenth century have long been recognized as occupying an important place in the recovery of Antiquity, but their specific social and cultural perspectives, and their unaffected, literalist prose, deserve more research especially as they appear in the creation of images of the Antique.

One last element must be explored before turning to du Choul's work itself: the bathing practices and sociability surrounding them at the time the work appeared. By the mid-sixteenth century, the *étuves*, those establishments of highly dubious moral standing, were being frequented less and less. Attacked by moralists and preachers not only for the fact that they were encounter zones for prostitution, the *étuves* and the bathing that took place there enhanced self consciousness of the body, and therefore the sins of the flesh, from the perspective of these preachers.[9]

While the *étuves* were public in the sense that they were open to anyone who could pay admission, they could scarcely have been thought of as public in the way du Choul would describe the later public baths of ancient Rome. It would not be historically sound to hinge an argument on just a semantic shift, or change of "real" public spaces for "imagined" public spaces, but it is important to note that du Choul inextricably linked public to baths and bathing as well as to exercise. This occurred in the technical description of spaces and activities hitherto scarcely imagined by the mid-sixteenth-century reader. The French Monarchy was, of course, the *res publica* for the French of the sixteenth century, thus the description of antique public spaces and manners did not undermine the royalism or absolutism that were ascendent during the Wars of Religion.[10] In the *longue durée*, the legal definition of public spaces would become very important not only for the relations between the state and society, but in the

que la majorité de l'élite forézienne apprit à aimer l'antiquité." 269. See the older, but still useful Emile Picot, *Les français italianisants an XVIe siecle* (Paris, Champion, 1906–1907) I, 165, 201, 208, 216. That Jacques d'Urfé was governor for the Dauphin, the future Francis II, suggests that du Choul's project had a "mirror of princes" dimension to it, and that this would be recognized when Héroard showed Louis XIII the treatise on *Castrametation. Journal*, ed. by M. Foisil (Paris, Fayard, 1989), 148.

9 Zerner, Henri, "La Dame au Bain" in *Le Corps à la Renaissance*, ed. by Jean Céard, Marie-Maeleine Fontaine, and Jean-Claude Margolin (Actes du XXXe Colloque de Tours, 1987), Paris, Aux Amateurs du Livres, 1990, 95–111, esp. 107. A. J. Krailsheimer, *Rabelais and the Franciscans* (Oxford, Clarendon Press, 1963), 56; Julian Bradshaw and Dorothy M. Jones, "Luxury, love and charity: Four paintings from the School of Fontainebleau" *Australian Journal of Art*, III (1983), 43.

10 Ballon, Hilary, *The Paris of Henry IV: Architecture and Urbanism* (Cambridge, Mass., MIT Press, 1991).

rise of a sense of *police*, that is surveillance of all social activities in public spaces in the name of keeping public order.[11]

We, in the twentieth century, must block out the images of ancient baths and athletes that we have inherited from Ingres, the pre-Raphaelites, Puvis de Chavannes, and the neo-neo classical gymnasiums of the 1930s, in order to assess the cultural impact that du Choul's prose descriptions of bathing and exercising may have had on the imaginations of his contemporaries. To be sure, the illustrations of ancient authors, notably Valerius Maximus, in illuminated manuscripts, and the genre scenes of women bathing together—an erotic theme already well established by the mid-sixteenth century—may already have titillated du Choul's readers.[12] But the Lyon Humanist that was du Choul had markedly different intentions when he described and illustrated ancient Roman religious, military and bathing practices. His aim was to recover at least something of the stoa, as the Romans understood it, and perhaps of the public nature of antique society, and perhaps the virtue which sustained it.

While certainly not the first historian to discuss ancient bathing, du Choul broke new ground by doing so systematically, and with illustrations. His idea of his project is to discourse upon the subject as completely as possible while addressing the perennial, all-time leisure-lacking reader, the king. The typical phrases about kings being too busy to read, and needing light reading matter to relax them as a result of the heavy burdens of their office, make du Choul's discourses characteristic of both Humanism and royalism in the early-modern centuries. By assembling every source he could find about bathing and exercising into a coherent, general description, du Choul gave a hitherto unknown relief and legitimacy to the subject. In superbly cut, elegant type, on paper with carefully measured margins, *Des Bains et Antiques Exercitations Grecques et Romaines* attracted some attention, as is evident from the number of the translations and editions in the sixteenth century. The fact that the discourse on bathing was coupled with a work on Roman military practice, and was carefully indexed with that text also lent *éclat* to the subject. For du Choul bathing and exercising were not titillating or lewd, but ancient practices that might shed light on the human condition, and more especially, the civic and military service of the *noblesse*.

Du Choul provides references to most of his sources in the margins, but if he was aware of differences of opinion or of borrowings by one ancient author from another, he does not bother to inform his reader about them. He is aware, however, not only of different practices among the Greeks, but of changes over the centuries. He does not note whether his sources are medical, architectural, etc., but he was aware that everything he was writing about touched on the

11 Brennan, Thomas, *Public Drinking and Popular Culture in Eighteenth-Century Paris* (Princeton University Press, 1988).

12 The French quickly created their version of the theme. See Jean Mignon's *Femmes au Bain*, reproduced in *Le Corps à la Renaissance*, figure 44.

domain of the physicians. He begins by describing the baths first, that is the arrangement of the tubs or pools, water temperatures, and "galleries or porticoes" that accompanied them in later Greek and Roman bathing. The spaces which Vitruvius describes obviously prompted wonder and excitement in du Choul, as he returns to them time after time. Simply put, the gardens, orchards, evergreen trees and topiary attracted him.[13]

He also senses something of the secretiveness or privacy of the ancient Greek bath that was an integral part of the house, and he becomes eloquent about how guests including virtuous princes might be entertained in these parts of the house. Here, he says, in the porticoes and galleries, learned men might be invited to discuss literature, painting, architecture, and "other excellent arts." In marked contrast to the real space of the *étuves*, where eating and drinking accompanied sexual encounters, du Choul never mentions food or drink in the ancient bath, thereby distancing the imagined ancient bath still further from the *luxuria* of the *étuves*. Did not the Romans bathe first and dine afterward?

Du Choul's distinction between the domestic bath and the public bath prompts no reflections. The Romans, as he says, "enjoyed the felicity of the world in the domestic baths, galleries, and porticoes, as well as in their *stribades*, those little vine-covered *cabinets* to which they could retire.

For the Romans the evolution in domestic bathing seemed evident to him.[14] Scipio had entered a small *réduit* to bathe in cold water after a day of toil, but in later times domestic baths became so vast that they had *contrefenestres*, and were "triumphantly lighted," but he does not moralize about this evolution. Du Choul does not see enjoyment, or *félicité du monde* as a symptom of Roman decline, but rather as the culmination of a quest to join the pleasures of the body with those of the mind.[15] The bath and its accompanying spaces in the house existed to provide honest pleasure, implicitly in all-male company, though du Choul observes that the Greeks "invited" their wives into the bathing area of the house.

Was du Choul's description of domestic bathing in late Antiquity a parallel with the spaces and sociability that he saw and imagined in the *apartement des bains* installed by Francis I at Fontainebleau? These baths were probably the

---

[13] See Linda Pellecchia, "Reconstructing the Greek House: Giuliano da Sangallo's Villa for the Medici in Florence" *Journal of the Society of Architectural Historians* LII (1993): 323–338, and "Architects Read Vitruvius: Renaissance Interpretations of the Atrium of the Ancient House" *Journal of the Society of Architectural Historians* LI (1992): 377–416.

[14] See Yvon Thébert's quick summary of the current scholarship on the question–for the Greeks, "Le bain n'était pas une pratique de propreté mais un plaisir complexe, comme chez nous la vie de plage." *Histoire de la Vie Privée*, ed. by G. Duby and P. Ariès (Paris, Seuil, 1985) I, 193. Fikret Yegül, in *Baths and Bathing in Classical Antiquity* (Cambridge, Mass., MIT Press, 1992) sums up from many of the same sources just the type of conversation-counseling space that du Choul was trying to capture, p. 187.

[15] *Discours des Bains . . .*, 153.

most elaborate and sumptuously decorated in Europe at the time.[16] Some of the most treasured works of art in the royal collection were on view in the bath apartment, presumably as a result of an attempt literally to create the physical spaces and sociability which Vitruvius described. Du Choul began his work with a compliment about the beauty of everything at Fontainebleau, so it would not come as a surprise if he was in effect describing through antique sources and in his own words what he had presumably seen and imagined participating in as a loyal servant to his king. The ambiguity lying between domestic or private bathing spaces, and public ones, was owing precisely to the union of the two in the prince, both in later Roman antiquity, and in the sixteenth century. Francis I's baths, like the baths of prominent Greeks and Romans, were domestic in the sense that they were in houses, yet they were also public in the sense that their owners and users were of the imperial family, senatorial families, and so forth.

As for the great public baths of later Rome, they became so common, says du Choul, that toward "the End" of the Empire princes bathed with the people. Still not moralizing, but simply recounting, as he knows he has a story that will please his readers, du Choul tells how Hadrian saw an old soldier whom he had known in earlier days in the *gendarmie*, scratching his back on a wall presumably to dry it, because he lacked a towel and servants. The emperor sent him servants and money.[17] On another occasion when the emperor was publicly bathing several *gens d'arms* came to bathe with him in hopes of a similar liberality. This time, however, instead of proffering gifts, Hadrian derisively dismissed them by ordering them to rub each others' backs.

Just as in his description of the sociability of the domestic bath, where a prince discusses philosophy and painting with the host and other guests, here again his gaze remains focused on the prince—in this case on Emperor Hadrian—and on his relations with the legionnaires. In other words, he makes a direct parallel between kings and nobles with Roman emperors and their elite military companies. To be sure, he also notes that the Romans bathed daily, and that some physicians had convinced the Romans that bathing facilitated the digestion of meat; but at no point does he seem to grasp the teeming humanity that frequented the ancient public baths, and the political bonds of gratitude created by the donation of baths by leading political figures in Rome itself and throughout the Empire.

By contrast, the Greek gymnasium receives much more attention. He re-marks that there were strong similarities between some Roman baths and those of the Greeks, but he becomes fascinated by the possibility of presenting all that he has learned about the *exedres*, or public schools, which he says were like the cloisters of "our religions," by which he meant the religious houses of his day.[18] Remarking with obvious approval the fact that the Greeks adorned their

---

[16] Zerner, 109, note 31.
[17] *Discours des Bains* . . ., 139.

[18] *Discours des Bains* . . ., 141.

gymnasiums with statues of athletes put there to incite youths to excel in exercise and games, he then dares to explore some Greek attitudes toward women. Plato does not reproach virgins for exercising completely naked when throwing the discus, du Choul says, or when they run or wrestle. Furthermore, women of all ages were encouraged to wrestle with men.[19] There follows a summary of the views of Lycurgus, Xenophon, and Cicero on exercise for women, which is particularly revealing of the ways du Choul could develop a topic once he had chosen to make more than a single comment about something. This is followed by a coldly erotic recitation from Propertius about how young Roman women could not be watched while exercising, though this had been customary in the Spartan *palestre*.[20] Again, instead of just the usual sentence or two found in an antique source, or *aside* in a sixteenth-century work about ethics, du Choul makes exercise for women a subject for reflection in his *Discours* . . .

Du Choul's description of the various recreational and educational spaces in the Greek gymnasium is an idealized composite of forcefully written verbal images. How did these strike the sixteenth-century reader? The synthesis of bodily exercise and mental learning almost inspires a sense of wonder in the antiquarian who was writing during the very years when the *ratio studiorum* of the Society of Jesus was attracting so many parents and city fathers who supplied funds for the new *collèges*.[21] Joining geometry and competitive racing in almost the same sentence, and in almost the same physical space, satisfied du Choul's deeply personal sense of pursuing the *curieux*.[22] He returns quickly to himself, however, and his social and political purview when he notes that princes in Ancient Greece came to see the athletes play their games, and listen to disputations by philosophers in the gymnasium. Always remarkably sensitive to what would almost be considered the exotic quality of the physical spaces described in the ancient texts, the Lyon nobleman pleasurefully expounds on the beauty of the trees, the gardens, the hedges, that surround the gymnasium— "giving shade, aroma, and green" as well as "comfort and consolation" to all who frequented them.[23] By associating comfort with nature, bathing, and edu-

---

[19] *Discours des Bains* . . ., 140.

[20] For the importance of Propertius to learned artists and antiquarians, see Thomas Da Costa Kaufmann, *The Mastery of Nature* (Princeton, Princeton University Press, 1993), 130.

[21] Huppert, George, *Public Schools in Renaissance France* (Ubana and Chicago, University of Illinois Press, 1984).

[22] Defaux, Gérard, *Le Curieux, le Glorieux et la Sagesse du Monde dans la première moitié du XVIe siècle* (Lexington, French Forum, 1982).

[23] "Il ne se trouve chose, que tant entretienne la bonne santé que l'exercitation. C'est le vray bain que le labeur, qui ne passe pour le sueur, car le labeur trop grand est mauvais . . . car commodement s'exerciter, lire haut, manier les armes, joüer à la paume, courir, se pourmener, et plus tost sous le Soleil qu'à l'ombre, sont toutes choses qui garde la bonne santé: que les philosophes ont estimé entre la félicité et biens divins." *Discours des Bains* . . ., 153. Note his ordering, reading before skill in the use of weapons—the more typical

cation, did du Choul make hitherto barely articulated feelings and associations available in words and images?

Almost as if this were not enough to inspire utopian pedagogical wonder, du Choul adds that the custom was for the Greeks to be naked in the gymnasium, and that they rubbed their bodies with a tremendous variety of oils to give them additional strength. After several pages describing oils and their properties as well as the difficulty in finding their French equivalents, he remarks that oil was also applied to make the body more *lubrique* for wrestling.[24] He reflects, in an almost off-hand manner: "The Greeks were the inventors of all vices." On this subject, however, he reflects no further. Even powders and sands of various types, and perfumes were also applied to fortify the body, making wrestling more challenging. There follows a lengthy discussion of the exercises and games that concludes with *plectiques,* or *pugiles* that is fist fighting. He illustrates this exercise, showing the use of cestes, the lead-filled leather gloves referred to in Book V of the *Aeniad.*

By making his inventory of games, oils, powders, and boxing the peroration for his *discours* on bathing and exercise, du Choul reached for an understanding of what could enhance the physical force and endurance of the human body, as the ancients knew it. The discourse becomes more intense when he stresses exercises and products that could be applied to the body, leaving the impression that he and perhaps the noblesse were anxious about bodily strength and dexterity.

In his work on masculine beauty Gabriel Pérouse discerns a similar preoccupation: physical strength, endurance, and dexterity were the essential qualities of manliness and beauty, not particular features or height, etc., in sixteenth-century France.[25] The male who could withstand the long military campaigns that made the reputations of Roman soldiers, and surviving the hardships of camp life were du Choul's general unstated preoccupations, and he thought it was useful for Henry II to know what the ancients did to strengthen their bodies. Joined to the perspective about in what spaces the noble compagnon could council his prince there remained the question of what could be done to strengthen the military class of the realm. The references to mathematics and philosophy are part of the whole ensemble of life in the ancient

ordering in the sixteenth century was to place arms before letters, especially by more clerkly and university trained commentators. I don't mean to suggest that du Choul was the first to try to capture in an illustration, ancient bathing as described by an ancient author. But just as an example, note that there is no attempt to create images of antique architecture in the 15th century illustrated copy of Valerius Maximus (Mss, 289, BN) from the 15th century, so well reproduced on the cover of *Communications* (1982) 35.

[24] *Discours des Bains . . .,* 146. It is tempting for the historian of the late 20th century to try to probe more deeply to try to discern still more of du Choul's feelings and views about sexuality, but to do so would be inconsistent with du Choul's overall intentions.

[25] "La Renaissance et la Beauté Masculine" in *Le Corps à la Renaissance,* 61–76.

FIGURE ONE

gymnasium, but never once does du Choul express curiosity about what mathematics were learned or philosophy taught.

It is, however, in the illustrations that du Choul reveals more about his not-conscious attitudes toward his readers. He assures them that he has personally supervised their creation.[26] Beginning with a portrayal of superposed founts located on a furnace (figure 1), each containing hot, tepid, and cold water, with the whole ensconced in a grand vaulted and columned space, du Choul attempted to put into images the very brief description of the baths that Vitruvius gives in his treatise on architecture. There would be many such attempts, all as vague and lacking specific notions about how they might work, but at least du Choul's has the advantage of portraying these heating "vases" as aesthetically

---

[26] He says about the *cuve* "l'une desquelles je representeray ci apres," *Discours des Bains* . . ., 125.

FIGURE TWO

grandiose and "classical," whereas some of his successors offered illustrations that looked more like inflated goat skins than devices in which water could be heated to different temperatures.[27]

---

[27] *Discours des Bains . . .*, 118. Compare with Jean Martin's translation of Vitruvius (Paris, Marness and Cavellat, 1572), 161, where the illustration certainly has a less antique feel. I wish to thank Nicole Fayel, Librarian in the Municipal Library of Rodez, for drawing my attention to this illustration. The copy of du Choul currently in the Rodez Library was part of the collections of the Rodez Jesuit College prior to the French Revolution. The illustration of the bather and his page going off to the baths has heavy ink spots at just the two locations where the genitals are depicted. The color of the ink is brown, which suggests that the blotting was done at some time in the Ancien Regime. Campaigns in favor of *pudeur*, and censorship of nudity in general intensified in the decades after the Council of Trent. The literature on the study of ancient baths by architects and antiquarians is vast. See Laetitia La Follette, "A Contribution of Andrea Palladio to the Study of Roman Thermae" *Journal of the Society of Architectural Historians* LI (1992): 189–198.

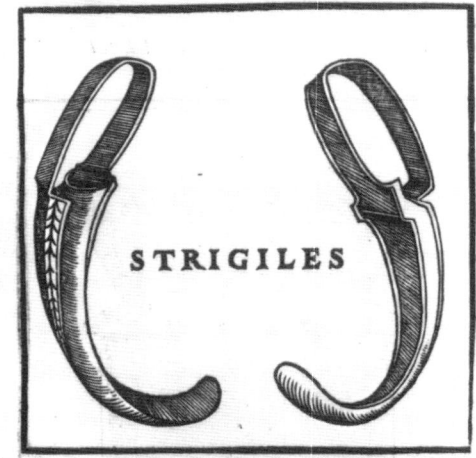

FIGURE THREE

There follows an illustration of a "roman" tub, or *cuve* (figure 2), which is followed by one of two strigils, or *étrilles* (figure 3). Du Choul reminds his reader, who is the king at this point, that he, du Choul, has given him a carefully made copy of an ancient strigil. Note that the copy, not the original, was given to the king, a fact that lets us suppose that du Choul either was eager to keep his own collection of artifacts as complete as possible, *or* that he had had the copy made for the king because he thought that the king might wish to use it while bathing. Had the gift been intended for a nascent royal curiosity cabinet would not du Choul have given the monarch the one which had been dug up, and had served as a model for the copy? Several other interpretations of this gesture immediately come to mind, but it is impossible to go beyond speculation at this point. After adding that Strabo, in Book V of his *Geographia* says that strigils were made of gold, silver, and bronze, and that the peoples of India made them from ebony, he remarks that the more *délicat* among the

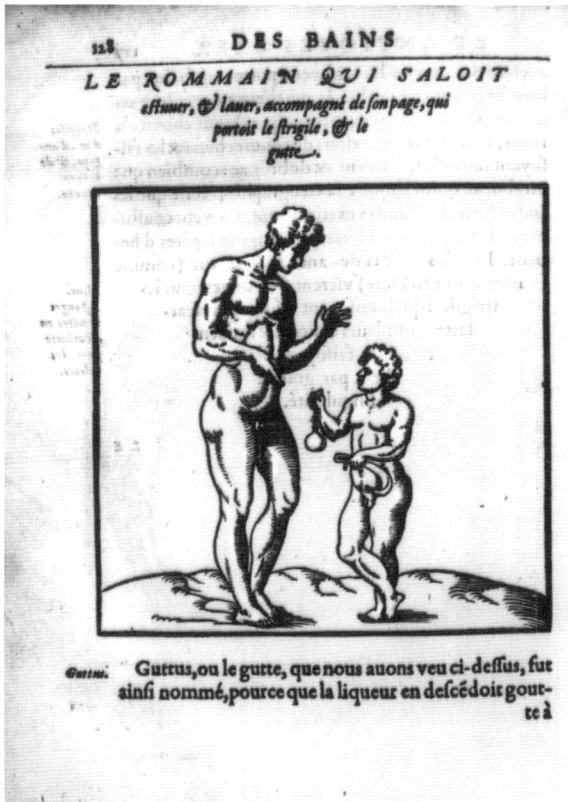

FIGURE FOUR

ancient Romans preferred sponges over strigils, and some had them dyed red for their "delectation."

The next illustration is of a Roman going off to bathe accompanied by his "page," who carries a strigil and oil flacon (figure 4). Both are depicted standing naked on the mound of earth with no buildings or person in sight. The bather's gestures indicate that the Roman is asking his page whether or not he has brought the strigil and oil, and the lad holds them up to show that he has remembered them.

The illustration of the actual bathing is almost overpowered by the architecture of the vaulted Baenum (figure 5). The bather's body seems decades older than the Roman who was heading for the bath in the previous illustration. He has a beard and quite long hair. Indeed, the illustrations are so different that it is possible to question whether they are the work of the same artist.

The final illustration is one to which we have already referred: Dares and

FIGURE FIVE

Entellus boxing, as described in the *Aeniad* (figure 6). They too are depicted on a simple mound of earth with no buildings or other individuals in view. The drawings of the figures is freer than in the illustration of the older Roman bather and his page. It is by the same artist as the one depicting the Roman and his page going off to bathe.

What is to be made of the fact that, in the illustrations involving architecture, the human figures seemed to be submerged by the vaults and columns? The obvious answer to this question merits our utmost attention, namely that there were two artists, with one skilled in the geometry required to show Roman vaulting *and* perspective, and the other excelled at drawing the human figure. Research to shed light on this difference in the illustrations would take us far afield, but it is interesting nonetheless to observe that it remained difficult to privilege both the human figure *and* the architectural setting when the latter was as much a subject of the book as the former. Baths and bathing

ET ANTIQVES EXER.   149
COMBAT DES CESTES ENTRE DARES
& Entellus, selon la description de Virgile.

FIGURE SIX

are obviously complimentary subjects, but for du Choul and his artist(s) not quite complimentary in the ways we might perceive them. After all, the size of the figures in donor portraits, and their relation to the size of their patron saint was still a matter for artists to reckon with,[28] and the perspectival problems depicting monumental Roman baths and individuals bathing in them were not all that different from this tradition.

In conclusion, let us return to the fact that in du Choul the Roman bather is assisted by his page. The debates over the etymology and semantic field of the word page are perhaps less revealing of its meaning for du Choul than the fact that for his age the social terms that were used by ancient writers could still be

---

[28] Wheaton, Robert, "Images of Kinship," *Journal of Family History*, XII (1987): 389–405. There is a tradition that dates at least from the 18th century that attributes these wood-cuts to Bernard Salomon. See Baudrier, as cited in Note 2.

quite easily translated into meaningful social roles in their own mid-sixteenth century. Like the *gens d'armes* for the Roman legionnaire (not *soudar*, the mercenary infantryman) the word page carried with it strong social and gender resonances. In late feudal society the page was still a young man of noble origins who was learning the ways of chivalry, but who was not old enough to be assigned the duties of a valet. If there survives a text from Antiquity that describes with care the hierarchy of duties on the male side of the household, du Choul does not mention it. Instead he chose to privilege this Roman bather-page relationship because it made explicit the bonds between elder and very young males, and possibly still between fathers who exchanged sons so that the youths might learn the ways of war. In describing what he calls the Roman game of Troy, du Choul adds: "we call it *tournay*." In spite of his interest in archeology, and his care in translating terms from Latin and Greek into French, du Choul reveals his need for a familiar and almost chivalric society in the history of ancient Roman bathing and warfare.[29]

At this point it is tempting to scoff at du Choul, and put on our philological spectacles in order to distance ourselves not only from his findings, but his ways of researching and writing. Indeed, du Choul's social and cultural blinders seem so evident that he scarcely deserves mention among the great Humanist scholars who were his contemporaries. Still, his research and books on bathing, military practice, and Roman religion augmented considerably the inventory of verbal and visual and gendered images available to readers in the sixteenth century. Du Choul also bears witness to the civic and philosophical attitudes of the more thoughtful of his class and generation. He turned to history in order to discern the ennobling spaces in which the subject-councilor might speak intimately with his prince. And his search for ways of making the male body more manifestly powerful in his culture rested on some doubt about the innate *virtù* of the French *noblesse*, in comparison to both ancient elite and military males, and contemporary Hapsburg enemies.[30] It may be suggested that beneath political ideology—in this instance classical republicanism as it was reconstructed by Machiavelli—there lay attitudes and feelings that had great cultural and social significance. Were his clerkly, or university trained contemporaries as sensitive as he was to the trees, gardens, hedges, pools, aromas, and oils that the ancients used to enhance their enjoyment of life?[31] Were they as attuned as

[29] *Discourse des Bains . . .*, 153.

[30] No doubt less formally philosophical, du Choul nonetheless shares with Lipsius some of the Roman notions summed up in *contubernium*, especially in the preoccupation with discovering appropriate spaces for teaching the virtuous military life. Mark Morford, *Stoics and Neo Stoics: Rubens and the Circle of Lipsius* (Princeton, Princeton University Press, 1991) 15.

[31] Mercurialis published his *Artis gymnasticae* in 1559, with illustrations that would yield some interesting comparisons with the written descriptions given by himself and du Choul. See Vivian Nutton "Les exercises de la Santé: Hieronymes Mercurialis et la gymnastique médicale" in *Le Corps à la Renaissance*, 295–308.

du Choul to capturing and conveying in words the imagined spaces in which the body and the mind might in unison reach their total fulfillment? The answers to these questions would require yet another paper on the social and cultural dimensions of Humanism.

PART TWO

Politics and the Law

4

Louis XII's Gallican Crisis of 1510–1513

FREDERIC J. BAUMGARTNER

In the era of Louis XII (1498–1515), the French Church was completely in the grips of Gallicanism. It can be defined as the theory that the French Church, of which the king was the head, was free from papal control over the administration of its offices and finances, while it accepted the pope's authority in matters of doctrine and discipline. There were, however, two versions of Gallicanism in the fifteenth century. Royal Gallicanism emphasized the authority of the king in the French Church, especially his right to appoint the occupants of its major offices; ecclesiastical Gallicanism placed that power in the hands of the clergy itself. The two competing theories of Gallicanism battled both the papacy and each other until Louis' bitter dispute with Julius II toward the end of his reign. One result of that affair was a clear victory for royal Gallicanism over both of its competitors in the question of who would control the French Church.

The "Gallican liberties" that the king defended against papal pretensions were left rather vague in the fifteenth century. The first expression of the concept dates to 1407 when Charles VI issued two cornerstone edicts on the relationship between the French Church and the papacy. He declared that the Gallican Church from the time of the conversion of Gaul had always enjoyed certain liberties from papal authority, which the pope of his time was denounced for allegedly violating. In particular, Gallican liberties involved the freedom of France from papal appointive power. The principle of local control over appointments to the French hierarchy was made explicit in the Pragmatic Sanction of 1438, a document drawn up by a national assembly of the French Church and promulgated by Charles VII. Both in the manner of its creation and in its content, it was the quintessential Gallican document, reflecting the idea that a French national council could legislate for the Gallican Church. It expounded the view that the king was able to call such assemblies and issue their decrees in his capacity as head of the French Church.

Also an essential part of the Pragmatic Sanction was the theory of church governance called conciliarism, arising out of the Great Schism and the scandal of the presence of three rival popes in the Church. Several French theologians, especially Jean Gerson and Pierre d'Ailly, had played major roles in formulating the theory in the early fifteenth century. Conciliarism was put into practice at the Council of Constance, not only in resolving the Great Schism but also in proclaiming two major decrees: *Sacrosancta*, declaring that everyone, including the pope, was obliged to obey a general council, and *Frequens*, establishing a timetable for regular meetings of the general council with the purpose of making it an essential part of church governance. In 1431 Pope Martin V called a council for Basel in accordance with *Frequens*. His death shortly after it opened placed Eugenius IV on the throne of St Peter. Far more hostile to the principles of conciliarism, he ordered the meeting moved to Ferrara. A large portion of the members, especially the French, refused to leave Basel and continued their work of reducing papal powers and prerogatives. It was largely these French prelates returned home from Basel who were responsible for the Pragmatic Sanction of Bourges, which put into effect in France the reforms and curbs on papal power expounded at Basel. For the next seventy-five years, Gallicanism and conciliarism were essentially inseparable.

The Pragmatic Sanction espoused in particular ecclesiastical Gallicanism, because its crucial clause returned to the French clergy the power to fill the major benefices (a clerical office with an income attached) of the French Church—the bishoprics and the major monasteries. The pope still had the right to accept or reject the nominees, since he continued to have the power of giving them their bulls of office. Royal Gallicanism, sometimes called *parlementaire* Gallicanism because the Parlement was its outspoken advocate, endorsed the right of the king to fill those benefices. The Pragmatic Sanction returned the naming of bishops and abbots to the cathedral and monastery chapters, the system that the popes had overturned in the previous two centuries. The king's rights in filling the major offices were restricted to the use of "sweet and kind prayers" that the chapters consider the worthy candidates whom he might wish to recommend to them. But when the royal chancellor showed up to promote the king's choice, as happened at Bourges in 1512, there was little question about who would be elected.[1] Last, the Pragmatic eliminated papal taxation on French benefices, especially a tax called the annates, the first year's revenues from a benefice when it was filled. The protection of the wealth of the French Church was an important goal of Gallicanism. The Pragmatic acknowledged that the pope could receive a gift of money from the French clergy but rejected the idea that he had a right to any funds from France.

By 1498 the Pragmatic Sanction had been in effect for sixty years, except for several years when Louis XI abrogated it in hope of currying favor with the pope, especially over the question of French rights in Avignon and the

---

[1]   E. de Ganay, *Un chancelier de France sous Louis XII: Jehan de Ganay* (Paris, 1932), p. 79. For a good summary of the problems of filling major benefices in this era, see R. de Maulde, *Les Origines de la Révolution française au commencement du XVIe siècle* (Paris, 1889), pp. 125–34.

kingdom of Naples. When Rome failed to respond as he wanted, Louis rein-stated it. Nonetheless, he put little stock in the Pragmatic's clauses. He rode roughshod over them by sending names to the chapters and demanding that the clerics elect his candidates. In numerous cases Louis XI simply named the new bishops and abbots, and the pope presented them with their bulls of office.[2]

During the drastic reduction of royal power marking Charles VIII's early years, the chapters reasserted their rights. When a more mature Charles sought to regain control, a bitter confrontation between monarch and churchmen resulted. While ultimate victory for the king was a foregone conclusion, the chapters fought stubbornly, and the decade before 1498 was a period of extraor-dinary confusion in the episcopate, as numerous sees had two candidates, one elected by the chapter and the other named by the king. In several cases there were three candidates, two put forward by factions in the chapter and a third by the king. An example of this occurred in the see of Sarlat in 1493. Of course, the king's choice eventually won the office, because the popes of the era, despite their offical position of hostility to the Pragmatic, which they regarded as a thoroughly schismatic document, usually cooperated with the king by granting the bulls of office to his candidates. No one disputed the fact that the papal approval was necessary for an episcopal or abbatial candidate, regardless of how he might have come to be nominated for the office, to exercise the authority of his office. If it were impossible for the popes to nominate French bishops and abbots, they clearly preferred to allow the kings to exercise the right of nomination instead of the chapters. Even papal approval, however, did not always end the disputes. The chapters and their candidates frequently refused to concede, and the disputes continued for years, with violence and force sometimes involved. The disorder and factionalism in the chapters and papal connivance in support of the monarchy resulted in the subversion of the Pragmatic's principles to the profit of the king.[3]

When Louis XII reached the throne, the good relations he quickly developed with Alexander VI boded ill for the system of chapter elections. Alexander routinely approved the king's candidates, and the chapters found they could not prevent the appointees from taking office. In 1501, Alexander gave Louis' right-hand man, Cardinal Georges d'Amboise, the office of papal legate in France. It gave the cardinal vast power over the French Church, but since it

---

[2] P. Ourliac, "The Concordat of 1472: An Essay on the Relations between Louis XI and Sixtus IV," in P. Lewis, ed., *The Recovery of France in the Fifteenth Century* (London, 1971), pp. 102–84.

[3] As Pierre Imbart de La Tour stated: "From 1483 to 1516 the history of [chapter] elections is to give an account of quarrels." *Les origines de la Réforme*, 3 vols. (Paris, 1905–35), II, 219. See also J. Thomas, *Le Concordat de 1516*, 4 vols. (Paris, 1910), I, 200–269; J. Vidal, "Une Crise épiscopale à Pamiers 1467–1524," *Revue de l'histoire de l'église de France*, 14(1928): 305–64.

was a papal office, it preserved the pretense of papal authority in France. The cardinal combined in himself broad royal and papal authority in the Gallican Church. It was the first and only time a French prelate held so much power.[4]

When word reached Louis in August 1503 that Alexander had died, he and Cardinal d'Amboise were ready for the coming conclave. The election of a French pope, or at least a French partisan among the Italian cardinals, was regarded as crucial to French interests in Italy, especially in the kingdom of Naples. The pope as the feudal lord of that realm invested the king with the power to rule. Investiture had eluded both Charles VIII and Louis XII, despite their victories in Naples. It would put a seal of legitimacy on the Valois right to rule the kingdom, which was becoming more and more urgent because Ferdinand of Aragon, who had been challenging French claims there since 1494, now had a powerful army in southern Italy. At the moment of Alexander's death, a large French force was passing by Rome on its way to Naples to reinforce the army already there. Louis ordered it to halt near Rome in order to influence the upcoming conclave.

Louis XII pulled out all the stops to get Cardinal d'Amboise elected. The king had released Ludovico Sforza's brother, Cardinal Ascanio, from captivity two years earlier, and he accompanied d'Amboise to Rome. There is no direct evidence that his release had followed a promise to vote for d'Amboise in the next conclave, but there were those who believed such a pledge had been required.[5] Louis promised to pay the expenses of the trip to Rome of the Cardinal of Aragon, a brother of the king of Naples, both of whom were in exile in France. The French also counted on the support of the very influential Cardinal Giuliano della Rovere, since he had spent ten years in exile in France because of his fierce opposition to Alexander. Louis also made a secret agreement with Alexander's son, Cesare Borgia, pledging to maintain him in his current possessions in exchange for his support for d'Amboise. Cesare, for his part, held the pledge of the eleven Spanish cardinals to vote for whomever he designated. On the other hand, there were only three other French cardinals besides d'Amboise.[6]

As a result of the large number of cardinals Alexander had created in his reign, there were thirty-seven cardinals at the conclave, the largest number to that time. The Italians numbered twenty-two, just short of the two-thirds needed to elect a new pope, but they were badly divided into factions. The pro-French among them were few, and only two French cardinals were able to

---

[4] Julius II's bull reappointing d'Amboise and describing his powers is in Bibliothèque nationale, Fonds Dupuy 83, fols. 1–9. See also Imbart de La Tour, *Origines*, II, 183–85. The most similar situation was that of Cardinal Wolsey in England.

[5] Francesco Guicciardini, *History of Italy*, 10 vols. (London, 1753–56), III, 104.

[6] Sources for the two papal elections of 1503 include J. Burchard, *Diarium*, 3 vols. (Paris, 1883), II, 245ff; M. Sanuto, *I Diarii*, 53 vols. (Venice, 1879), V, 78ff; L. von Pastor, *History of the Popes from the Close of the Middle Ages*, 40 vols. (St Louis, 1938–53), VI, 185–216.

take part, one being d'Amboise. Nonetheless, Louis left no stone unturned to make his friend pope. As the Venetian ambassador in Rome reported: "The representative of the king of France has received a written instruction from his master to exhort all the cardinals to consult his pleasure and make the cardinal of Rouen Pope. Every possible blandishment, promise, and inducement is employed, together with implied threats against those who may ignore the request."[7] The ambassador went on to say that the Italian cardinals intended to foil Louis by hurrying the conclave without waiting for the French cardinals, but he expected that the French king would use his army in the vicinity of Rome to prevent that from happening. Meanwhile d'Amboise left for Rome on August 28 "with silver à *largesse*" and 200 royal guards.[8]

In spite of all that, d'Amboise's bid was doomed to fail. Cesare Borgia fell ill, preventing him from taking an active part in ensuring that his clients among the cardinals voted for the French candidate. Without his direct involvement, the Spanish cardinals followed the dictates of Isabella and Ferdinand, who made it clear they did not want a French pope and moved Spanish forces into the vicinity of Rome. Neither Ascanio Sforza nor della Rovere were as supportive as the French expected. Della Rovere said that he was going to look after his own interests and would not vote for d'Amboise unless the Frenchman already had enough votes to win. Before it became clear to d'Amboise that della Rovere was working against him, della Rovere persuaded him to order the French troops to move from Rome.[9]

Six days after d'Amboise reached Rome, the conclave opened in the Vatican Palace. From the first vote it was clear that the conclave was stalemated. D'Amboise, like the other leading candidates, looked for a cardinal both for whom he could vote and who was not likely to live very long. A Venetian reported: "When the Cardinal of Rouen saw that he could not be elected, he thought that if he could not be pope himself, he had better avoid the humiliation of having one elected of whom he disapproved. So . . . he went with the stream and sought the glory of making it appear that the pope was his choice."[10] The pope-makers settled on Francesco Piccolimini, the nephew of Pius II, who was sixty-four years of age, in poor health, and as neutral a candidate as could be had. He was acclaimed pope on September 22.

Pius III had been elected largely because the other candidates did not expect him to reign long. He greatly exceeded their expectations. Worn out by the lengthy coronation ceremonies, he died only twenty-six days after his election. The cardinals had hardly begun to disperse when Pius died, and all were able to

---

7 A. Giustinian, *Dispacci*, ed. by P. Villari, 3 vols. (Florence, 1876), II, 175–77.

8 Jean d'Auton, *Chroniques de Louis XII*, 4 vols. (Paris, 1889–95), III, 202; BN, Fonds français 25718, fol. 90.

9 Guicciardini, *History of Italy*, III, 239; d'Auton, *Chroniques*, III, 250; Giustinian, *Dispacci*, II, 181.

10 Giustinian, *Dispacci*, II, 200–01; Pastor, *History of the Popes*, VI, 195n.

return to Rome for the new election. However, della Rovere had already secured the votes needed, whether by promises and persuasion or outright bribery. In the same evening as the conclave opened on October 31, della Rovere was acclaimed pope, the shortest conclave ever under the procedures adopted in the twelfth century and still today largely in effect. He took the name Julius II, more in reference to Julius Caesar, it has been argued, than to the obscure Julius I. The new pope was sixty years old but in excellent health, and his energy and activity were those of a much younger man. Armed with a powerful will and a fierce temper, he was a formidable opponent, especially since his diplomatic skills matched his determination to dominate.

The French thought Julius was acceptable, because they expected the ten years he had spent in France had made him a French partisan. Louis' special envoy who arrived in Rome in April 1505 to render his obedience told Julius that the king had felt great joy and hope when his friend of so many years became pontiff.[11] Julius II appeared very accommodating to the French in the first several years of his pontificate, but in fact, from the moment Julius became pope, he was scheming about how to drive the French out of his homeland. Largely because the papal treasury was empty from Alexander's mismanagement, Julius could not move quickly against the French, but he bided his time and worked to refill his treasury and reestablish his control over the Papal States before he confronted the French. Being the shrewd diplomat that he was, he was able even to get the French to cooperate in several of his schemes against other powers in Italy, in particular Venice. But soon enough it was the turn of the French and Louis XII to feel the sting of the powerful mind and will of Julius II, *Papa Terribilis*.

There were several causes for the violent confrontation between pope and king. One was the pope's refusal to grant the cardinal's red hat to several French prelates to whom Louis believed it had been promised. When Julius named twelve new cardinals in early 1510, none were Frenchmen. It is clear that Julius was determined to prevent the election of a French pope after his death by naming cardinals hostile to France. In turn Louis infuriated Julius by proceeding to make appointments to church benefices in Milan without papal approval. Then there was the matter of the League of Cambrai, which Louis XII and several other princes had organized to help the pope recover a number of places in the Romagna occupied by Venice. Louis personally led his army to victory over Venice at Agnadello in 1509, allowing the pope to recover his cities. That done, Julius unilaterally made peace with Venice. Louis, who after twelve years of dealing with the Italians should have known better, was taken by surprise. He lamented that the pope had stuck a dagger in his heart by his peace with Venice. The most important cause of the animosity between king and pope was Julius' zeal to free Italy of the barbarians—by whom he meant all

---

[11] K. Setton, *The Papacy and The Levant*, 3 vols. (Philadelphia, 1976–84), III, 35.

non-Italians—starting with the French because they controlled more of Italy than the others. When Georges d'Amboise died in May 1510, the one person capable of both devising a workable strategy against Julius and mediating between him and Louis was removed from the scene.

By early 1510, Julius was challenging Louis on many fronts. In June, he told the Venetians: "These French are trying to reduce me to being nothing but their king's chaplain; but I mean to be pope, as they will find out." A month later he told the French ambassador: "I look upon your king as my personal enemy and do not wish to hear anything more."[13] He then ordered the ambassador out of Rome. Meanwhile, Julius had arrested Cardinal François de Clermont, archbishop of Auch, for attempting to leave Rome without his permission.[14] At the same time he arranged to have 10,000 Swiss mercenaries assemble on the frontier with Milan. He provided money and encouragement to the Fregosi to lead a rebellion in Genoa, which France then controlled. From France's point of view the most annoying of Julius' actions was his mistreatment of Alfonso d'Este, Duke of Ferrara, Louis' firmest ally in Italy. When Julius excommunicated the duke for allegedly having plotted to depose him and place d'Amboise on the papal throne, it was a serious challenge to Louis' ability to protect his friends.[15]

Niccolo Machiavelli, who came to France in June 1510 in hope of persuading Louis to stop pressing Florence to declare against the pope, has a good account of Louis' response to all these provocations. Machiavelli felt that after d'Amboise's death Louis was indecisive over how to respond to the pope. One day he was ready to lead an army to Rome and depose Julius; the next he was resolved to stay in France and depose the pope through the structures of the Church. Louis' new right-hand man, Florimond Robertet, wrote to the French ambassador at Rome that the pope's behavior was causing the king "horrible pain."[16]

By early summer of 1510, Louis had decided to confront Julius II with a national synod of the French clergy.[17] In June he sent Robertet to Lyon to preside over an assembly of theologians and jurists, who set out the principles of Gallicanism and the papal violations of them. A month later, he convoked an assembly of the French clergy to meet at Orléans in September.[18] He gave as the

[12] Guicciardini, History of Italy, V, 53–54; Pastor, History of the Popes, VI, 323.

[13] Quoted in Pastor, History of the Popes, VI, 326–27.

[14] A. Renaudet, Le concile gallican de Pise–Milan: Documents florentins (Paris, 1922), pp. 2–3.

[15] Calendar of State Papers Existing in the Archives of Venice and Northern Italy, ed. R. Brown (reprint Nendeln, Liechtenstein, 1967), II, 33; Sanuto, Diarii, XI, 108–439, passim.

[16] P. Villari, The Life and Times of Niccolò Machiavelli, 2 vols. (reprint New York, 1968), I, 509–10; Renaudet, Le concile gallican, pp. 4–6; Maulde, Diplomatie, III, 457.

[17] O. de La Brosse, Le Pape et le Concile (Paris, 1965), pp. 51–55; La Brosse, Latran V et Trente (Paris, 1975), 36–38.

[18] BN, Fonds latin 1559, fol. 2.

reason for the convocation only his desire to communicate with his clergy, but two weeks later he issued a manifesto explaining that he was assembling the clergy in order to get its advice on how to deal with the hostile and provocative policy of the pope. He forbade the clergy from sending money to Rome or seeking benefices from the pope. While Louis sought papal bulls for his nominee to fill the vacancy at Rouen created by d'Amboise's death, he also told his court that if the pope refused them, he would seat the new archbishop anyway. The king later transferred the assembly site to Tours, where the deputies of the clergy gathered on September 13. Five archbishops, fifty-seven bishops, some fifty theologians and representatives of the universities, and the presidents of four parlements made up the assembly.[19]

A committee of theologians from the University of Paris was commissioned to draw up a document to present to the assembly. On September 15, Chancellor Ganay formally opened the meeting by presenting its report. It was largely a series of questions about the pope's authority in Church and state.[20] Could the pope declare war on a Christian prince when the papal lands or the faith were not under attack? Could the prince defend himself in such an event? In that situation, could the prince withdraw his obedience from the papacy; and if he could, how was the national church to be governed? In a clear reference to the duke of Ferrara, the prelates were asked whether a Christian prince could go to the aid of an ally whom the pope had unjustly attacked. The next day Louis arrived in Tours and presided over the assembly while Ganay addressed it in his name. The chancellor announced that the meeting had three matters before it—the quarrel with the papacy, the disorder in the benefices in the French Church, and church reform in general—but the first had priority. He declared that Pope Julius was guilty of perfidy in his handling of the League of Cambrai and for urging the king of England to assert his claim to France. The French had intercepted papal letters to Henry VIII in July prompting him to take that step.[21] Other charges included his illegal financial demands on the French clergy and his failure to keep the oath taken at his election to call a general council in two years.[22]

The French clergy quickly agreed that the king ought to ask the pope to

[19] The number of attendees varies from source to source. These are given in a letter to Margaret of Austria from her ambassador in France. *Lettres du Roy Louis XII et du Cardinal d'Amboise*, 4 vols. (Brussels, 1712), II, 29. See also Sanuto, *Diarii*, X, 113–297 passim; and Renaudet, *Le concile gallican*, pp. 6–7.

[20] A record of the proceedings at Tours is in BN, Fonds Latin 1559. See also Ganay, *Un chancelier*, p. 6ff; and Renaudet, *Préréforme et Humanisme à Paris pendant les premières guerres d'Italie* (Paris, 1953).

[21] Calendar of State Papers Venice, II, 33–36; Calendar of State Papers Spain, II, 53.

[22] In 1510–11 France provided 10,716 ducats to the papal treasury; in 1511–12 the sum dropped to 2,163. Imbart de La Tour, *Origines*, II, 35n. For W. Ullman, "Julius II and the Schismatic Cardinals," *Studies in Church History*, 9 (1972): 177–93, Julius' failure to fulfill his oath was the strongest justification for the Council of Pisa.

convoke a general council and tell him in a spirit of fraternal charity to cease his warmongering. If he did not, then the king would be justified in using force against him and withdrawing from obedience. The monarch should then appoint a patriarch for the Gallican Church and request the emperor to call a general council to depose the pope. The clergy also voted to provide Louis with a *décime* of 300,000 *livres*, 60,000 of which were to go for the expenses of the general council. The interesting point about the *décime* of 1510 was that it was directed to the general expenses of the king rather than for a war or a phantom crusade, as all previous ones had been. It was an important step in establishing the *décime* as an annual levy on the clergy, as happened under Francis I. On September 30, the clergy dispersed without having anything further to say on the reform of the Church. The gathering agreed to meet again in the spring. Louis' anger at the pope was revealed in the letter he wrote the next day to Julius demanding a general council. The pope's reply was curt: he did not take orders from princes in regard to the Church and would summon a council when his conscience told him to do it.[23]

On the diplomatic front Louis' position was being seriously undermined, although he did not realize it for some time to come. He remained convinced that Ferdinand was still his staunch ally. The wily Aragonese was doing his best to "behave as though the greatest friendship prevailed between him and the king of France," but his diplomats to England, the pope, and the emperor were directed to arrange an anti-French league. His ambassador in England was told to go through Queen Catherine, Ferdinand's daughter, if Henry was not receptive, and if she were not willing to cooperate, to use her confessor to persuade her to influence her husband.[24]

With Ferdinand's ambassador in Rome making clear his eagerness to break with France, Julius became much more aggressive. He ordered his army into action against Ferrara, and occupied several towns in the duchy in early September 1510. A small Spanish force joined the papal army as it prepared to invest Ferrara, although Ferdinand argued that he was simply fulfilling his feudal obligation to his suzerain in Naples. Louis in turn sent 3,500 men to help Ferrara. Julius had gone to Bologna to be closer to his army, and Charles d'Amboise, Louis' governor in Milan, marched there with a potent force. When he appeared before the walls, Julius excommunicated him and his men. The wielding of that spiritual weapon was Julius' major advantage. D'Amboise lost his nerve, withdrew his forces, and began to negotiate. Negotiations went nowhere, but the French had lost valuable time.[25]

Respect for the pope as the head of the Church and fear of his spiritual power were great obstacles for Louis in his struggle with Julius. Ferdinand wrote to his ambassador in England: "Should the King of France really depose the Pope,

23 *Lettres de Louis XII*, II, 48.
24 Calendar of State Papers Spain, II, 46, 52.
25 Sanuto, *Diarii*, XI, 250ff; J. Tailhé, *Histoire de Louis XII*, 3 vols. (Paris, 1755), II, 250.

such an insult to all Christian peoples and to all the princes of Christendom would be even a greater offence than an attack on their dominions, and they would be forced to oppose France with all their might."[26] Julius' sense of the immunity of the papal person from attack, along with his impetuous nature, helps to explain why he went in person to command his forces at the siege of Mirandola, regarded as the key to Ferrara. He reached Mirandola in early January 1511 and took an active part in the conduct of the siege. He took up quarters so close to the walls that enemy shot hit his rooms several times, once killing two of his servants. When the city agreed to surrender at the end of January, Julius, wearing armor and carrying a weapon, refused to wait for the gate to be opened and entered the city with his troops through a breach. He was ready to give the city over to sack but was dissuaded by his aides, who emphasized the scandal it would have caused. Guicciardini commented that it was a notable thing that the king of France, "of an age not yet past its vigor and in a good state of health [a questionable assertion] trained from his youth in handling arms should at present be taking his repose, . . . and on the other side to see the highest priest, Vicar of Christ on Earth, old and infirm, now involved in person in waging a war stirred up by him against Christians . . . as leader of soldiers he exposed himself to hardships and perils, retaining nothing of the pontiff but the name and the garb."[27]

Meanwhile, Louis had recalled the Gallican national synod, which met again at Lyon in April 1511. He invited the clergy of Flanders to attend, but Maximilian refused to allow them to go. The convocation at Lyon passed several edicts on Church reform and reaffirmed the decrees on canonical elections of the Council of Basel. It agreed to make all decisions passed by a council called to counter Julius binding on the French Church.[28] Louis' scheme of holding a council to depose Julius had received a major boost in December 1510 when five cardinals—two French, two Spaniards, and one Italian—fled to Milan. These five, and four more, issued an invitation on May 16, 1511 in the name of the emperor and the king of France to the princes of Europe to attend a council and send their clergy. Two more cardinals announced their intention to attend the council. It was scheduled to begin on September 1, 1511, in Pisa, which had been under the control of Florence since 1507. Louis had pushed Florence hard into agreeing to hold the council in Pisa. The invitation included a sharp attack on Julius II, whom it accused of causing great scandal in the Church. Nonetheless, it also invited him to attend.[29] Placards with the call

[26] Calendar of State Papers Spain, II, 52.

[27] History of Italy, V, 149. For the siege see also Pastor, History of the Popes, VI, 340–42; Sanuto, Diarii, XI, 712–783, passim. Believing that Julius was dying in late 1511, Louis was prepared to send a large sum of money to Rome to win the election of Cardinal Briçonnet as pope.

[28] BN, Fonds latin 1559, fols. 20–26; Lettres de Louis XII, II, 45, 142. See also Imbart de La Tour, Origines, II, 145–46; and La Brosse, Le Pape et le Concile, pp. 54–66.

[29] The invitation to Charles of Habsburg is in Lettres de Louis XII, II, 235–41. See also

for the council were placed across Europe; Julius saw one on the cathedral door in Ravenna. He responded by calling his own council for Rome the following spring. Those who attended the French council, "schismatics already separated from the flock," were threatened with excommunication, and the place where it was held, put under interdict.[30]

Louis was eager to ensure that his people were solidly behind the two-fold military and spiritual attack on the pope. To attack the pope in either fashion was terrifying to the people of Christendom, since it posed a very real threat to their eternal salvation. Charles d'Amboise was reported to have begged papal forgiveness as he lay dying, and Queen Anne was so opposed to any rupture with the papacy that she, as the duchess of Brittany, refused to allow the archbishop of Nantes, Cardinal Guibé, to go to Pisa. In fact, she sent him to Rome for Julius' council. Louis retaliated by seizing his episcopal revenues, but Julius then gave him the income from Avignon.[31] Louis was also aware of his people's resistance to more taxes, which were necessary if war with Julius' alliance occurred.

The French people, therefore, had to be convinced of the righteousness of Louis' case against the pope. Royal propaganda to persuade the broad public was spread through placards, pamphlets, poetry, and plays. One placard carried a caricature of the pope, surrounded by corpses and his flag lying on the ground. The papal throne is empty, over which France is keeping guard.[32] A group of poets, many in the pay of the king, who included Jean Lemaire de Belges, Jean d'Auton, Guillaume Crétin, and Jean Bouchet, produced poems lambasting Julius and praising Louis as the defender of the Church.[33] But the plays reached the largest number of people. There was a group of authors in place, the Basoche, who could be called upon to write the kind of satirical play desired. The best of them, Pierre Gringore, put himself completely to royal service, probably at Louis' request, but there is no evidence he was on Louis' payroll.[34] Gringore's first anti-Julius piece was a poem, "La chasse du cerf des cerfs," printed at the beginning of 1511. The title is a parody on the papal title

BN, Fonds Dupuy 85, fols. 28–29; Sanuto, Diarii, XII, 249–54; Renaudet, Le concile gallican, pp. 18–19.

[30] Guicciardini, History of Italy, V, 248–51; Sanuto, Diarii, XI, 203–223; Pastor, History of the Popes, VI, 352–54. L. Landucci, A Florentine Diary from 1450 to 1516, trans. A. De Rosen Jervis (Freeport, New York, 1971), pp. 254–47, indicates that Florence was under interdict for several months.

[31] Sanuto, Diarii, XII, 56; E. Gabory, Anne de Bretagne Duchesse et Reine (Paris, 1941), pp. 213–14. The Breton Church was still autonomous in this era.

[32] Maulde, Origines, p. 273. Maulde indicated that several such placards were in the Hermitage Museum in St Petersburg.

[33] J. Britnell, Jean Bouchet (Edinburgh, 1986), pp. 160–71.

[34] Gringore did receive money from the city of Paris on several occasions for his plays and poems. E. Picot, Recueil des sotties, 3 vols. (Paris, 1909–12), II, 111. See also the introduction to Gringore, Oeuvres complètes, ed. by C. d'Hericault et al., 2 vols. (Paris, 1858–77).

of "Servant of the Servants of God." Gringore quickly followed it with *L'Espoir de la paix*, which received the royal privilege-to-print on February 8, 1511. Less cleverly satirical and more bluntly hostile to Julius, the piece is largely a history of the papacy. Gringore acknowledged that there had been a number of bad popes, but Julius clearly was the worst. Louis XII must serve as the scourge of God against him.

The most important of Gringore's attacks against Julius was the *sottie* (farce), "Le jeu du Prince des sotz."[35] It was performed at Les Halles, the main market-place in Paris, on Mardi gras in 1512. Highly praised as one of the best medieval plays for its drama and eloquence, it combined a cutting attack on Julius with satirical asides on nearly all elements of society. Louis XII is the one person who escapes unscathed. His goodness and kindness toward his people are strongly portrayed. The war against the pope is fully justified, but Gringore is very sympathetic toward those who cringe at a violent confrontation with the pope. The paradox of defying the bad pope while loving the head of the Church is resolved for Gringore by having Julius appear in disguise in the play, showing that he is a wolf in sheep's skin.

There were also several serious works published to justify Louis' policy. Among them the most powerful was Jean Lemaire de Belges' *Le Traicté de la difference des schismes et des conciles de l'église*, which was printed in May 1511.[36] After giving a long history of both church councils and schisms, Lemaire concluded that the meeting called for Pisa was a true council, and the papacy had caused most schisms. The author had strong words in favor of the Prag-matic Sanction as vital for the "great good honor and profit of our Christian religion." Julius was accused of planning his own schism through the council he called. Lemaire concluded that Louis would triumph and bring peace to the Church and Christian princes and then lead them in a great crusade to exter-minate the Muslims.

Rome, of course, was not silent in the face of these Gallican salvos. Tommaso di Vio, general of the Dominicans, the Cardinal Cajetan of later Reformation controversies, wrote a work in late 1511, which condemned any council not called by the pope, even those called in an emergency situation, as was claimed for Louis' Council of Pisa. The leaders of the council sent the book for rebuttal to the faculty of theology of Paris, always a stronghold of conciliarism, sup-ported by a letter from the king. Uncertainty about the validity of Louis' council made the theologians of Paris reluctant to take on the task. Louis had to write to the faculty of theology on February 19, 1512, insisting that a

---

35 In Picot, *Recueil des sotties*, II, 132–73.
36 In J. Lemaire de Belges, *Oeuvres*, ed. by J. Stecher (Geneva, 1969), III, 231–359. For a lengthy analysis of the work, see J. Britnell, "The Antipapalism of Jean Lemaire de Belges' *Le Traicté de la difference des schismes et des conciles de l'église*," *Sixteenth Century Journal*, 24(1993): 783–800.

refutation be produced.[37] The task was given to Jacques Almain, who, although he had just received his doctorate in theology, already had a reputation as a conciliarist and a good theologian. He quickly produced the *Tractatus de auctoritate Ecclesiae et Conciliorum generalium* (1512). It was published under his own name rather than in the name of the faculty of theology, which supports the view that the faculty was badly divided on the issue of the Council of Pisa. And in fact, a near majority of the faculty favored telling the king in January 1513, that the Council of Pisa was potentially schismatic. Almain's principal point was that the power given to the pope was not absolute; if the pope fell into heresy or open sin, the secular authorities had an obligation to oversee the Church until he repented. A Christian king had the right to assemble a council in a suitable place and invite the other national churches to send delegates. Even if few churches were represented, it would still be a legitimate council. Almain also argued that papal authority did not extend to the civil realm except through the force of moral persuasion.[38] The effectiveness of this propaganda is difficult to ascertain except in so far as the French people accepted the higher taxes without rebelling. There were few defections in France despite the pope's willingness to wield the most powerful spiritual weapons in his arsenal—interdict and excommunication.

The council called for Pisa, however, proved to be a bitter disappointment for Louis. The Florentine government objected strenuously, and the people of Pisa, a place that had been chosen largely because it was close enough to Rome to annoy Julius, refused to extend any hospitality. Maximilian did not approve of Pisa, as he wanted a site in the imperial lands of north Italy. Louis hoped for prelates to come from the Empire, but the emperor would not allow any from the Low Countries to attend, since only the pope could call a council.[39] The French king had no illusions that the Spanish and English clergy would appear, but many of the French prelates evaded going as well.

After a long delay to assemble a strong French escort for the clergy going to Pisa, the council formally opened on November 1 with only four cardinals, two archbishops, sixteen bishops, and a small group of abbots and theologians;

---

[37] Louis's letter is in BN, Fonds latin 16576, fol. 34. The theology faculty's discussions are given in J. Clerval, ed., *Registre des procès-verbaux de la faculté de théologie 1505–1523* (Paris, 1917), pp. 111–23. See also J. Farge, *Orthodoxy and Reform in Early Reformation France: The Faculty of Theology of Paris, 1500–1543* (Leiden, 1985), pp. 222–25.

[38] La Brosse, *Le Pape et le Concile*, pp. 147–210; F. Oakley, "Almain and Major: Conciliar Theory on the Eve of the Reformation," *American Historical Review*, 70 (1965): 673–690; Oakley, "Conciliarism in the Sixteenth Century: Jacques Almain Again," *Archiv für Reformationsgeschichte*, 68 (1977): 111–31. John Major's conciliarist work was written in the context of Pisa, but first published in 1518. The political theory found in their works is regarded as important to the development of modern political theory as "the background of constitutionalism." See Q. Skinner, *The foundations of modern political thought*, 2 vols. (Cambridge, 1978), II, 117–23.

[39] *Lettres de Louis XII*, II, 421–22.

nearly all of those attending were French.[40] The Pisans, who were about to suffer an interdict for a decision over which they had no control, were decidedly unfriendly. The council members were not allowed to use the cathedral of Pisa or borrow the vestments of the local clergy for their opening Mass. Cardinal Carvajal, a Spaniard, was elected president of the council. The members declared theirs to be the only valid council and denounced as schismatic the one that Julius, "a pope who is a friend of violence," was planning for Rome. Before the council could proceed far in its agenda, a violent confrontation between French soldiers of the prelates' escort and Pisans revealed the hostility of the townspeople. On November 12, the council leaders agreed to go to Milan, as Louis had promised Machiavelli they would after several face-saving sessions in Pisa. Their reception in Milan, despite being under French control, was hardly better.[41]

The council resumed its business in January with a small increase in attendance. It was largely concerned with denouncing Julius and the council he was organizing. When the news of the crushing French victory at Ravenna in April 1512 reached Pisa, the anti-Julius council quickly voted to depose the pope. It called on the clergy, princes, universities, and people of Christendom no longer to obey Pope Julius, "because he is a disturber of the peace and an obstinate and daring author of schism."[42] They had for some time been debating whom they would elect as pope in his place; Louis XII preferred Carvajal.

The harsh words and schemes had no effect, because the French army, badly over-extended in Italy and deprived of its brilliant young commander Gaston de Foix when he was killed at Ravenna, could not hold its gains. By June, it was in full retreat across northern Italy, abandoning Milan and Genoa. The council fled with it to Lyon. On July 20, 1512, what was left of the council agreed to grant Louis a *décime* of 300,000 livres from the French clergy.[43] It then faded away.

By the end of of 1512, Julius II was victorious on both the political and the spiritual fronts. His council, the Fifth Lateran, attracted representation from across Europe except France, although its achievements were limited. The collapse of the Council of Pisa revealed what observers had been arguing all along: a successful anti-Julius council was completely dependent on French military success. As Louis' military and diplomatic advantages eroded, Julius regained his stride after the defeat at Ravenna and resumed his aggressive position toward France. An alliance encompassing the papacy, Spain, and Venice was signed, which committed its members to defending the Papal States

---

[40] On the Council of Pisa, see Renaudet, *Le concile gallican*, especially pp. 529–57; and L. Sandret, "Le Concile de Pise," *Revue des questions historiques*, 34 (1883): 425–56. In July 1511, Louis had delegated twenty-four bishops to go to Pisa. Renaudet, p. 71.

[41] Renaudet, *Le concile gallican*, pp. 494–512.

[42] Quoted by Sandret, "Le concile de Pise," p. 451.

[43] Maulde, *Origines*, p. 325n.

and recovering Bologna for the pope. Ferdinand's efforts to include his son-in-law, Henry VIII, paid off when the ambassadors of the two kings signed a separate treaty directed specifically against France. They declared that since appeals to Louis XII failed to move him, they were now obliged to defend the Church. The signatories agreed to oppose the "schismatic" council at Pisa and support the one the pope had convoked. These two treaties created the Holy League. The Swiss were not formally members, but they acted in concert with it. Maximilian did not join because he was angry at Venice, despite intense diplomatic pressure from the members.[44]

With both England and Spain rushing preparations to invade France, Louis chose to try to negotiate with Julius. Despite all of the assurances of his prelates and theologians, the king harbored deep concerns about what the conflict with the irascible old pope meant for his soul and those of his people. Queen Anne continued to press Louis to make peace with the papacy to prevent further damage to the Church. He sent an envoy to Rome whom Julius, pushed by the cardinals, agreed to receive, but he told the Venetian ambassador that he only intended to fool the French. Encouraged by the news that the French position was much weaker than could have been imagined right after Ravenna, he redoubled his labors at getting the Swiss and the emperor involved against Louis. A month after the Battle of Ravenna, the pope's spirits had risen to the point that he said he expected soon to go to Paris and place the French crown on the head of the king of England. He had already prepared a secret bull depriving Louis of his title as king of France and giving Henry the rule of France if he invaded that realm.[45] In July 1512, the pope proclaimed the deprivation in a meeting of cardinals, although Henry VIII still had to conquer France to win papal investiture with the French crown.[46]

Louis continued to receive bad news: Maximilian finally had committed himself to the anti-French alliance. On November 19, 1512 a treaty between the emperor and the members of the Holy League was proclaimed at Rome. France would be nearly dismembered: England would take Gascony, Guyenne, and Normandy; Maximilian would recover Picardy and Burgundy; the pope would do with Provence as he pleased; and Dauphiné and Lyon would be divided between pope and emperor. The allied forces would subsist by foraging in France and "do the schismatical French as much harm as possible." The signatories of the treaty were at liberty to go beyond the listed appropriations to destroy or conquer France entirely, "no matter however long the war may last." Julius was optimistic enough about the success of the war against France to include a clause calling for the conquest of the Ottoman Empire after it was

---

44 Calendar of State Papers Spain, II, 57–59.
45 Sanuto, Diarii, XIV, 185, 202; Bridge, History of France, IV, 161.
46 BN, Fonds Baluze 14, fol. 159. See also D. Chambers, Cardinal Bainbridge in the Court of Rome, 1509–1514 (Oxford, 1965), pp. 38–39.

over. In December 1512, the Lateran Council approved a bull placing France under interdict.[47]

Yet, not all was lost for France. Louis was able to reach an agreement with Venice in March 1513. Only five days later, ambassadors for Louis and Ferdinand put together a truce of one year's duration. Although Henry refused to be bound by it, the truce did give Louis some breathing space.[48] The event that most reduced the pressure on the king of France was the death of Julius II on February 21, 1513. In the last days of his reign he had refused to accept ambassadors from Louis unless the king handed over the prelates associated with the Council of Pisa for punishment, although he did receive a special envoy from Queen Anne.[49] At the conclave for the papal election, the Breton Cardinal Guibé was only the French cardinal present among the twenty-five who participated, but the results were well received at the French court. On March 11, after a conclave of a week, Cardinal Giovanni de Medici, the second son of Lorenzo the Magnificent, was elected Pope Leo X.[50] The French were euphoric when the news reached Blois three days and sixteen hours later. Since a Florentine courier brought the news, the ambassador from Florence had the honor of announcing it to the king and queen. They received it "with such obvious pleasure that it was plain no other selection could have been more pleasing to them. . . . The king repeatedly said, 'He is someone to my taste, because he is a good man; from someone good only good can be expected.' "[51] Nonetheless, he could not be regarded as an automatic friend of France. He belonged to a family that the French had helped to oust from power in Florence, and he had been held captive by French troops for several months after the Battle of Ravenna. However, his more pacific nature allowed him to be more conciliatory to Louis than Julius could ever have been.

But the naturally cautious Leo was slow to offer an olive branch to Louis. Before any negotiations could begin between them, France suffered an invasion of Picardy by Henry VIII, which resulted in the loss of Tournai, and a Swiss siege of Dijon, which was lifted only upon the pledge of a huge bribe. Meanwhile, the new pope gave signals that he was ready to make peace with the French king. He did not celebrate several French defeats in early 1513 and was quick to accept the submission in June 1513 of two of the cardinals involved in the Council of Pisa. By July pope and king had exchanged envoys (Louis' was Claude de Seyssel), but a successful conclusion to the schism eluded the diplo-

---

[47] La Brosse, *Latran V*, pp. 54, 416.

[48] Calendar of State Papers Spain, II, 79–105; Le Glay, *Négociations*, I, 513; Sanuto, *Diarii*, XVI, 119–23; Guicciardini, *History of Italy*, VI, 95–96; Archives Nationales, Fonds KK 1639, fol. 36.

[49] Sanuto, *Diarii*, XV, 557; Guicciardini, *History of Italy*, VI, 108–09.

[50] Sanuto, *Diarii*, XVI, 26–29; *Lettres de Louis XII*, IV, 63–97; Chambers, *Cardinal Bainbridge*, pp. 41–45. Bainbridge was the first English cardinal to attend a conclave since 1370.

[51] Sanuto, *Diarii*, XVI, 133–34.

mats as long as Louis refused to repudiate his council. Louis' reluctance to make the humiliating concession that the council had been schismatic delayed a final resolution until Girolamo Aleandro, an Italian humanist serving as rector of the University of Paris, who had been one of the most outspoken advocates of Louis' right to call a council, declared that it had been illegal.[52] In late October, the king signed a statement drawn up at Rome repudiating the Council of Pisa and recognizing the Council of the Lateran. Leo accepted a clause stating that Louis had never been included in the excommunication Julius II had issued against supporters of the false council. On December 19, 1513, Seyssel presented the signed document to the pope, while ten French churchmen who had been at Pisa requested absolution for themselves and their absent colleagues.[53]

In accepting the decrees of the Council of the Lateran, Louis agreed to its denunciation of the Pragmatic Sanction. At the fourth session of the council, its members had approved Julius' declaration that the Pragmatic Sanction was offensive to God, pernicious to the Church, and null and void. Two sessions later, the council again had denounced the Pragmatic Sanction specifically and Gallicanism in general.[54] Thus, Louis made the formal first move toward its replacement. Discussions took place in Rome about replacing it, but Leo's claim that the pope had the power to fill all major French benefices prevented a solution before Louis' death. The pope was far more willing to compromise after Francis I's great victory at Marignano in 1515, which led to the Concordat of Bologna of the next year.[55]

The failure of Louis' Council of Pisa was also a devastating blow to the theory of conciliarism. Its existence had been predicated on the theory that the Catholic princes, or at least the Holy Roman Emperor, had the right to convoke a council without the consent of the pope. When Maximilian refused to send his clergy to Pisa but did dispatch them to Rome, he signalled his rejection of the theory. It was harmed even more by the failure of the Council of Pisa to accomplish anything at all, and Louis' denunciation of it as a price of reconciliation with the papacy was the final blow. Francis Oakley has written: "The mainstream of Conciliar thought . . . was still flowing strong on the very eve of the Reformation itself;"[56] but largely because of the failure of Louis XII and his council, it had nearly dried up when the Reformation did begin. The Lutherans and some Catholics did try to resuscitate it after 1517, but there was no life in the theory by then. France had always been the mainstay of conciliarism.

---

[52] According to Aleandro's letter of February 1512, to Erasmus, he had been chosen to represent the university at the Council of Pisa. R. Mynors, et al., eds., *The Collected Works of Erasmus* (Toronto, 1975), II, 218. Aleandro resigned the post only three days later.

[53] Dumont, *Corps diplomatique*, IV, 175; Pastor, *History of the Popes*, VII, 55–72.

[54] The decree is in La Brosse, *Latran V*, pp. 97–98.

[55] Thomas, *Le Concordat de 1516*, I, 289–95.

[56] Oakley, "Almain Again," p. 132.

When the French rejected it, there was little chance it would take root again elsewhere, although ideas derived from it would flicker through the resistance theory of the later sixteenth century.[57]

Louis XII's feud with the papacy by no means destroyed Gallicanism, but it was changed substantially. The Pragmatic Sanction had been largely a product of ecclesiastical Gallicanism: both had developed out of the principle that the clergy, through its representatives, had a superior right to direct the affairs of the Church over pope and king. By forcing the French king to negotiate with the papacy, Louis' quarrel with Julius II opened the way for the Concordat of Bologna, which was the official repudiation of that principle and both its manifestations. True, there was strong opposition to the Concordat for a time after 1516 from the University of Paris, always a stronghold of ecclesiastical Gallicanism, and from the Parlement of Paris, because the magistrates felt it gave away too much to the papacy. Expressions of opposition lingered through the sixteenth century. Nonetheless, the events of 1510–1513 allowed royal Gallicanism to emerge victorious and hold sway until 1789. As for Louis XII, the principal legacy of his feud with Julius II was the creation of an image of the quintessential Gallican king, who had braved papal excommunication to protect the rights and liberties of the French Church.

[57] J. H. M. Salmon, "An alternative theory of popular resistance: Buchanan, Rossaeus, and Locke," *Renaissance and Revolt* (Cambridge, 1987), 136–54.

5

A Day in the Life of the Third Estate: Blois, 26th December 1576

M. GREENGRASS

Historians of English Parliaments in the sixteenth and seventeenth centuries have developed a distinctive way of writing the political history of the English state.* The sophisticated analysis of the Parliaments of the 1620s by Lord Russell is one distinguished example in a tradition stretching back to Sir John Neale.[1] Its exponents recreate each nuance of debate, each half-remembered institutional precedent. They evoke the memories of past political successes and failures, the personal and corporate ambitions of the men of business as well as the sometimes ill-expressed anxieties of a disparate squirarchy. Hardly a stone on the High Road to the English civil war has been left unturned.

Across the Channel there is no such equivalent historical tradition. Close political analysis—of the kind which seeks to rekindle the excitement of the political moment—can scarcely be said to exist. But then the French absolute monarchy did not nurture the kind of representative institutions, and thus the particular evidence, on which such studies may profitably be pursued. And anyone who has worked on the high politics of the last century of the Valois monarchy knows how difficult it is to provide anything like a coherent account of the formation of policy, of the dominant voices of counsel, of the conflicting concerns of counsellors, even of the nature and patterns of the meetings of its councils of state. In the traditions of the judicious and prudential French

---

* An earlier and emaciated version of this paper was presented to the *Colloque international du centre de la Renaissance* in Tours in October 1989. It is a pleasure to record a debt of gratitude to its director, Robert Sauzet, for his hospitality and the colloquium's lively debate.

[1] C. S. R. Russell, *Parliaments and English Politics, 1621–1629* (Oxford, 1979). The introduction and essays in *Conflict in Early Stuart England. Studies in Religion and Politics, 1603–1642*, eds. Richard Cust and Ann Hughes (London, 1989) provide a good introduction to the substantial research and publications on and around the subject.

monarchy of the sixteenth century, it was not the custom to record much, if at all, about what went on in the 'cuisine des grands'.[2] Secrecy was a princely virtue.[3] We are left, like the ambassadors to the French court on whom we mainly rely for our information, keeping our ears and eyes open, piecing together the fragments which come our way. The result is an inevitable and frustrating gap in the historiography of France's civil wars. It is a weakness not of narrative history (in the sense that Lawrence Stone has suggested it) but of the capacity to re-*present* the raw scent, the dangerous savour of the political moment.[4]

Yet hardly a year passed during the French civil wars when high politics was not of preeminent concern. The sudden and unpredictable shifts of political fortune were recorded along with other acts of God in contemporary diaries. The decision of the estates of Blois in 1576 to propose to the king that he should reunify the realm under the one, Catholic faith, and the way in which that decision was exploited in the political circumstances of late 1576, was one such matter of inexplicable process but inevitably profound and manifest consequence. How was it that an estates general, summoned into being by clause 53 of the edict of pacification with the protestants in May 1576 should, as one of its first public acts, abrogate the edict and the principles behind it?[5] How was it that a king who had sworn solemnly in his *lit de justice* before the assembled judges of the *parlement* of Paris to uphold that edict of pacification should, seven months later, be so readily prepared to accept the wayward advice of the estates and forswear such an act?[6] And how did an assembly which was convoked to embody the corporate will of the realm in the only way that was possible in sixteenth-century France in order to initiate the reforms which were seen as the best way of cementing the new-found fragile pacification, seek as its first endeavour to enact a measure which, above all, would threaten renewed war and the end of reform?

---

[2] A phrase used by Antoine de Laval, who prided himself on his 30 years of service as a secretary to the duc de Montpensier and the Bourbons when he wrote the preface to his *Desseigns de professions nobles & publiques* . . . (Paris, 1605) in 1602. A secretary, he reminded his readers, was someone who guarded the secrets of the great.

[3] Jean Bodin, *The Six Books of a Commonweal*, trans. Richard Knolles, ed. Kenneth D. McRae (Cambridge, Mass., 1962), pp. 253–4.

[4] L. Stone, "The revival of narrative: reflections on a new old history", *Past and Present*, no. 85 (1979), 3–24.

[5] Clause 53 of the Edict of Beaulieu, May 1576—printed in *Mémoires de Monsieur le duc de Nevers*, 2 vols. (Paris, 1665), I, 117–35 (henceforth cited as *Nevers*).

[6] According to S. Hanley, *The* Lits de Justice *of the King of France. Constitutional Ideology in Legend, Ritual and Discourse* (Princeton, 1983), p. 212, Henri III "never convoked a *Lit de Justice* assembly". Yet the formal visit to the *parlement* on Monday 15 May when, according to Estoile, he "fit homologuer et publier l'édit de pacification, l'entretenement duquel il jura et fit jurer par les assistants" (Estoile, *Journal du règne de Henri III*, ed. L.-R. Lefèvre (Paris, 1943), p. 115) was generally regarded and spoken of as a "lit de justice" (e.g. *Nevers*, I, 182).

The political drama of the hapless estates of Blois brings the historian face to face with the frustrated, contradictory yearnings and fundamental divisions in French society. The sources are, as always, irritatingly inadequate. The ambassadors to the French court were kept some eight miles outside Blois at the village by the Loire of St Dié. They made what they could of the fragments of news which leaked out to them.[7] Each estate swore, as was the custom, to preserve the secrecy of their deliberations and not to keep notes on what happened.[8] Fortunately, we have the *procès-verbaux* of the proceedings for the clerical and third estates, the formal record of their sessions and conclusions. More excitingly there are four extant private diaries for the period. That of Guillaume de Taix records the atmosphere and inclinations of the first estate from the perspective of an intelligent but modest *chanoine*.[9] The diary of Pierre de Blanchefort is a rich and circumstantially detailed account of the sessions of the noble estate from a delegate who was by no means convinced of the wisdom of attempting to reunite the kingdom under one religion. The full manuscript has recently been used by Mack Holt to demonstrate that, contrary to received wisdom, the second estate was more interested in the restoration of their traditional role in government and society than in a return to war.[10] Blanchefort refused to sign any formula of association when he was in Blois on the grounds that it might commit him to undertaking an unjust and illegal war. He pushed to (and possibly beyond) the limits of what he was instructed to represent as the views of the nobility of his circumscription on the matter of religious unification. As a deputy from the Nivernois and Donzonois, Blanchefort's election (and, probably, his continuing local good standing) was in the hands of Louis de Gonzaga, duc de Nevers. By his actions at Blois, Blanchefort could scarcely have crossed the duke in a clearer or more calculated fashion; keeping his diary was doubtless a way of protection against likely recrimination when he arrived back in Nevers.

---

[7] See the various reports from the newly arrived English ambassador, Sir Amias Paulet, in *Public Record Office* SP 70/140–142. Cf. the reports from the Papal nuncio, Antonio Maria Salviati, calendared in P. Hurtubise and R. Toupin (eds.), *Correspondance du nonce en France: Antonio Maria Salviati*, 2 vols. (Rome, 1975), I, 561 et seq. Paulet regarded the real reason for their being lodged outside Blois as part of the delicate orchestration of the estates: ". . . they will not want many complaints, many quarrels, many accusations yea against the King himself . . ." (SP 70/141 fol. 883). But St Dié was, Professor R. J. Knecht tells me, the village which was used to provide accommodation for visiting dignitaries to Chambord in the earlier sixteenth century; its surviving oversized church and surprisingly ample sixteenth-century buildings testify to this part of its history.

[8] See, for example, the decision recorded in the *procès-verbal* of the third estate in one of its earliest sessions—Lalourcé and Duval, *Recueil des pièces originales et authentiques concernant la tenue des Etats Generaux*, 9 vols. (Paris, 1789), III, 190 (henceforth cited as *Recueil*).

[9] The diary is reprinted in *Recueil*, II.

[10] Mack P. Holt, "Attitudes of the French Nobility at the Estates-General of 1576," *The Sixteenth Century Journal*, 18 (1987), 489–504.

Similar reasons are likely to have prompted Jean Bodin, the delegate for the third estate from the *bailliage* of Vermandois, who also had views at odds with the decisions of his estate. He went one better, however, and published his diary the following year.[11] Historians have not been slow to see the possible 'paradox' between the views on sovereignty which he expressed in the *République*, published in its first French edition only a few months prior to the estates general and Bodin's role at the estates of Blois.[12] They have been more reluctant to exploit the potential interest of matching his views on the ideal ways of creating 'harmony' within a polity with his experience of representative institutions more generally.[13] One further diary is of exceptional interest; the extracts from that kept by the duc de Nevers during the period that he was at court in Blois in 1576–7 are a unique record from the *petit conseil* of the king, and from someone who was surely determining the swing of events.[14] Nevers takes us close to the high tension cables at the heart of royal government. He recounts the debating points of conscience, sharpened into rapiers as dangerous as the points of honour which did for the seigneur de Saint-Sulpice in the basse-cour of the *château* on 20 December. We are as near as we are likely to get to the 'débonnaire' and 'très fine' subtleties of the king, adroitly seizing the short-term advantages of the moment as surely as he turned the longer-term future into a hostage to fortune.

Accompanying this diary is the detailed *Advis donnez au Roy par escrit, par son commandement*.[15] This is apparently the only surviving written conciliar advice presented to the king on a major matter of policy, a rare form of *consulta* prepared after the contemporary Spanish fashion. In it, sixteen prominent figures from the king's *petit conseil*, the king's key strategic, administrative and diplomatic advisors, were invited in the last week or so of 1576 to present their views on how to proceed in the light of the decision to reunify the kingdom under one religion. The resulting series of memoranda are, in the main, chillingly realistic. It was, perhaps, its naked *realpolitik* which explains, at least in part, why so many copies of this manuscript were in circulation during the *ancien régime*.[16] The last document to be mentioned here is one which appears

---

[11] J. Bodin, *Recueil de tout ce qui s'est negotié en la compagnie du tiers estat de France* (Paris, 1577) (Henceforth, cited as *Bodin*).

[12] O. Ulph, "Jean Bodin and the Estates General of 1576" in *Journal of Modern History*, 19 (1947), 289–96.

[13] See, however, R. Crahay, "Jean Bodin aux états généraux de 1576" in *Assemblee di stati e istituzioni rapresentative. Convegno internationale* (Perugia, 1983), pp. 85–120.

[14] The *petit conseil*, or *conseil d'en haut*, so-called because it generally met in the royal apartments on the first floor of royal châteaux. It was a very informal body, meeting (during this period) at least once a week, generally after dinner on a Saturday evening each week.

[15] Reprinted in *Nevers*, I, 181–237.

[16] Manuscript copies so far located in Paris include: BN MS Dupuy 24 (an early seventeenth-century copy); BN MS Fr 17299 (a seventeenth-century copy from the Séguier collection) and 6548 (an eighteenth-century copy). In addition, various copies of particular memoranda survive in BN MS Fr 20341 (duc de Nevers); BN MS Fr nouv acq

not to have been utilised by historians at all, despite its evident significance. It is a *précis* of the debates at the third estate on religious reunification. Unlike the *procès-verbal* or Bodin's diary, this gives us what may well be in some parts quite close to the *ipsissima verba* of the speeches of delegates.[17] The document repays careful scrutiny.

The background to the summoning of the estates general in the wake of the edict of pacification and under the shadow of catholic reaction has already been evoked by J.H.M. Salmon.[18] By St Stephen's Day, Wednesday 26 December 1576, the third estate had been in session for four and a half weeks and the estates general formally convened for almost three weeks. There had been time enough for all but one of the 171 delegates whose procurations would be accepted by the king to make their way to Blois.[19] The estate was well-attended. In only seven circumscriptions did a protestant boycott of its elections result in an absentee delegation.[20] At the formal opening of the estates, the king had flattered his audience, 'composed', he said, 'of men of standing, respect and experience'.[21] The procurations of third estate delegates, however, suggest that this was hardly an exaggeration. Well over a third of the delegates were royal officeholders. (*See Table One*)

Although the majority were magistrates in lower courts, a significant minority were distinguished individuals from the sovereign courts or presidents of secondary jurisdictions. Alongside, but distinct from, the royal officers at the third estate, should be placed the substantial contingent of lawyers. Altogether, the *gens de justice* made up over half the third estate. Such a predominance reflected the fact that the electoral procedures at the *bailliage* and *sénéchaussée* levels were often held under the influence of local courts. A petition presented to the third estate at Blois from the *bailliage* of Troyes claimed, in fact, to represent the views of its inhabitants which had been deliberately excluded from the *cahier* by the 'gens de justice'—'dautant que les cinq pars dont les six

---

7,145 (Catherine de Médicis) and BN MS Fr 3177 fol. 120 (Jean de Morvillier, bishop of Orléans).

[17] BN MS Dupuy 428 fols. 82–89v.

[18] J.H.M. Salmon, *Society in Crisis. France in the Sixteenth Century* (E. Benn, London, 1975), p. 202.

[19] The deputy from the *bailliage* of St Quentin was only accepted by the third estate on 18 January 1577. His Ile de France compatriot from the *bailliage* of La Ferté managed to arrive on 24 December 1576. Those from the southern provinces, by contrast, were almost all in Blois by the end of the first week of December.

[20] The *sénéchaussées* of Haute-Marche, Montpellier, Beaucaire, Armagnac, Dax, the *pays* and adjoined *jugeries* of Rivière-Verdun etc., the town and government of La Rochelle.

[21] *Recueil*, II, 35. The text was widely distributed in this published form: see *Proposition faicte par le Roy en l'assemblee des Estats . . .* (Paris, F. Morel, 1576).

Table One: Analysis of the Procurations of
the Third Estate, 1576[22]

Total Number of Procurations accepted: 171

of which

Officeholders:	Senior Magistrates	9	5.26%
	Junior Magistrates	51	29.82%
	Others (gens de finance)	2	1.17%
	Total:	**62**	**36.25%**
Lawyers:	Avocats	27	15.79%
	Procureurs	4	2.34%
	Total:	**31**	**18.13%**
Municipal Officials,			
Syndics and Greffiers:	Civic Officers	29	16.96%
	Syndics and Greffiers	11	6.43%
	Total:	**40**	**23.39%**
Bourgeois, Habitants etc:	Bourgeois	9	5.26%
	Merchants	2	1.17%
	Physicians	4	2.34%
	Habitants or *Laboureurs*	2	1.17%
	Total:	**17**	**9.94%**
No relevant information:		**Total:**	**30**	**17.54%**

font le tout des deputez de ladicte province sont gens de Justice . . .'.[23] But the lawyers of the third estate were also often elected civic officials (*capitouls, échevins, maires, majeurs, châtelains* etc.) or syndics and scribes of local representative institutions. They enjoyed a substantial knowledge and experience of public affairs in a variety of contexts. Only a relatively small fraction of the third estate was prepared to be described on its procuration as a merchant or a bourgeois, and only two owned to being *laboureurs*.[24]

The third estate had been assigned the *hôtel de ville* in Blois for its deliberations; its council chamber was not large and, with the exception of its elected

[22] The social status referred to in the procurations is doubtless far from the complete truth; much more work is needed to confirm the initial impressions this data create. The social categories are not exclusive of each other and therefore the percentages are not intended to sum to 100%.

[23] BN MS 500 Colbert 8 fols. 366–7 ("Remonstrances tres humbles extraictes du cahyer du bailliage de Troyes . . .").

[24] Florant Gayant, "laboureur", delegate for the *bailliage* of Roye in Picardy; and Grégoire Audiger, "marchand, laboureur", delegate for the *duché* and *sénéchaussée* of La Ferté.

officers delegates stood, rather than sat, for its plenary sessions, grouped behind the spokesmen for the relevant 'governments' of the kingdom.[25] The meeting on 26 December was the fourteenth plenary session and the first where a substantive matter arising from the various *cahiers de doléances* was discussed. There had been plenty of time for delegations to 'se recognoistre' and, more importantly, for the rhythm of the vital separate meetings of the deputies from the various individual governments held in lodgings around the city.

The overall objective of these deliberations was clear enough. They were progressively to distill the views of the *cahiers*, giving due weight to the social status of the petitioners. It was a process of pyramidal harmonisation and homologation from the thousands of locally generated *cahiers* to the engrossed *cahiers* of just over a hundred circumscriptions, which were in turn refined down to the *cahiers* of the twelve 'governments' before being encapsulated in the bulky final *cahier* of the whole third estate. Jean Bodin would have doubtless mused that this loosely reflected the kind of geometric proportionality to be expected in a well-tempered polity: 'the form of a well ordered commonweal shall so long be firm and sure, as it shall keep right consent and tune, well agreeing unto the sweet delight of the ear'.[26] Three estates in a realm was, he had written, itself a reflection of such politic proportionality.[27]

The principle was simple enough. The practice was more complex and it is difficult to discover much about how deputies sought to reflect the disparate views of the various *cahiers*. In such a vast realm with its varying customs and traditions, rooted regional identities and relatively fixed social divisions it cannot have been an easy task. It was still more delicate in a period of intense politico-religious discord. Using two surviving sets of local *cahiers* for the third estate in 1576, one from Chartres and the other from Troyes, Jean-Marie Constant has analysed the various petitions which were submitted.[28] There were, of course, some familiar refrains, well-rehearsed resentments: against the *taille* and the tax-collectors, against the *gabelles*, against the sergeants at law and

---

25 The assembly had elected, in accordance with custom, the senior delegate from the Ile de France as its president—Nicolas Luillier, merchant provost of the city of Paris. Pierre Boulenger, an advocate from the *parlement* of Rennes, syndic and *procureur général* of that city, was confirmed as its secretary. At the same time, two "assesseurs évangélistes" were appointed, whose tasks included summoning the various delegations to the plenary sessions of the estate and ensuring that debates were conducted in accordance with custom and precedent. For many of the relevant details on how the estates functioned, see E. Charleville, *Les Etats Généraux de 1576* (Paris, 1901).

26 J. Bodin, *The Six Books*, p. 455. Cf M. Villey, "La justice harmonique selon Bodin" in *Jean Bodin*, ed. H. Denzer (Munich, 1973).

27 Bodin, *Six Books*, pp. 403–4.

28 Jean-Marie Constant, "Le langage politique paysan en 1576: les cahiers de doléances des bailliages de Chartres et de Troyes" in *Représentation & vouloir politiques autour des états-généraux de 1614*, eds. Roger Chartier and Denis Richet (Paris, 1982), pp. 25–50. The *cahiers* from the *châtellenies* of Troyes were partially published by E. Boutiot, *Documents inédits tirés des archives de Troyes et relatifs aux états généraux* (Troyes, 1878).

the bailiffs. There were also reflections of recent miseries; all but one of the 50 *cahiers* from around Chartres (open, rich countryside, ripe for rapine) included an article against the war-crimes of the soldiery.[29] At the same time, the clamour for reform was remarkably disparate, interestingly reflective of debates current amongst the chattering classes: foreigners were to be removed from government, women to be banned from public life, government was to be in the hands of a council of notables. How did the *rédacteurs* of the *bailliages* reflect adequately these sometimes contradictory demands in order to convey them onwards to the estates? The difficulty was most acute when it came to religious change. 'Pas de diversité religieuse' was the key phrase, articulated in 22% of the individual *cahiers* of Chartres, 26% of those of Troyes. Such sentiments were to be found in those zones most affected by the sectarian tensions of the civil wars and most engulfed by the collective conscience which these had engendered.[30] It was mostly registered in the zones under the influence of the towns—south of Chartres and in the Beauce, and down the valleys of the Seine and the Yonne around Troyes. It was least in evidence in the regions most out of their reach—in the pays d'Othe in Troyes, where the Huguenots had their church, and in the Perche in Chartres.[31] When faced with this minority view in favour of religious unification, however, we may take it that the *rédacteurs* tended to incorporate a strongly-held article on a matter of conscience into their engrossed *cahier*, wherever it came from, and especially when it was expressed by the urban, literate and 'sanior pars'.

What were the delegates at Blois to do with the various articles on religious unity? According to the diary of Jean Bodin, it was an issue which gave rise to persistent controversy in the separate meetings of the delegates from the Ile de France up to 26 December. The debate began on Monday 3 December in a session which lasted the whole day. It was opened by Pierre Versoris, the articulate, intelligent, socially ambitious and dévot advocate from Paris.[32] 'Il ouvrit le cahier de Paris, où l'article de la Religion fut leu, par lequel il estoit requis qu'il pleust au Roy, voir tous les suiets en vne Religion Catholique Romaine.'[33] The deputy of the *prévôté* of Paris followed with support from his

[29] Constant, art.cit., p. 34; only 27 of the 36 *cahiers* of Troyes contained a similar article.

[30] As analysed in Denis Crouzet, *Les guerriers de Dieu*, 2 vols. (Paris, 1991).

[31] As Jean-Marie Constant observed, it was significant that the one explicitly protestant *cahier* from Illiers, in the *bailliage* of Chartres, reflected this distinction in its article against "l'audace des villes qui retirent toute la graisse du plat pays . . ." (Constant, art.cit., p. 37).

[32] The essential biographical detail is presented by Robert Descimon in *Qui étaient les Seize? Mythes et réalités de la Ligue parisienne (1585–1594)* in *Mémoires de la fédération des sociétés historiques et archéologiques de Paris et de l'Ile de France*, 34 (1983), 226–7. Versoris died on 26 December 1588, twelve years to the day after the decision of the third estate at Blois, mortified at the assassinations there of the duke and cardinal of Guise, to whom he had been a principal advisor. He was interred amidst the super-sanctity of the Chartreux of Paris.

[33] *Bodin*, p.9.

cahier 'nonobstant tous edicts'. Then came Bodin himself, the first deputy from the *bailliages* outside Paris. He read out the first and twelfth articles of his *cahier* 'qui portoit qu'il pleust au Roy maintenir ses suiets en bonne paix et dedans deux ans tenir vn Concile general ou national, pour regler le faict de la Religion: et puis, apres avoir longuement discouru sur les incommoditez de la guerre, fut interrompu par Versoris . . .'. The result was a vigorous discussion which continued through the afternoon session, with interventions from other delegates. Senlis sided with Paris, Mantes wished to add the words 'par douces & sainctes voyes' to any proposed article and Valois proposed that they should postpone any final decision until the other delegations of the government had arrived. So they returned to the issue on the 15 December. Once again, the debate was lively, even (reading between the lines) contentious. Pierre Luillier, president of the government of the Ile de France (as well as elected president of the third estate) had some difficulty in securing the necessary concord.[34] Bodin stood by the terms of his *cahier* 'suyvant sa charge' but eventually an agreement was reached around the Paris formula with the vital additional phrase 'par les plus douces et sainctes voyes que sa Maiesté aviseroit'. The deputies agreed and, with relief and an intended note of irony, the president echoed the *Nunc dimittis* as he brought the session to a conclusion.

Similar debates doubtless also went on amongst the delegations from the other eleven governments. Although the deputies from Burgundy—used to working with each other at the provincial estates—were apparently able to reach agreement on the issue at their first meeting on Monday 3 December, those from the Lyonnais had greater difficulty.[35] The *cahier* from the city of Lyon was uncompromisingly phrased.[36] The delegates of the *plat pays* had already been in dispute on 1 December and they were still at odds on 26 December.[37] After the spokesman for the government had presented their conclusion on religious unification, one of his compatriots from the Lyonnais

[34] For the biographical details of Nicolas Luillier, sieur de Boulancourt and Saint Mesmin, *prévôt des marchands* of the city of Paris and a *président* of the Paris *chambre des comptes* since 1567, see Barbara B. Diefendorf, *Paris City Councillors in the Sixteenth Century* (Princeton, 1983), pp. 9, 22, 37, 141–2, 178, 284.

[35] *Bodin*, p. 10. Cf. H. Drouot, *Notes sur la première Ligue en Bourgogne. Les débuts de Mayenne* (Dijon, 1937), p. 45.

[36] The *cahier* for the city of Lyon is reprinted in A. Péricard, *Notes et documents pour servir à l'histoire de Lyon*, 2 vols. (Lyon, 1838), II, 17–24. The king should return the kingdom to the catholic religion of his holy predecessors. Protestant ministers should be expelled from the kingdom. Protestants should be required to frequent catholic sermons regularly on pain of banishment. Failure to attend a Catholic Easter office should be automatically notified to the secular authorities. The king should immediately abrogate the edict of pacification of 1576 because it had been signed under duress and without the consent of the estates of the realm.

[37] *Bodin*, pp. 7–8.

insisted on registering the strong contrary views in his *cahier*, much to the displeasure of the assembled estate.[38]

So the spokesmen for each government prepared to present the conclusions which they had reached on the issue. The debate began, as usual, at 8am on 26 December. *Portes-parolles* were supposed to stick closely to the mandate they had been given although, as Bodin noted in the second edition of *The Six Books*, when there was dissension, their task was harder.[39] Luillier began by reading out the conclusion of the government of the Ile de France. Significantly, and not for the last time in the construction of a petition on this subject at Blois, he omitted the agreed amendment: 'by gentle and holy means'.[40] Then the spokesmen for each of the governments followed in the established order of precedence. Jean le Quieu, the spokesman for the government of Picardy third estate, offered a crucial addition to the article proposed by the Ile de France. Religious unification was easily the subject for the high moral ground, empty of practical purpose—in this respect it was ideal for a lofty but vacuous article at the estates general. Le Quieu gave religious reunification a hard cutting edge. All protestant ministers, deacons, elders and schoolmasters, or anyone who had ever acted as such, should be required to leave the kingdom within a set period or face the death penalty. At the same time, every inhabitant of the realm above the age of fifteen should be required to take an oath of profession to the Catholic church.

It is not difficult to see the Picard additions as emanating from the Picardy League which had begun amongst its frontier nobility in May 1576.[41] From the beginning, however, it had engaged various elements of the third estate in its fortress towns. The proposals were perhaps framed with at least one eye on the recent events over the frontier from Picardy in Flanders, where, or so deputies were told on 15 December, a similar policy was just about to be adopted. It

---

38 The delegate from the *bailliage* of St Pierre de Moustier insisted on being heard: "J'ay charge de ceux de mon Bailliage unaniment de supplier treshumblement le Roy quil soit son bon plaisir de faire garder et observer Inviolablement l'edict de pacification et que pour cet effect soit faict commandement a un chascun de poser les armes, lors Il fut rabrue et hue de presque toute lassemblee". (BN MS Dupuy 428 fols. 88v –89).

39 Bodin, *The Six Books*, p. 403.

40 BN MS Dupuy 428 fol. 83: "Le Roy Reunira tous ses subiectz a une certaine et seule Religion Assavoir a celle de l'Eglise Catholique Apostolique et Romaine laquelle Il a receue des feus Rois ses predecesseurs de main en main depuis Clovis premier Roy Chrestien, Et laquelle Il a jure de tenir garder et observer de point en point lors quil fut dernierement sacre a Reims et celle faire garder et observer a tous ses subiectz Suivant laquelles les feuz Roys ont acquis le tiltre de tres Chrestien et rendus puissant Invincibles et formidables a toute l'Europe".

41 M. Orlea, *La noblesse aux états généraux de 1576 et de 1588* (Paris, 1980), pp. 36–41. The contentious election of noble deputies to the estates general from Picardy at Montdidier on 30 October are revealed in BN MS Fr 3329 fol. 38 et seq. A protestant noble presented an alternative *cahier* and started a debate on the clause proposing forcible exile for those who refused to return to the catholic fold. The debate lasted over two days.

already had been successfully implemented in the Palatinate, where the new Count Palatine, Ludwig I, had just succeeded his father Frederick III. He had authorised the expulsion of 500–600 Calvinist ministers and others who refused to accept a Lutheran confession.[42]

This proposal split the delegates more clearly. The spokesman from Normandy, whose turn was next, took refuge in the high moral ground. He spoke at length and, in the end, offered the delegation's adhesion to the Ile de France's proposition. The Picardy additions were tactfully left to one side.[43] Pierre Belin, the mayor of Troyes and *bête noire* of the protestant *érudit* of Troyes, Nicolas Pithou, took the same, rather prudential line. As Pithou's diary records for 1576, there were signs in Troyes that the League was by no means universally popular.[44] Aware of the divisions in his own government, Belin explicitly repudiated the Picard article whilst aligning himself with a rather emollient version of the Ile de France's article.[45]

The next speaker offered an entirely different perspective. Joseph Eymar, a *président* in the *parlement* of Bordeaux and its mayor, had lived long enough to remember the failure of the persecution of heresy in the 1550s, when he was already a junior magistrate in the *parlement*.[46] He had seen the damage inflicted by the civil wars in his province and spoke with a combination of passion and practicality. He affirmed his own fundamental catholicity and reminded deputies of the risks which he had run to sustain the traditional religion in a southern province. He accused deputies from governments north of the Loire of taking decisions from their comparative security which would have tragic

---

[42] SP 70/141 fol 945 (24 December 1576): On 15 December, the third estate deputies were told "that those of the Low Countries have capitulated with their King and refused the Prince of Orange, would endure no other religion than the Romish, and would banish all that professed any contrary religion and all their adherents; that the new Count Palatine had already banished all the ministers placed by his father . . .".

[43] "Il parla assez longuement de l'honneur de dieu Et que du mespris d'icelluy et de l'Eglise Catholique estoient proceddez les maux de la france. Il adheroit a l'article susdit de l'Isle de France".

[44] In his manuscript history of the civil wars in Troyes Nicolas Pithou copied out an "Advertissement tres salutaire a Messieurs de Troyes, et autres villes du pays" which circulated in the city towards the end of 1576. It urged the third estate to give the League a wide birth—"ce cheval de bois", a latter-day Trojan horse. Pithou himself, of course, was entirely dismissive of the league and estates general: "Qui ne voit donc que ceste ligue est vne vraye pipee, pour avec le temps nous envoyer tous a la besace?" (BN MS Dupuy 698 fols. 427v–428v).

[45] "Nous demandons que quant au General de ceux de la Religion pretendue reformee, Que le Roy recoive en sa protection et sauvegarde tous et ungs chacuns faisans profession d'icelle les garde et maintienne en toute seurete avec liberte de consciences en leurs maisons sans qu'il leur fust mesfaict ny mesdict a eux leurs familles biens et heritages en quelque sorte ou facon que ce fust et y pourvoir aucunement par les moiens les plus doux et salutaires". (BN MS Dupuy 428 fol. 84).

[46] Fleury Vindry, *Les parlementaires français au XVIe siècle* (Bergerac, 1901), p. 46. He was born in 1530 and became a *conseiller* in the *parlement* in c.1554.

consequences for those less fortunate than themselves.[47] Even a stranger to France, a barbarian, would sympathise with the plight of his province.[48] If the two proposals were accepted, it would put an end to any hopes of pacification.[49] The protestants have retained their defensive strategy. Their military base was intact. Only that morning the news had broken that the vicomte de Turenne had taken up arms in the lower Limousin. If the assembly did not support the edict of pacification, the results would be potentially catastrophic.[50] Its reforming endeavours in justice, royal finances and the church would be utterly wasted.[51] The regions not immediately affected by warfare would eventually suffer as well.[52] Warfare only encouraged the vice and immorality which had brought France to its civil strife in the first place. The Old Testament and the history of the Church taught that heresy could not be defeated by force of arms.[53] All legitimate means should be attempted to unite the kingdom under one religion but in such a way that warfare did not result.[54]

The Breton delegation's spokesman was Pierre Martin, the *procureur du roi* in the *parlement* at Rennes. He evoked rather less emotionally the destructive effects of war and agreed that, as a result of the civil wars, the catholic religion had suffered whilst protestants had become more hardened in their opinions. Nevertheless, his government would vote for the Ile de France proposition providing that the proposed reunion of the realm was undertaken purely by peaceful means.[55] Burgundy's delegation was even more judicious and prudent.

---

[47] "Vous me faictes souvenir de ceux qui se promeinent sur le pont IN TUTUM et voient en haute mer Ung navire tourmenté d'orages et en danger de Naufrage. Chacun en dict son advis et sont bien aisé non du malheur d'autruy Mais de leur bonne fortune." (BN MS Dupuy 428 fol. 85).

[48] "Mais un estranger, ung Schite, les plus barbares hommes du monde seroient muz a pitié et commiseration, et comme ie croy mettroient la main pour nous aider et secourir". He reminded deputies that "venant de Bourdeaulx Icy en poste Iusques a Orleans Ie nay veu Eglise quelconque debout Tellement que les lieux dediez pour le service de dieu servent maintenant d'estables a chevaux et de toitz à pourceaux".

[49] "Car si elle a lieu Nous sommes a la guerre comme devant".

[50] "Si vous ne changez ceste conclusion nous sommes perdus. Il fault que je vous dis que vous faictes aujourdhuy cinquante mille femmes feves, cent mille enfans orphelins, et tant d'autres maux et calamitez".

[51] "Vous estes icy assemblez pour regler [*to reform the kingdom*] et vous pellemeslez et confondez toutes choses. Vous voulez mettre ordre au miserable estat de ce Royaume et vous le desordonnez".

[52] "Nous sommes trop vos voisins, nous nous touchons de trop pres. Quelle stupidite seroit cela de voir brusler la maison de son voisin et n'avoir point peur de la sienne". (Ibid., fol. 86).

[53] "Et on ne trouvera pas que quant Il est survenu quelque heresie en l'Eglise qu'elle ait este ostee & extirpe par les armes et par les remedes extremes ains par les larmes, par les jeusnes et oraison des pauvres fidelles Chrétiens qui Impetroient la grace et misericorde de dieu". (Ibid., fol. 86v).

[54] "Mais tellement que nous ne venons iamais a la guerre ny aux malheurs desquelz par la Clemence et bonte de sa Majeste nous sommes nagueres eschappez".

[55] ". . . y pourveoir avec Conseil et le plus doucement et sagement que faire ce pourra si

It recognised reunification as a laudable objective. But the province would hardly venture its opinion as to the means of achieving it and preferred to leave the whole matter to the king's wisdom and discretion. By contrast, the Orléannais, 'touched by its zeal for God's honour and that of his Church' strongly supported the articles proposed by both the Ile de France and Picardy.

By the afternoon session, and with four governments still to declare their hand, the issue was still in the balance. Bernard de Supersanctis, the leading delegate from the province of Languedoc, chose to paint an alternative view to that presented in the morning from Guyenne.[56] He reminded deputies that Toulouse was virtually a Catholic frontier garrison, its inhabitants forced to watch from its walls as they saw their farms and barns burnt to the ground.[57] They had suffered so much for the honour of God and the conservation of his church and they should not give up the struggle now. Languedoc would support all the proposed articles. The deputy from the Lyonnais reminded the assembly that his province was so poor and debilitated by the recent troubles that it could see no prospect of reuniting the realm under one faith save by peaceful means. The delegation from Dauphiné was represented by the vice-senechal from the Valentinois, Jacques Colas.[58] The surviving *cahier* from the provincial estates of Dauphiné, drafted by Jean du Bourg, was more interested, it would seem, by the question of 'égalisation' (interpreted in a Bodinian fashion) than 'unification'.[59] Jacques Colas echoed the opinions of Guyenne, although he added an authentic Dauphinois dimension with an excursus on the problem of communal indebtedness.[60]

Even at this stage, it was possible that the third estate would have ended without a clear majority view. Everything depended on the declaration of the last spokesman, that of Provence. Antoine Thoron, a lawyer from Digne, was an advocate in the *parlement* of Aix whose ultra-catholic tendencies were

que nous ne revenons plus a la guerre civile le feu de laquelle n'est pas a grand peine amorty".

[56] Bernard de Supersanctis, a *capitoul* of the city of Toulouse, a *docteur* and *avocat* was serving in his second period in office as *capitoul.* His first period in office had been in the aftermath of the failed protestant coup of May 1562. He had engineered a local Catholic League there in early 1563 and was repeatedly chosen by the city to undertake special delegations to court. See AM Toulouse BB 172 fol. 165; AA 14 No. 55 (1563). BB 175 fol. 335: AA 16 fol. 133v (1568).

[57] "Combien de foys auons nous veu la fumee de nos fermes et mestairies que l'on brusleroit lors que nous faisions la garde sur les murs de notre ville". (Ibid., fol. 88)

[58] For the extraordinary and baroque career of Jacques Colas, see E. Colas de la Noue, *Jacques Colas* (Paris, 1892).

[59] See the analysis of the surviving *cahier* in E. Le Roy Ladurie, *Le Carnaval de Romans* (Paris, 1979), chap. III.

[60] "L'oppression et calamitez que son pais auait souffert pendant les autres guerres qui auoient duré dix sept ans que le plat pays estoit depeuplé et totallement destruict qu'il n'y auoit que les villes qui fussent debout Mais tellement pauures que tout leur bien ne souffiroit pas a payer les debtes qu'il a convenu faire pour soustenir la despense de la Guerre et entretenement des soldats".

well-documented.[61] He reminded the assembly that he had represented his province in the past at the court, asking the king to expel the protestants from the province. On that occasion, he had suggested that his co-religionists in Provence would be prepared to buy the protestants out of their property in order to assist their expulsion. With support from the deputies in Marseille, whose *cahier* was also integrist, he aligned the province with the views already expressed by the Languedoc spokesman.[62]

So, towards late afternoon, the *greffier* announced the result of the day's deliberations, counting the 'opinans' for and against the proposed articles. He declared the Ile de France article carried without opposition and the Picardy articles 'tendans au ban des ministres' carried by seven votes to five.[63] The third estate had avoided a damaging split with the other orders at the estate and had followed them in voting both for the principle of reunification and also one central plank of the means by which it should be undertaken. Jean Bodin was left to muse on the arithmetic behind geometric proportionality.[64]

It is often assumed that the third estate at the estates of Blois, under the influence of the Catholic League, had easily been persuaded and readily adopted the articles on reunification. That was clearly far from the case. The third estate's reluctance is evident at every turn. On the other hand, there is no doubt that the third estate had been, and were being, manipulated ('entendu sous main' is Estoile's expression), a wilful puppet in the hands of the king.[65] The 26 December 1576 was a day of dupes in an estates general which has been described as 'a prolonged day of dupes'.[66]

What was Henri III up to? It is hard to be precise and he intended it to be so. From the meeting of the *petit conseil* over the weekend of the 1–2 December 1576 onwards, however, the evidence of Nevers' journal points in only one direction.[67] In the privacy of princely strategem, Henri III had begun to glimpse a way, 'vne si saincte oeuvre' whereby he might neuter the dangerous elements of the provincial Leagues and turn them to his advantage. He would put

---

[61] G. Lambert, *Histoire des guerres de religion en Provence (1530–1598)*, 2 vols. (Marseille, reprinted 1972), I, 307–8.

[62] The Marseille *cahier* is to be found in AM Marseille, AC AA 117.

[63] The Picardy article had thus received the support of the delegations from the Ile de France, Normandy, Champagne, Languedoc, the Orléannais, Picardy and Provence. The rest had voted against it.

[64] "Il est à noter", he wrote, "que le gouvernement de Guyenne avoit dix sept deputez, & le gouvernement de Provence n'en avoit que deux". Various deputies from the Marche, Lyonnais and the Auvergne were sufficiently unhappy at the outcome to apply for a written note of the view presented by their government spokesman "pour leur servir de descharge envers ceux qui les avoyent deputez".

[65] Estoile, op.cit., p. 130. In January 1577, his expression was stronger: "Le peuple, qui de soi-même, n'a mouvement que celui que le vent des grands lui fait prendre, s'emeut où le premier vent le pousse, et ordinairement contre son utilité manifeste". (Ibid., p. 166).

[66] P. Chevallier, *Henri III* (Paris, 1985), p. 341.

himself at their head and be the principal beneficiary of the explicit oaths of association and loyalty which they would embody. With their support, the estates general would become the true incorporation of the will of the realm. If each estate were to commit itself solemnly and irrevocably to Catholic reunification, then (in due course) each estate would have to will the resources, military, moral and financial, with which to carry it out. The king would graciously assent to the petitions of the estates and declare the promises which he had made in May 1576 counter to his coronation oath and the express will of his people. The protestant military leadership would have to take note of the incorporated will of the realm which was of one resolve on the matter, rallied in resources, strategy and initiative behind the king. Spain could hardly complain, despite rumours of French meddling in the affairs of Flanders. The Guises would be firmly sat on. Henri III would be resolute, not bellicose, and a truly catholic prince; it would be for the protestant leadership, not the king, to decide whether the realm was plunged into further warfare.

To carry this forward, however, Henri III would need the cunning of a princely fox. Dissimulation was vital; the strategem must needs be implicit 'pour ne pas precipiter un dernier Remede'.[68] The risks of another St Bartholomew massacre as a result of ill-judged remarks about catholicity were all too great. The rumours were already circulating; a general massacre was planned for the 15 December. Henri III issued a formal denial: 'Je n'ay autre plus grand désir et volonté que de faire vivre mes dits sujets en amitié, union et concorde, les uns avec les autres'.[69] Anjou, the king's brother, would need to be carried along, kept at court, given promises to feed to his former companions in revolt. So, too, would 'ma bonne mère' and the Chancellor. Failure on these scores would mean that the whole strategem would have to be aborted; better, then, to proceed underhand, stage by stage.[70]

The provincial Leagues, too, had to be encouraged (in a royalist framework) but by stealth. There must be no hint of the king bowing to the inevitable, still less of creating an instrument by which individuals would, in the fullness of time, be committing themslves and their wealth to a cause, the full implications of which would not be immediately evident to them. The formula did not explicitly commit the League to a mechanism for reunification; but, in one revealing phrase, the implicit strategem was made apparent.[71] The formula for

---

[67] *Nevers*, I, 166. If Nevers is to be believed, reunification was already on the agenda— 'pour voir comme il auroit à se gouverner, pour faire qu'il y eut qu'vne Religion en son Royaume".

[68] Ibid., 167.

[69] Chevallier, *op.cit.*, p. 345.

[70] Among the subjects for discussion at the king's palace academy at Blois in December 1576 was, however, "De la Vérité et du mensonge"—see Robert J. Sealy, *The Palace Academy of Henry III* (Droz, Geneva, 1981), pp. 62–4.

[71] Protestants were to be left in peace "pourveu qu'ilz ne contreviennent aucunement a ce qui sera par Sa Majesté ordonné après la conclusion des Estatz generaulx".

such associations was drafted around 2 December and circulated to the provinces.[72] Deputies at the estates only knew of it through individual approaches by aristocratic governors to sign up to such associations at Blois.[73] Many deputies, including Blanchefort, were unsure whether these associations were proposed with the king's approval or not. There was already much talk of treason, according to the English ambassador.[74] Entirely unsure of what was happening, preachers put the Advent Gospel to good use: 'On earth nations will stand helpless, not knowing which way to turn . . .'.

Meanwhile, the estates general had to make the right noises about reunification, but without the king seeming to offer them any open encouragement to do so. In his opening discourse, Henri III was at his cleverest; each phrase delicately placed to suggest, but without any explicit commitment, that the estates general had been convoked to cement the work of pacification begun in the edict of Beaulieu, even as he was preparing to abrogate it.[75] Meanwhile, the nobility had to be persuaded. Nevers' diary indicates some of the ways in which it was done. Some explicit pressure was placed on the president of the estate on 12 December. A draft of his speech to the delegates was seen and corrected. Nevers promised to deal with Blanchefort. The required decision was arrived at by the nobility on 19 December. In the meantime, the presidents of the governments of the third estate were being worked over. Nevers himself saw the deputies from the Lyonnais on 14 December.[76] The president of the estate was told they had to reach a decision promptly. The king must have been reasonably secure that things were going in the right direction by the *petit conseil* of the weekend before Christmas Day. Anjou had offered him a public promise of loyalty before the estates. On 24 December he announced his decision to the council of the queen mother: 'qu'il ne vouloit plus qu'il y eust deux religions en France, & qu'il ne pouvoit aller contre son premier serment fait au sacre'.[77] On the same day as the third estate's debate, arrangements were being set in hand for Nevers to write the speech which would announce the king's decision in public and for the Grand Almoner to make it. In the event the king made the announcement himself on the 1st January 1577.[78]

By then, the sixteen privy councillors who were invited to submit advice to

[72] *Lettres d'Henri III*, ed. M. François, 4 vols. in progress (Paris, 1965–), III, 85–8.

[73] E.g. the association agreed amongst the deputies from Champagne at Blois on 11 December 1576, reprinted in *Nevers*, I, 114. This was not according to the formula proposed by the king. It included a sinister clause on religious unification: those inhabitants who refused to sign up to the association "sera estimé en tout le pays ennemy de Dieu & deserteur de sa Religion, rebelle à son Roy, traistre & proditeur de sa Patrie: & du common consentement de tous les gens de bien abandonné de tous".

[74] SP70/140 fol. 832.

[75] *Recueil*, II, 35.

[76] "Je gagnay les deputez du Lionnais le matin pour mettre vne seule Religion". (*Nevers*, I, 167).

[77] Ibid., 168.

[78] Estoile, op.cit., p. 138.

the king on how to proceed, following this announcement, were almost completed. The resulting documents are fascinating because they reveal how much the king's advisors were trying to learn the lessons of the civil wars and, in the process, to seize back the military, diplomatic and strategic initiative. The king should combine with the estates general to show the protestants the express will of the kingdom to return to catholicism. He should specifically guarantee the safety of those who did not revolt against his authority. At the same time, he should prepare to enforce his will by force, organising diligently the supplies, payment and defined strategic objectives of his forces.

Events were to show the king's advisors how much they still had to learn about these matters. The protestant military leadership was not impressed by the show of solidarity achieved at the estates by these means. Deputies were chosen from the estates and despatched with ambassadors from the king to present the case separately to Navarre, Condé and Damville in their respective provinces.[79] Those sent to the prince of Condé at La Rochelle returned the soonest, reporting back to the separate estates on 8 February 1577. He had refused to receive them formally.[80] Instead, he treated them to a sustained harangue. The estates general were a puppet assembly, manipulated into being by the *gens du roi* and then corrupted, perverted, sollicited and duped. He drew on the reservoirs of righteous indignation, the harbinger of righteous revolt amongst the French higher nobility.[81] There were shades, too, of the contemporary protestant commentaries which had accused the French protestant court of following Machiavellian precepts. Had not, so the first and third parts of the subtle and underrated pamphlet, *La France-Turquie* (published in 1576) intimated, their rulers a subtle Florentine strategy to emasculate the old constitution of France and turn it into an oriental despotism?[82]

Meanwhile, at the estates general, the king attempted to turn the debates towards providing the funds for the war which, should the protestant military leaders reject their peace overtures, must necessary follow the unanimous decision to return France to its catholic roots. The deputies of the third estate saw clearly which way things were going on 15 January. Preparing for the plenary session on 17 January, they instructed their spokesman, Pierre Versoris, to emphasise that they had only committed themselves to reunification 'par doux

[79] Bodin, p. 30.

[80] Condé's "protestation" of 23 January is summarised, without date, in La Popelinière, *l'Histoire de France*, 2 vols. (1581), II, fols. 333v–334. For another, dated, version, see SP 70/142 fol. 143.

[81] See A. Jouanna, *Le devoir de révolte* (Fayard, Paris, 1989).

[82] *La France-Tvrqvie. C'est à dire, Conseils et Moyens tenus par les ennemies de la Couronne de France, povr redvire le royaume en tel estat que la Tyrannie Turqvesque* (Orléans, 1576). The strategy was attributed in the pamphlet to the chevalier Pcncet, a confidant of the queen mother who had spent some time in Florence and the Ottoman empire. The eponymous Poncet would in due course appear before the estates general in January 1577 with a neat idea for a universal poll tax to solve all the monarchy's financial woes.

moyens & sans guerre'.[83] Whether he put the qualification strongly enough in his 90 minute harangue before the plenary session was a matter of conjecture and argument which erupted in the third estate session of 30 January.[84] Deputies threatened one another with fists and the president had to retire by the back door from the *hôtel de ville*. Bodin would shortly remind the king that, if the debates about religious reunification had really been about peace and war, then they were unconstitutional, since such decisions were 'cas réservés', indisputably matters of sovereignty and not ones to be decided in the forum of an estates. It was the classic application of his sovereignty thesis and it would cost him both the promised mastership of requests and the favour in which he had been briefly held by Henri III.

In so many ways, then, the debates and arguments at the third estate on 26 December 1576 portrayed a France which was torn apart by the legacy of the civil wars. The debates of that day only served to reinforce those divisions and to expose the enforced duplicities of a king whose authority was in question. Both in protestant propaganda, and in reality, this proved to be France's 'Machiavellian moment'. A French graffiti, spotted when I first worked in archives in Paris over twenty years ago, seems an appropriate conclusion: 'In the kingdom of gulls, the king is a fool'.

[83] *Bodin*, p. 44.
[84] Ibid., pp. 48; 59.

6

Meddling Chaperons:
The Involvement of the Parlement of Paris in the Estates General of 1593

ADRIANNA E. BAKOS

In 1753/4 Louis Adrien Lepaige, an *avocat* with Jansenist sympathies, published his *Lettres historiques sur les fonctions essentielles du parlement* amidst the so-called "refusal of sacraments" controversy. In an attempt to intimidate Jansenists, orthodox clergy were refusing to administer the last rites to suspected heretics, unless the unfortunate soul in question could produce a "billet de confession" attesting to his orthodoxy. The Parlement of Paris, many of whose members were Jansenists, issued *arrêt* after *arrêt*, attempting to force the clergy to perform last rites. The *Lettres historiques*, along with another treatise by Lepaige on the parlementaire assemblies known as "lits de justice," sought to legitimize the parlement's involvement in the controversy by pointing out the historic role the parlement had always played in French government. Lepaige argued that in fact the institution which he calls the "Parlement Général" was born in the same instant as the monarchy itself. The functions of this ancient assembly, combined with those of the smaller conciliar body known as the "cour de roi", were currently exercised, in Lepaige's view, by the Parlement of Paris.[1]

By way of a footnote to this discussion, Lepaige makes a clear and, for our purposes, crucial distinction between assemblies held under the first and second race of French kings, "Parlemens Généraux," and the later institutional innovation known as the estates general:

> The estates general, which began under Philippe le Bel, are in no way the ancient parlements; they are only an imperfect copy of them. The authority

---

[1] Louis Adrien Lepaige, *Lettres historiques sur les fonctions essentielles du parlement*, 2 vols. (Amsterdam, 1753–54), 1:124. ". . .C'est la réunion des anciennes fonctions de la Cour du Roi, avec celles des anciens Parlemens Généraux, qui constitue la nature actuelle du Parlement . . ."

and the functions of these ancient assemblies remained so securely in the parlement that, far from ceasing to exercise them during the assembly of the estates, on the contrary it exercises this authority over the estates themselves; it represses, by its *arrêts* that which was attempted to be passed contrary to the laws of the kingdom, of which [the parlement] is the depository and the guardian, as representing alone the ancient parlements. One sees proofs of this at the estates of 1615 and those of 1594 [sic] . . .[2]

In his article discussing the Jansenist influence on parlementaire theory during the eighteenth century, Daniel Joynes has argued that the refusal of sacraments controversy crystallized the aspirations of the Parlement of Paris to, as he put it, "transform itself from a corporate judicial body, visibly dependent upon the monarch for its authority, into a body endowed with independent legislative and political power, and constitutionally coequal with the crown."[3] Joynes' work, and that of other historians studying the political ambitions of the Parlement of Paris during the eighteenth century, has much to commend it.[4] A critical lacuna nevertheless exists in the scholarship: an examination of how the Parlement of Paris construed its relationship with the estates general, the only other institution that could claim political involvement on the national level. Given the fact that the estates general had not been convoked since 1614/15, it is perhaps surprising that eighteenth-century parlementaires seem concerned to establish the exact nature of the relationship between these two institutions. If we turn to the second half of the sixteenth century when the estates general met with relative frequency, the rivalry between the estates and the Parlement of Paris is all the more evident.

While a number of historians have recognized that this rivalry existed throughout the sixteenth century, few have demonstrated more than a passing interest in this struggle, focussing instead on how these two institutions came into conflict with the crown.[5] This focus both emerges from and confirms the

---

[2] Ibid., 1:142 "Les Etats Generaux qui ont commencé sous Philippe le Bel, ne sont point les anciens Parlemens; ils n'en sont qu'une copie imparfaite. L'autorité et les fonctions de ces anciennes Assemblées, sont tellement demeurées réunies dans le Parlement, que loin de cesser de les exercer, pendant la tenue des Etats, il les exerce au contraire sur les Etats eux-mêmes; il réprime par ses Arrêts, ce qui s'y peut passer de contraire aux Loix du Royaume, dont il est le dépositaire et le gardien, comme représentant seul les anciens Parlemens. One en a vû des preuves pour les Etats de 1615 et pour ceux de 1594, et c'est ce qui a conservé la Couronne à la Maison de Bourbon."

[3] Daniel C. Joynes, "Parlementaires, Peers and the *Parti Janseniste*: The Refusal of Sacraments and the Revival of the Ancient Constitution in Eighteenth-century France," *Proceedings of the Annual Meeting of the Western Society for French History* 8 (1980): 229–38.

[4] Among these, see especially Keith Baker, *Inventing the French Revolution: Essays on French Political Culture* (Cambridge, 1990) and Dale Van Kley, *The Damiens Affair and the Unraveling of the Ancien Regime, 1750–1770* (Princeton, 1984).

[5] See for example the cursory manner in which the topic is treated by, among others, J. Russell Major, *The Estates General of 1560* (Princeton, 1951), pp. 39–40. The notable exception is Sarah Hanley, *The 'Lit de Justice' of the Kings of France* (Princeton, 1983).

long-held schema that articulates a neat division of early modern political thought into the opposing ideological strands of absolutism and constitutionalism. The conflicts between the crown and the Parlement of Paris or the estates general are thus interpreted as struggles between those holding absolutist and constitutionalist views of French government. Challenges to this schema of constitutionalist/absolutist dichotomy have been frequent and persuasive, although perhaps not entirely successful.[6] An examination of the involvement of the Parlement of Paris at the estates general of 1593, as part of a larger investigation into the institutional and ideological tensions between the two bodies may, paradoxically, save that schema by complicating it.

The fracas that occurred at the estates general of 1593 was the culmination of long-standing rivalry and repeated disputes over the participation of magistrates in the estates general. As early as 1413 there was debate as to whether members from the Parlement of Paris ought to be deputed to the estates general. The Parlement of Paris was required to register laws, edicts and ordinances and was, moreover, able to temporarily obstruct the registration of such laws if it deemed them to be either unjust or incongruent with existing French law.[7] The parlement refused to send deputies to the assembly held in 1413 on the grounds that it would be improper for the court to act as both plaintiff and judge; the parlement maintained that it could not rule on the justness of edicts based on deliberations in which some of its members had taken part.[8] The parlement was also asked to send some of its members to assemblies of the estates general in 1467 and 1484, but apparently only complied in 1467, sending first president Boulanger and a dozen councillors. Signicantly, this group of magistrates was sent "not as a body, but in order to give counsel."[9] The emphatic denial of corporate representation was meant to protect the parlement's cherished right of registration.

Although the estates general did not meet again until 1560, there are several instances in the first half of the sixteenth century when the lines distinguishing the Parlement of Paris from an ostensibly representative institution like the

Hanley makes several excellent points about the relationship between the parlement and the estates general, especially regarding the parlement's claim to be an abridged version of the larger assembly. Most of her comments are, however, more narrowly focussed on the identification of the *lit de justice* with the estates general.

   6 For reviews of recent scholarship addressing the issue of absolutism see Richard Bonney, "Absolutism: What's in a Name?" *French History* 1 (1987): 93–117 and James Eastgate Brink, "Provincial Assemblies and Parlement in Early Modern France: A Review of Historical Scholarship," *Legislative Studies Quarterly* 11 (1986): 429–53.

   7 For a discussion of the right of registration see J. H. Shennan, *The Parlement of Paris* (Ithaca, 1968), chapter 5.

   8 Gerard F. Denault, "The Legitimation of the Parlement of Paris and the Estates-General of France, 1560–1614." Ph.D. Dissertation, Washington University, 1975, p. 243.

   9 Edouard Maugis, *Histoire du parlement de Paris de l'avènement des rois Valois à la mort d'Henri IV*, 2 vols. (Paris, 1913), 1:656.

estates general began to blur.[10] One of the most significant encounters between the Parlement of Paris and the estates general occurred after the disastrous defeat of French forces at Saint Quentin in 1557. As we shall see, the assembly was later cited in support of magisterial involvement in the estates general of 1593 because of the peculiar organization of the meeting in 1558: to the usual three estates of the clergy, the nobility and the third estate was added a fourth order, composed of members from the sovereign courts. A few short years after the assembly of 1558, the struggle between the Parlement of Paris and the estates general centered once again around the issue of the parlement's role in legislative registration. During the assembly of the estates at Pontoise, the crown found its efforts to secure subsidies stymied when deputies refused to consider finances until the ordinance advocating administrative reform, based on the deliberations of the estates of Orléans, was duly registered by the Parlement of Paris. When pressed for a reason as to the sovereign court's tardiness in registering the ordinance, first president Le Maistre argued that since the parlement does not participate in the deliberations of the assembly, it must take due time to consider all the articles of the ordinance.[11]

The estates held at Blois in 1576, and again in 1588, were relatively free from the sort of institutional wrangling which plagued the relationship between the parlement and the estates general for much of the sixteenth century. But by the end of the 1580s, the concatenation of circumstances had created a situation in which the problematic self-definition of the parlement was bound to come into conflict with the aspirations of the estates general convoked to Paris in 1593. If we turn now to an examination of the estates general of 1593 we shall find that the issues touched upon so far are explicit in the confrontations between the Parlement of Paris and members of both the clerical and third estates.

There is, of course, the important consideration of whether either the Parlement of Paris or the estates general were lawful entities by 1593. The last

---

10 During the captivity of Francis I, for example, a shortlived institutional experiment was implemented when the Parlement of Paris organized a committee to oversee the defense of Paris. The *Assemblée da la salle verte*, as it was called, was to be only a "simple commission of information and initiative," but began to refer to itself as an assembly of the three estates after only three weeks in existence. Out of twenty-three members, nine were from the parlement, along with three from another sovereign court, the *chambre des comptes*. Only six members came from the town of Paris and five from the university and the Church. The composition of the commission appears to have caused some consternation, eliciting debate over exactly which institution, the Parlement of Paris or the estates general, possessed jurisdiction over the committee. Maugis, 1:639.

11 One of the most interesting points put forward by Le Maistre is that the parlement is required to make sure that the articles do in fact correspond to the *cahiers* of the people upon which they are supposed to be based. Le Maistre went on to argue that in an earlier period it was not necessary for the parlement to register edicts because the king responded to the "plaintes du peuple" from the field of the assembly itself. Since this method had fallen out of practice, it was now up to the parlement to ensure that the "plaintes" were answered. B.N. Ms. N.A. 8060, 386r–v.

years of the 1580s witnessed something of a magisterial crisis when the Parlement became increasingly factionalized over the issue of support for the ultra-
catholic League. After the assassination of the Duc de Guise at the estates of
1588, the sovereign court found itself in the horns of a dilemma: if it supported
the League, it would lose the support of the crown. Could its other sources of
legitimation bear the heavier burden?

The widening split between the moderates and the radicals within the
Leaguer faction, which had taken over the municipal government after the
barricades of May 1588, resulted in a purge of the parlement which took place
in 1589. Twenty-two magistrates were arrested. In March of 1589 Henri III
moved the Parlement of Paris to Tours; royalist magistrates followed the king
while their Leaguer counterparts remained in Paris.[12] Even the rump body
which continued to function in Paris was riven by internal division. The
ongoing radicalization of the municipal government of Paris was manifested
when Barnabé Brisson, who had become first president of the Parlement of
Paris in the wake of the initial purge in 1589, was himself executed along with
two other counsellors in 1591.[13] By 1593 the Parlement of Paris's claims for
institutional legitimacy were tenuous indeed.

As for the estates general assembled in Paris in 1593, scholars generally
discount their legitimacy because of the manner in which they were convoked,
the limited geographical representation and the overt ideological foundation
which all but precluded the participation of deputies unsympathetic to the
Leaguer platform. An awareness that they were open to charges of illegality
prompted the deputies themselves not to refer to the assembly as an estates
general in their communications with the Navarre faction, taking place concurrently with the holding of the assembly in the first six months of 1593.[14]
Nevertheless, the question of legitimacy does not obscure the importance of the
interaction between the parlement and the estates general. In their exchanges,
neither the parlementaires nor the deputies cast doubt on the legitimacy of the
estates general or the Parlement of Paris, respectively. To do so would, of
course, cast aspersions on their common Leaguer pedigree. One could argue,
as well, that arguments about the relative authority of these two institutions

[12] Shennan, p. 227. I am grateful to Michel de Waele for drawing my attention to the
fact that the royalist parlement at Tours, like its Parisian counterpart, struggled with issues
of legitimation. In contrast to the Leaguer parlement in Paris, however, the parlement at
Tour, not surprisingly, placed rather more emphasis on the monarchical foundation of the
sovereign court.

[13] For a discussion of the Catholic League in Paris, see Elie Barnavi, *Le Parti de Dieu:
étude sociale et politique des chefs de la Ligue* (Brussels, 1980) and J. H. M. Salmon, "The Paris
Sixteen, 1584–1594: the Social Analysis of a Revolutionary Movement," *Journal of Modern
History* 44 (1972): 540–76. Specifically concerning the successive purges culminating in
the assassination of Barnabé Brisson, see Elie Barnavi and Robert Descimon, *La Sainte
Ligue: le juge et la potence: l'assassinat du président Brisson* (Paris, 1985).

[14] Georges Picot, *Histoire des états généraux*, 4 vols. (Paris, 1872), 3:229.

would have to be all the more cogent and persuasive in order to successfully counteract challenges to their legitimacy.

The proceedings of the 1593 assembly amply demonstrate the rivalry between the Parlement of Paris and the estates general and the essential uncertainty about each institution's relationship to the law, the king and the people from which that rivalry stemmed. The estates had been convoked to Paris for the purpose of electing a Catholic king in an effort to prevent the accession of the heir presumptive, Protestant Henri de Navarre. The extent to which the parlement should participate in the deliberations of the estates general, a contentious issue for much of the century, was again the topic of debate. Corporate representation aside, magistrates were often present at assemblies of the estates through the incidental election of individual deputies who were members of the courts. Such was the case at the estates of 1593; Guillaume du Vair, who played such an important role in the debate concerning the succession and the Salic Law, was elected as a deputy from Paris.

There was, in fact, an attempt to send a group of delegates to the estates of 1593 as representatives of the parlement *per se*. After some initial hesitation, based on fears that attendance at the assembly might interfere with their role as judges of all actions and declarations made therein and might undermine their superiority over the estates, at the end of January the parlement agreed to send a deputation of ten magistrates, two presidents and eight counsellors, to the assembly, "in order to assist the estates destined to bring an end to the interregnum through the election of a king."[15]

According to Bernard, the editor of the *Procès-verbaux des États-Généraux de 1593*, a great hue and cry went up from the third estate when it was learned that the parlement intended to send some of its members to the assembly. The deputies maintained that such an innovation would profoundly alter the assembly because these new deputies would not be from any order. The members of the court were not permitted to participate as delegates of the parlement. It was decided, however, that the Duc de Mayenne could invite parlementaires to provide him with counsel on an informal basis.

The controversy over the formation of a fourth chamber erupted again in May amidst the consideration of a proposal made by the Spanish ambassador, the Duc de Feria that the Infanta of Spain be elected queen of France. The issue was inextricably bound up with debates concerning the succession and the validity of the Salic law which barred accession to the throne of any potential heir descended through a female line. When, in a general assembly of the three estates on the morning of 28 May, the *procureur-général* Molé spoke with vigour and eloquence against the Spanish proposition, he was denounced for meddling. Molé condemned the proposition as "notably repugnant and contrary to

15 E. Glasson, *Le Parlement de Paris. Son rôle politique depuis le regne de Charles VII jusqu'à la révolution*, 2 vols. (Paris, 1901), 2:63–4. See also B.N. Ms. Fr. 8091 "Extrait des registres du Conseil," pp. 344(r)–345(v).

the laws of the kingdom." Molé further called upon other members of the sovereign court who were present at the assembly (in a non-corporate capacity) to follow his example and stand in adamant opposition to the illicit proposal. The Archbishop of Lyon retorted that Molé had not been called to the estates to exercise his function as *procureur-général*; that to have done so, "would be too scandalous in so solemn a situation and the estates would not have permitted it"[16] More wrangling ensued, at the end of which another parlementaire delegate, president de Hacqueville commented petulantly that perhaps it would be more expedient if parlementaire deputies did not participate at all in the assembly, to which the deputies of the third estate responded with a hearty good riddance!

The exchange in the morning session resulted in considerable discussion at the sessions held separately by each estate in the afternoon. The clergy's session was particularly lively where the bishop of Amiens recounted a meeting with the Duc de Mayenne at which time the idea of a fourth chamber was addressed. It seems that Mayenne, who possessed his own majestic ambitions, wanted to imbue the assembly with more authority and consequently advocated the formalized involvement of members of the courts as well as "grands officiers."[17] The bishop of Amiens objected strenuously to such a plan, arguing that the Catholic faith and the authority of the estates must be preserved inviolate, claiming that the organization of the assembly was governed by fundamental law. It is ironic that an appeal to fundamental law was used to derail the plan for corporate representation of the parlement in the estates given the sovereign court's claim to be sole guardian (and interpreter) of fundamental law. The bishop of Amiens denounced the proposal in the most forceful language, saying that to add a further order would "deform this body and form a monster in our estate as strange and wondrous to see as if we had made a monster of nature."[18] Mayenne responded that he himself was concerned to protect the prerogative and authority of the estates but that such a weighty matter as the election of a king required the advice of the parlement. Furthermore, a precedent for the parlement's involvement could be found in the assembly of 1558.

Desperate to raise much-needed funds in order to continue the fight, Henri II had decided to gather together an assembly of notables to meet in Paris during the first months of 1558. The assembly has sometimes been called an estates general because although Henri II had asked the towns to send their mayors, some towns decided to delegate whomever they wanted, in contravention of Henri's instructions.[19] The assembly of 1558 was singled out by Mayenne

[16] Auguste Bernard, ed., *Procès-verbaux des États Généraux de 1593* (Paris, 1842), p. 483.

[17] Alexandre Vivien, "Memoire historique sur les etats generaux de 1593," *Compte rendu de l'Academie des sciences morales et politiques* 19 (1851): 23.

[18] B.N. Ms. Fr. 17534, "Assemblé des estatz de la Ligue tenus à Paris l'an 1593," p. 39(v).

[19] J. Russell Major, *Representative Institutions in Renaissance France 1421–1559* (Madison, 1960), pp. 144–7. Primary sources about the "estates" of 1558 are scarce; the most useful account of the assembly is *Discours des estats tenuz à Paris par le tres Chrestien roy de France,*

because of its unusual structure, composed of four estates rather than three.[20] In response to Mayenne's point, the bishop of Amiens argued that the example cited was not valid since the 1558 meeting was not a true assembly of the estates and that, moreover, all those in attendance in 1558 recognized the inclusion of magistrates to be extraordinary.

At this point, some of Mayenne's counsellors suggested that all the various elements that would make up a fourth chamber be dispersed among their respective estates. Even this was deemed unacceptable because, in the view of the third estate,

> No one had the right to be admitted to the estates without being elected by the provinces; one must not suffer that the liberties of so notable an assembly, which claimed to be above the king, be diminished and diluted during this interregnum by persons inferior to the king.[21]

Meanwhile, in the assembly of the third estate, after hearing of the meeting with Mayenne, all the deputies from the provinces gave their opinions, after which it was resolved that the "messieurs des cours de parlement" could not be admitted to the estates with a resolutive and conclusive voice. Mayenne was allowed to seek the advice of such counsellors as he saw fit, retaining them only in a consultative capacity. Thus Mayenne was asked to conserve "l'auctorité et dignité des estats."[22] The decision of the third estate was echoed in the other two chambers. The attempt to create a fourth chamber, composed primarily of members of the sovereign courts, was effectively quashed.

The debate is parodied in the *Satyre Menippée*. In one of the most famous satires of the period, the author(s) present the major figures involved in the estates general unwittingly incriminating themselves after ingesting a concoction which forces them to speak only the truth. So, for example, the Duc de Mayenne, under the influence of this truth serum, refers to the assembly which he convoked as, "une mommerie d'estats."[23] Other important participants are

---

Henry second, au moys de Ianvier, ceste presente annee, Mil cinq cens cinquante huict (Paris, 1558).

20 The *Discours des estats tenuz à Paris* recounts the seating plan in the Chambre de Saint Louis (in the Palais de Justice) as follows: the archbishops, bishops and other prelates were seated beneath the window. On an elevated platform to the right were seated the bailiffs, senechals and others from the nobility. "And on a bench decorated with *fleurs de lys* were the presidents of the parlements. And below the said bench, on another small bench on the same side were the *gens du Roy* of the Parlement of Paris, the two advocates and the *procureur du Roy* in the middle."

21 "Nul n'avait le droit d'être admis aux Etats sans être elu par les provinces, il ne fallait pas souffrir que les libertés d'une si notable assemblee, qui pretendait être par-dessus le roi, fussent diminuees et amoindries pendant cet interregne par des personnes inferieures au roi." *Procès-verbaux*, p. 485.

22 *Procès-verbaux*, p. 223.

23 Ch. Marcilly, ed., *Satyre Ménippée de la vertue du Catholicon d'Espagne et de la tenue des estatz de Paris* (Paris, n.d.), p. 64.

similarly lampooned. During the speech made on behalf of the nobility, the Sieur de Rieux attacks the magistrates as "chaperons" foisted on the estates by the Parlement of Paris who play at being gentlemen and who meddle in affairs of state without true cognizance.[24] The magisterial pomposity to which the Sieur de Rieux refers is confirmed when a member of "la noblesse nouvelle" rises to begin a harangue calling for the creation of a fourth chamber. The speaker, a certain Sieur d'Angoulevent (the name referring to a bird with a raucous call), is satirized mercilessly. The Sieur d'Angoulevent rises to speak prior to the representative of the third estate because, in his view, the third estate is only composed of "les manants." He begins his harangue, "Monsieur, le douzieme . . ." but is prevented from continuing by a clamor among the peasants standing behind the deputies. Although he tries repeatedly to make his speech, he is never able to get beyond the words, "Monsieur, le douzieme . . ."[25]

Finally, the Sieur d'Aubray rises to speak on behalf of the third estate. Under the influence of the truth serum, d'Aubray says that he would consider the estates legitimate if there were serious men of sufficient probity and stature in attendance. "But I see only self-interested foreigners."[26] D'Aubray denied that d'Angoulevent possessed the right to speak at all; it had always been the custom to have only three estates and he, d'Aubray, has been charged to speak on behalf of the third estate. According to the *Satyre*, the argument became so heated that it was thought the matter might end in the exchange of blows. The debate is tabled, however, as the hour is late and it is past the papal legate's dinner time! Angoulevent is enjoined to cease his endless attempts to speak and, instead, to commit his ideas to paper.

Although the proposal to create a fourth chamber was soundly defeated, parlementaire involvement in the deliberations of the estates was only just beginning. Indeed, as already noted, the controversy over the participation of the magistrates was an integral part of the larger debate over the succession. Throughout the early months of the assembly, the Duc de Feria put forward several variants of a proposal which involved the election of the Infanta as queen of France. The estates were divided: the staunchest Leaguers, placing faith above country, were willing to accept a Spanish monarch, while the more moderate, some of whom were members of the courts, found the idea of foreign

---

[24] Ibid., p. 156.

[25] The anecdote is included in the *Satyre* to poke fun at the Sieur d'Amours, a counsellor in the Parlement of Paris, who had been sent to welcome back that section of the sovereign court that had gone to Tours with Henri de Navarre after the death of Henri III. According to the story bruited at the time, d'Amours began his speech before de Harlay, the only first president present. He started, "Monsieur, le douzieme . . ." but was repeatedly interrupted by the successive entrance of other presidents and only after the last president had entered could he complete the phrase, "Monsieur, le douzieme de mai . . ." Ibid., p. 163, n. 1.

[26] Ibid., p. 247.

control repugnant. It should be noted, moreover, that the negotiations with Henri de Navarre, taking place concurrently with the assembly, were proceeding apace, and there were strong intimations that Henri was ready and willing to convert to Catholicism. This, combined with revulsion at the thought of Spanish overlordship, convinced some deputies that they ought to work against the Spanish proposals.

Throughout the month of June, negotiations with both Spain and Henri de Navarre were on-going. Towards the end of the month, despite an eloquent speech given by Guillaume du Vair on behalf of "la patrie et la loi fondamentale," it seemed that the assembly was leaning toward the acceptance of the Spanish proposal to elect the Infanta as queen and to marry her to a French prince who would rule jointly with her. When the battle appeared lost, du Vair and the entire delegation from the Ile-de-France left the assembly.[27] A nineteenth-century biographer of du Vair, in a fervor of admiration for his subject, wrote that, considering du Vair's speech to the assembly and his subsequent withdrawal, "one could say that he saved monarchy."[28]

This is certainly a debatable point, but it is clear that the actions of the parlementaires elicited hostility from the estates. The Satyre Menippee illustrates the antipathy of the deputies in the harangue of the Sieur de Rieux, the representative of the nobility. Rieux launches into an attack on the magistrates and what he sees as an unreasonable fixation on the Salic Law. When news regarding the actual acceptance of the Spanish proposal by the estates reached the parlement, the sovereign court resolved to act. On 28 June 1593, the Parlement of Paris passed an arrêt, declaring all attempts on the part of the estates general to transfer the crown of France to a foreign potentate to be contrary to the laws of France and consequently null and void.[29] The arrêt itself makes no radical claims regarding the authority of the parlement. It merely states that parlement possesses both the responsibility and the authority to protect the laws of the realm. A more powerful exposition of the parlement's authority can be found in Guillaume du Vair's Suasion de l'arrest donné au parlement pour la manutention de la loy salique. Speaking in support of the proposed arrêt, du Vair recounts the events at the estates and says to his colleagues, "I see your faces pale and a murmur of astonishment is raised among you, and not without cause, for perhaps never has one dared to speak so freely, so brazenly . . . about the fortune of such a great and powerful kingdom."[30] He points out to the members that if they remain silent in the face of such an

---

27 Picot, 3:245.

28 C. A. Sapey, Essai sur la vie et les ouvrages de Guillaume Du Vair (Paris, 1847), p. 15.

29 See F. A. Isambert, ed., Recueil Général des anciennes lois françaises depuis l'an 420 jusqu'à la révolution de 1789, 29 vols. (Paris, 1822–1833), 15:71.

30 "Je voy voz visages pallir, et un murmure plein d'estonnement se lever parmy vous, et non sans cause, car jamais peut-estre il ne s'ouyt dire que si licentieusement, si effrontément on se jouäst de la fortune d'un si grand et puissant Royaume . . ." Guillaume du Vair, Actions et Traictez Oratoires, edited by René Radouant (Paris, 1911), p. 126.

assault on the laws of the kingdom, they will be as culpable as those actively engaged in the unlawful actions. One *arrêt* is all that is needed to stop this criminal design in its tracks. Du Vair expounds on the authority of the court to take such action against the resolution of the estates:

> One cannot doubt that you have the power to do this, you who have the stewardship of the laws and the guardianship of the kingdom in your hands, you, by the authority of which this assembly is made; seeing that that which is customarily resolved in the estates general of France duly and legitimately assembled has no force or vigour until after it is verified by you seated at the throne of kings, on the bed of their justice, in the court of peers. If these things legitimately deliberated, justly resolved and passed by general consent, possess force only with your approbation, how much more true is it of those things discussed by monopolies and proposed contrary to the laws and the good of the state, to which all good men, and generally all those who still call themselves Frenchmen and who have some sense of decency openly oppose themselves, can be condemned by you and prevented by your judgment, in order to stop the disastrous course of their pernicious designs.[31]

Du Vair is quite clearly asserting the parlement's superiority over the estates. Perhaps influenced by du Vair's impassioned speech, the parlement passed the *arrêt* and it was taken to Mayenne by president Le Maistre and some twenty other magistrates in the evening of the twenty-eighth of May.

In his meeting with Mayenne, Le Maistre maintained that there were three reasons for the *arrêt*: the obligation of the court to conserve and maintain the fundamental laws of the realm, the fear that all Frenchmen feel at the thought of Spanish domination and the pleas made by the Parisian populace to the parlement to act against the transmission of the crown into foreign hands. With regard to the parlement's role in the protection of the laws, Le Maistre stated that members of the court were obliged to undertake this duty "as much by the institution of the parlement as by the oath that each of them had made to the said court."[32]

The Parlement of Paris was not alone in attempting to extend its authority

---

31 "On ne peut pas douter que vous n'ayés le pouvoir de ce faire, vous qui avez la garde des loix et la tutelle du Royaume en voz mains, vous, par l'authorité desquels est faicte cette assemblée; veu que ce qui a accoustumé de se resoudre aux Estats generaux de la France bien et legitimement assemblez n'a force ny vigeurs qu'apres qu'il a esté verifié par vous seans au throsne des Rois, au lict de leur justice, en la cour des Pairs. Que si les choses legitimement deliberées, justement resoluës et passées par un general consentement, ne prennent leur force que de vostre approbation, à combien plus forte raison celles qui ne sont traictées que par monopoles, et qui sont proposées contre les loix et le salut de l'Estat, ausquelles tous les gens de bien, et generallement tous ceux qui se disent encores François et qui ont quelque rest de pudeur, reluctent ouvertement, peuvent-elles estre par vous condamnées et prevenuës par vostre jugement, pour arrester le funeste cours de leurs pernicieux desseins." Ibid., p. 126.

32 *Procès-verbaux*, p. 743.

by interpreting the gray area of contested powers to its own advantage. While parlementaires asserted that the sovereign court had a right to participate in legislation, there were writers who sought rather to expand the authority of the estates general by arguing that it ought to be involved in the judicial process. In a pamphlet from 1588, *Articles pour proposer aux estatz et faire passer en loy fondamentalle du Royaume*, the author propounded the constitutionalist argument that the monarch's authority cannot be so absolute that it is not contained within the fundamental laws of the realm. If the exercise of "royalle majeste" exceeds these boundaries, the estates general as "Iuges competants" is empowered to bring the king back in line.[33] It seems almost as if the estates are to take over the remonstrative duties which the Parlement of Paris had always claimed as its own.

Of perhaps even more importance is the author's suggestion that each sovereign court contain a chamber "composed of persons elevated by the estates to which the complaints of the people and the contraventions of ordinances [promulgated] by the estates would be reported and considered . . ."[34] The notion that the estates general would be directly represented in the sovereign court and would oversee the judicial activities taking place therein is a truly radical concept. It is an illustrative counterpart to the proposal to incorporate the Parlement of Paris as a separate chamber in the estates of 1593.

It is significant that the author is referring in this pamphlet both to the creation of fundamental law and to its protection, controversial points very much at the center of the conflict between the magistrates and the deputies at the estates of 1593. Both constitutionalist and absolutist writers focussed much of their attention on the fundamental laws, rules of government that many believed had been established at the very beginning of the French monarchy. One historian of political thought has quite rightly pointed out that the concern about the status of fundamental law manifested by constitutionalist writers should be seen as distinct from their emphasis on popular sovereignty.[35] I believe that the rivalry between the estates general and the Parlement of Paris had a great deal to do with the way in which two distinct strands within

---

[33] *Articles pour proposer aux estatz et faire passer en loy fondamentalle du Royaume* (n.p., 1588).

[34] Ibid., p. 12. ". . . Composée de personnes esleuës par lesdicts Estatz à laquelle les plaintes du peuple et les contraventions aux ordonnances desdictz Estatz généraux seront raportées et en cognoistront en dernier ressort." With regard to the Leaguer arguments that the estates were empowered to create new fundamental laws, see André Lemaire, *Les Lois fondamentales de la monarchie française* (Paris, 1907), pp. 133–141.

[35] The emergence of the notion of fundamental law is discussed by Harro Höpfl, "Fundamental Law and the Constitution of Early Modern France," in *Die Rolle der Juristen bei der Enstehung des modernen Staates*, ed. Roman Schnur (Berlin, 1986), p. 347. See also Martin Thompson, "The History of Fundamental Law in Political Thought from the French Wars of Religion to the American Revolution," *American Historical Review* 91 (1986): 1103–1128.

constitutionalist thought, notions about the primacy of fundamental law and an emphasis on popular sovereignty became entangled one with another.

It was generally accepted that fundamental laws, such as the law prohibiting the alienation of the royal domain, were irrevocable. Not even a reigning monarch could alter or suspend such a law. Nevertheless, considerable debate existed over whether fundamental laws were created or discovered. The issue of whether fundamental laws are made or found is of utmost importance since it largely determines the authoritative weight given to each of our rival institutions. If fundamental laws are discovered, the Parlement of Paris is assigned the pre-eminent constitutional function because of its generally acknowledged role as guardian of the laws of the kingdom. On the other hand, the notion that fundamental laws are created would add weight to the claims of legislative authority made on behalf of the estates general.

According to the *Journal de l'Estoile*, the Duc de Mayenne was distressed at the passage of the *arrêt* and expressed his irritation that he was not consulted by the parlement prior to its issuance. He enjoined the parlementaires to reconsider their position "that they must change their *arrêt* out of friendship, as he pleaded with them to do, or force would be employed, to his great regret . . ." In an attempt to be diplomatic, president Le Maistre responded that parlement believed Mayenne to be so wise and well-advised that he would never descend to the use of force, but should he attempt to violently coerce parlement, God would always be for justice, which the court had simply followed in its *arrêt*.[36] The antagonism of the estates both to the pretensions of parlement to "meddle" in affairs of state in general, and parlementaire defence of the Salic law in particular, dwindled rapidly after the passage of the *arrêt*, due at least in part to renewed assurances that Henri de Navarre would abjure. All three estates agreed to accept the *arrêt* and consequently reject the Spanish proposals.

The success of the *arrêt* in forestalling a possible agreement between the estates and Spain has led some scholars to argue that the parlement scored a significant victory over the estates-general. In his *Histoire du parlement de Paris*, Edouard Maugis maintains that the parlement ". . . a fait triompher, avec la principe de son entière distinction d'avec les Etats Généraux, celui de sa jurisdiction superieure, de son droit de révision et de verification des ordonnances issues de leurs cahiers."[37] Ernest Glasson also argues that in defending the fundamental laws of the realm, the parlement was placing itself in opposition to the authority of the estates.[38] On the other hand, Auguste Bernard, the editor of the *Procès-verbaux*, asserts that the estates general's attempt to interpret fundamental law and the assembly's unwillingness to admit delegates from the parlement did the court grievous injury. The court, newly re-unified with the parlementaires who had gone to Tours, was able to retaliate when Henri IV

---

36 *Mémoires-Journaux de Pierre de l'Estoile*, 12 vols. (Paris, 1896), 6:43.
37 Maugis, 1:670.
38 Glasson, 2:71.

commanded that all ordinances and declarations made to the detriment of royal authority since December of 1589 be revoked.[39] Several individual members were also involved in the physical destruction of all documents and materials pertaining to, and emerging from, the assembly.[40]

Whether or not parlement struck a blow against the estates-general is difficult to conclude. The blurring of jurisdictions overseen by the estates-general and the Parlement of Paris forms the basis both for possible cooperation and for rivalry.[41] By what Maugis has called "leur entente secrète," the assembly and the court possessed the potential to initiate and execute programs of reform.[42] But because the extent of each institution's authority was never clearly delineated, the gray area of shared responsibility caused disputes considerably more often than co-operative efforts. Indeed, the attempts of both the parlementaires and proponents of the estates general to claim superior authority over the other institution created deep divisions among those devoted to the idea of monarchical limitation which may have contributed to Henri IV's success in emerging from that chaotic period at the end of the religious wars with so firm a grip on the reins of power.

In its bid to displace or undercut the estates general, the Parlement of Paris dramatically demonstrated the essential ambivalence of its position; it desired at once to be a pillar of royal authority and the guardian against the abuse of that authority. A study of the relationship between the estates general and the Parlement of Paris points to a multi-faceted interaction of absolutist and constitutionalist discourse in early modern France. Such an investigation illustrates the fact that corporate efforts to attain political legitimation never relied exclusively on royal, legal or popular foundations. Rather, both the estates general and the Parlement of Paris used shifting strategies of legitimation citing institutional connection with the king, the people and/or the law as the political circumstances warranted. Nor were these strategies insincere in their application. The ability of magistrates and parlementaire theorists to draw upon different, even at times opposing, sources of legitimation testifies to genuine

---

[39] See *arrêt* of 30 March 1594, in Isambert, 15:86–7.

[40] Guillaume du Vair and Jean Pithou were charged to oversee the suppression of documents produced by the assembly. Claude Malingre, *Extrait des registres du parlement* (Rouen, 1652) cited by Bernard in the preface to the *Procès-verbaux*, p. lxiii.

[41] It must be remembered that early modern French government demonstrated no real "separation of powers." Even in Jean Bodin's famous exposition of sovereignty in which he emphasized legislative authority, we find the incorporation of judicial power (through the right of final appeal) and administrative control (through the appointment of officers). In his early book on *The Estates General of 1560*, Russell Major notes that the estates were sometimes characterized by comtemporaries as possessing the quality of a court distinguished from the parlement in that the latter dealt with private cases while the estates heard "public" ones (pp. 94–95). Conversely, in *La France moderne: l'esprit des institutions* (Paris, 1973), p. 31, Denis Richet points out that the standard contrast made between English parliament and French parlement ignores the legislative quality of latter.

[42] Maugis, 1:667.

uncertainty about the exact basis of each institution's authority and therefore the recipient of its ultimate loyalty. An examination of parlementaire involvement in the estates general of 1593 and other such occasions of interplay between the Parlement of Paris and the estates general highlights how, out of the alloy of institutional history and the history of political thought, a more nuanced understanding of constitutionalism and absolutism might be wrought.

7

The Monarchic State in Early Modern France: Marital Regime Government and Male Right

SARAH HANLEY *

From the medieval feudal era of growing national consciousness through the early modern period of nascent state building and into modern times, state formation in France has been circumscribed by negative juridical frameworks that excluded women from political rule: first, by an alleged *Salic Law Ordinance*, then by an influential *French Law Canon*, which dictated female exclusion from rule and privileged male right alone. As rendered in the original Merovingian text (500s) and Carolingian redaction (800s), the Salic Law Ordinance found in the Franco-Germanic Salic Law Code (Title *de allodio*) actually regulated inheritance to lands in families (allodial lands). As transformed into a national myth (600s–800s) and later lost for some time in both text and memory, revived only in hazy memory (1100s–1350s) and then rediscovered, textually interpolated, and forged (1350s and 1400s), the text of that Salic Law Ordinance was reproduced fraudulently as a "French Salic Law" that excluded women from succession to monarchic office in the kingdom. Many chroniclers, historians, and encyclopedists have held that the Salic Law established female exclusion from monarchic office and thus legitimized the male right to rule in France. The case is quite the contrary. The medieval invention of a fraudulent French Salic Law, accompanied by the misogynist litany of moral injunctions (clerical and humanist), presented a troublesome text repeatedly manipulated in attempts to sustain juridical grounds for female exclusion from rule.[1] And that is not all. In the early 1500s when new generations of

* My great appreciation to colleagues and staff at the National Humanities Center, where this chapter first took form; to the Guggenheim Foundation; and to colleagues at the New York Area French Seminar and the Institute for Advanced Study, where it was revised.

1 The relevant passage is Title 59 "Concerning Allodial Lands (*de alodis*)," article 6, in

scholars and legists realized the extent of this deception, they acknowledged the serious fraud but approved its substantive thrust. Abandoning the mythical Salic Law, which no longer validated female exclusion from monarchic office, they developed a French Law Canon, which legitimated the male right to rule in both political state (as king) and marital household (as husband).[2] Across many centuries, these varied efforts to exclude women and legitimize male right bear witness to the high stakes of a national political enterprise supposedly grounded in law but actually based on gender contraries inscribed in juridical and moral precepts and committed to human memory and history. An instructive example of the historical process through which political and social relations are negotiated and new definitions of reality comprehended, the manner of propagating male right in the early modern French monarchic state is worth unravelling.

From the 1500s legists and historians who were well trained in the new *mos gallicus* method of historical research recovered original documents from French archives. Adept at philology, they discovered Carolingian capitularies, including uncorrupted texts of the ancient Salic Law, and published annotated editions that revealed the earlier emendations and forgeries. Shocked and embarrassed by the evident fraud, one after another laughed at the Salic Law myth and wrote devastating critiques of its makeshift history. They boldly undermined its spurious juridical foundations in French Public Law and judged instead that past practice excluding women from monarchic office in France was a "salic" or feudal custom, not a law of the ancient French constitution.[3]

---

the 65-title version of the Code, *Pactus Legis Salicae* (c.507–511), from the later reign of Clovis (c.481–511); and is Title 34 "Concerning Land held by Allodial Tenure (*de alode*)," article 6, in the 70-title Systematic Version of the Code, *Lex Salica Karolina* (802–803) from the reign of Charlemagne (771–814) cited in later times: "Indeed, concerning Salic land, no part of the inheritance shall pass to a woman but all the inheritance of land goes to the virile [male] sex;" Katherine Fischer Drew, trans., *The Laws of the Salian Franks* (Philadelphia, Pa., University of Pennsylvania Press, 1991), pp. 122–123 and 198; and for the Latin: "De terra vero Salica nulla portio hereditatis mulieri veniat, sed ad virilem sexum tota terrae hereditas perveniat," in Karl August Eckhardt, *Monumenta Germaniae Historica, Leges Nationum Germanicarum*, 4:2, *Lex Salica* (Hanover, 1969), p. 214. Sarah Hanley, *State Building in Early Modern France: Law, Litigation, and Local Knowledge* (forthcoming, Princeton University Press) treats the political consequences of this legal fraud; and for commentary on a French edition, see Sarah Hanley, *Des Femmes dans l'Histoire: La Loi Salique*, preface (Paris: Côte-femmes éditions, 1994); and "La Loi Salique," *Encyclopédie politique et historique des femmes*, ed. Christine Fauré, 2 vols. (Paris: Presses Universitaires de France, 1995–1996). See Colette Beaune, *The Birth of an Ideology: Myths and Symbols of Nation in Late-Medieval France* (Berkeley, Ca.: University of California Press, 1991), chap. 9, appendix A, for early chronicle sources on the law; and Ralph E. Giesey, "The Juristic Basis of Dynastic Right to the French Throne," *Transactions of the American Philosophical Society* (Philadelphia, Pa., 1961), new ser. 51:5, pp. 17–22, for later juristic sources.

[2] The complete study, including the interaction of structure and event (patterns of laws and cases litigated in court) is in Hanley, *State Building in Early Modern France.*

[3] Donald R. Kelley, *Foundations of Modern Historical Scholarship: Language, Law, and*

This was a crucial period. The French juridical case for female exclusion was tainted for lack of demonstrable legal evidence and moral force, and customs could change. The rule of queens as monarchs was not the exception but the norm in Europe (Isabella of Spain, Mary of England, Elizabeth of England, Mary of Scotland, and later, Christina of Sweden); and the appointment of queens as regents was common practice in France (Louise of Savoy, Catherine de Médicis, Marie de Médicis, and later, Anne of Austria).[4] Even so, these scholars, legists, and *parlementaires* were not bold enough to reassess the case on its own merits. They failed to transcend the glaring legal and moral problems, because legitimation of male right in the early modern nascent French state was no longer simply a legal or constitutional matter. It had become a singular obsession aimed at defining all authority to govern as fundamentally masculine in nature during a time of interrelated family formation and state building.

From the early 1500s to the decades around the 1650s, legists and *parlementaires* propagated a *French Law Canon*,[5] which secured legal foundations for the male right to govern along the lines of a *Marital Regime* in law. This Law Canon finally attained what jurists and kings had sought for centuries: an indigenous French body of laws quite able to contend with law codes cited competitively by other European states and papacy. On political grounds, the French Law Canon functioned through particular French principles: *Public Law* precepts instanced in political maxims and articulated in newly ordained *Lit de Justice* assemblies convoked from 1527 as constitutional forums to regulate state building; and *Civil Law* edicts instanced in the *Marital Law Compact* promulgated to regulate family formation. On philosophical grounds, the French Law Canon stood on a universal principle: *Natural Law* instanced in *biogenetic seminal notions of male generative capacity* that informed political power. On cultural grounds, the French Law Canon drew on moral customs: *Moral Law*, or social mores (*moeurs*), instanced in *legal, social, and political lessons defaming women.*

History in the French Renaissance (New York, N.Y.: Columbia University Press, 1970), chaps. 7–11, discusses the new design for history and critical legists: Bernard Girard du Haillan, François Hotman, Charondas Le Caron, Pierre Pithou, and Etienne Pasquier; and Sarah Hanley, *The Lit de Justice of the Kings of France: Constitutional Ideology in Legend, Ritual, and Discourse* (Princeton, NJ: Princeton University Press, 1983; French ed., Paris: Aubier, 1991), chaps. 2–9, traces historical views politically articulated in Parlements.

4 Monarchs: Isabella I (1479–1504), with husband, Ferdinand II); Mary I Tudor (1550–1558); Elizabeth I (1558–1603); Mary I Stuart (1560–1567); Christina (1632–1654). Regents: Louise (Francis I, absent at war 1515, imprisoned in Spain 1525); Catherine (Charles IX, minor, 1560–1563); Marie (Louis XIII, minor, 1610–1614); Anne (Louis XIV, minor, 1643–1651).

5 Some historians maintain that France had no state constitution until the first written one (1791) and that French law was not codified until the Code Civil (1804), or Code Napoléon (1807). Yet those suppositions do not hold if we consider the many ways Public Law was articulated in the early modern state and the way legists compiled, printed, and used patterns of laws and case precedents to formulate what I have entitled here the "*French Law Canon;*" Hanley, *The Lit de Justice of the Kings of France*, and *State Building in Early Modern France* make this case.

Constituted with requisite epistemological roots in the universal and the particular, this French Law Canon underwrote both monarchic state building and family formation by resort to a juridical Marital Regime system of governance.

At each step of state building from the 1520s through the 1650s, the development of the Marital Regime system marched apace with the law. The first rubric of the French Law Canon, Public Law, which addressed the constitutional foundations of the monarchic state, articulated precepts of Marital Regime government through political maxims ritually demonstrated. From the 1520s on, the public appearance of a powerful new metonymic device,[6] the French marital maxim, encapsulated the principle of male right in a legal fiction readily comprehended through analogic equivalencies. On the surface enigmatic, the marital maxim when probed provides access to the conceptual framework that enabled the singular legitimation of male right. From the outset French legists discarded the familiar but limited political frame for the polity offered by the medieval marriage metaphor, which discreetly depicted the political marriage of ruler and realm by reference to the spiritual marriage of bishop and church.[7] They created instead the marital maxim, which linked family formation and state building by contractually uniting king and kingdom in a political state marriage likened legally to that of husband and wife in a social civil marriage: *The king is the husband and political spouse of the kingdom.*[8] And they drew into its orbit other legal axioms that brought family and state governance under the Marital Regime.

The marital maxim was extended through a domain-dowry analogy that equated the royal domain of the kingdom, ritually brought to a king at the Coronation and rendered inalienable by Public Law; with the family dowry of a wife, ritually brought to a husband in a civil marriage and likewise rendered inalienable (as *propres*) by Civil Law: "The kingdom brings to him [the king] the said domain as the dowry of his Crown; which dowry kings at their Sacre and Coronation swear solemnly never to alienate." As further extended along

---

6   For the way implications are drawn from metaphors and other imaginative aspects of reasoning, see George Lakoff, *Women, Fire, and Dangerous Things: What Categories Reveal about the Mind* (Chicago, Il: University of Chicago Press, 1987), xi–xvii.

7   The likely medieval source is Lucas de Penna (1320–c.1390), *Commentaria in Tres Libros Codicis*: "Just as there is contracted a spiritual and divine marriage between a church and its prelate, so there is contracted a temporal and terrestrial marriage between the prince and the realm. . . . The man is the head of the wife, and the wife the body of the man. . . . After the same fashion, the prince is the head of the realm, and the realm the body of the prince;" Ernst H. Kantorowicz, *The King's Two Bodies: A Study in Medieval Political Theology* (Princeton, NJ: Princeton University Press, 1957), pp. 207–223, cites this and other medieval formulations.

8   [All italics on maxims are mine]. French jurists who propagated the new marital maxim, *Le roi est le mari et epoux politique de la chose publique* (and other versions), in *Lit de Justice* assemblies, Royal Séances, Coronations, Royal Entries, and legal treatises knew De Penna's popular work (6 French editions from 1509); Hanley, *The Lit de Justice of the Kings of France*, chaps. 2–7, and index, *maxims*.

seminal lines to include autogenetic male generative acts, the maxim identified royal sons as political progeny born of the progenitor king and kingdom: "They are children of the French people and of the kingdom."[9] Still further extended to incorporate the realms of state and family succession to royal domain and family property, monarchic office and government offices, the maxim drew upon two other axioms: the new Public Law maxim, *The king never dies* (signifying immediate male succession to monarchic office in the kingdom; hence state continuity),[9] and the old Civil Law maxim on family inheritance, *The dead [person] seizes the living [one]* (signifying immediate male succession to estates, including government offices, in families; hence family continuity).[10] Finally brought full circle and ritually connected with civil marriage in society, the politicized marital maxim declared that kings at Coronation swear by oath (at the moment the marriage ring is bestowed) to uphold Public (i.e. Constitutional) Laws: "He [the king] is obliged to maintain the [Public] Laws of the Crown; apropos of that a marriage is made between the said lord and his said subjects."[11]

As an explanatory legal fiction, *The king is the husband of the kingdom*, drew upon allusions encompassed in the marriage contract, the ring and oath, the inalienable dowry, autogenetic male generation of progeny, and male suzerainty in office and property. The medieval marriage metaphor had posited an ideal political-spiritual relationship for ruler and realm befitting the analogic celibate equivalent, bishop and church. It allowed rule by a queen.[12] To the contrary, the early modern French marital maxim posited a contractual political-legal relationship for king and kingdom matching the conjugal equivalent, husband and wife. It disallowed rule by a queen. Featured in political discourse and ritually demonstrated in the magnificent new *Lit de Justice* assemblies convoked for the first time in 1527, again in 1537 by Francis I, and in 1563 by Charles IX; the marital maxim, *The king is the husband of the kingdom*, and its metonymic allusions was written into the Coronation ceremonies for Henry II in 1547 and

---

[9] Ibid., chaps. 7, 9, 11, and 13: *Le roi ne meurt jamais*, invented by Jean Bodin and propagated in the 1600s by Charles Loyseau, Antoine Loisel, Nicolas Bergier, Pierre Dupuy, and many others.

[10] Ibid., chaps. 7 and 11, for the parlementary context: early in the 1500s André Tiraqueau set forth this maxim on family inheritance, *Le mort saisit le vif*, which harks back to the Feudal Law of *seizin*; at times it was associated with an older axiom of Baldus de Ubaldis from the late 1300s, *Mortuus aperit oculos viventis* (The dead [person] opens the eyes of the living [one]), as at n. 36 below.

[11] Ibid., chaps. 2, 3, 5, 7, and 9.

[12] Well within the spiritual celibate parameters of the medieval marriage metaphor, Elizabeth I responded to critics of her unmarried condition: "I am already bound unto an Husband, which is the Kingdome of England . . . (And . . . shee shewed them the Ring with which shee was given in marriage, and inaugurated to her Kingdome . . .)"; in William Camden, *Annales* (London, 1625), p. 28, cited by Marie Axton, *The Queen's Two Bodies: Drama and the Elizabethan Succession* (London: Royal Historical Society, 1977), p. 39, noting jurists' distress over chosen celibacy.

Henry IV in 1594 along with the ritual bestowal of a marriage ring. Programati-
cally rendered in the unprecedented Inaugural *Lit de Justice* of 1610 in the
Parlement of Paris declaring Louis XIII (a minor) king and also in the Royal
Entry tableaus set up for the Coronation (now ritually inverted) that followed,
the marital maxim was prominently cast also in legal and political treatises from
1538 through the 1650s.[13]

Here it is critical to note that the marital maxim did not stand alone as a
discursive entity: it was socially sited in French laws that actually conveyed
governing authority to male heads of political and social bodies (state and
family) as *king* and *husband* (not as king and father) for two reasons. First, the
legal prerequisite, marital status (creating a husband), was assured, whereas the
derivative biological condition, parental status (creating a father), was not.
Second, in national terms, marital governing power was recognized as legitimately French, whereas paternal power was Roman. Many jurists—Jean Bodin in
the 1570s, Antoine Loisel in the early 1600s, Robert-Joseph Pothier in the
1750s—made this French connection clear. They commented on the related
ruling power of husbands and kings and distinguished marital power (as French
law) from paternal power (as Roman Law) in the maxim, *The law of paternal
power is not applicable [in France].*[14] As a result, they legally structured a formidable Marital Regime model of government that drew under its singular aegis
both family and state units. Guaranteed a long conceptual life through concise

13 For rituals, including the first two *Lit de Justice* assemblies of 1527 (which were
officially defined as constitutional assemblies and differentiated from ordinary Royal
Séances held in Parlement), and legal treatises, Charles de Grassaille, René Choppin,
François Hotman, Pierre Gregoire, and Jean Bodin; see Hanley, *The Lit de Justice of the
Kings of France*, chaps. 2–9, Table 1, and engravings.

14 At the beginning of this study, I made the tentative suggestion in the closing sentence of an article that there may have issued from the Family-State negotiation of a
Compact of Civil Laws (which was a Marital Compact) a political "family model of
authority" for the state but gave no further definition; see Sarah Hanley, "Engendering the
State: Family Formation and State Building in Early Modern France, *French Historical
Studies*, 16:1 (1989), 4–27. Now further study of legal sources makes it necessary to under-
score several important points in this regard. First, the pattern of laws negotiated by
officeholding families and the government was a "Marital Law Compact" that empowered
husbands. Second, since the power to rule in families was invested maritally in husbands
(not fathers), this governing system is best defined not as a "family model" (as earlier
suggested) but as a "*Marital Regime*" model that encompassed both family and state units.
In fact, husbands (who might also be fathers) wielded the right to rule *as* husbands,
whereas fathers simply *as* fathers had no authority as in the case of family bastards born of
non-husbands and in Louis XIV's failed attempt to place his male bastards in line for royal
succession. Third, neither family formation nor state building issued one from the other;
the two proceeded apace as *parallel* endeavors. For Bodin and Pothier, see nn. 38 and 45
below; for Loisel, *Institutes Coutumières*, ed. M. Dupin (new ed., Paris: Videcoq Père et Fils
Libraires, 1846), Book 1, no. 55. See also Book 1, no. 122 denoting married women (in
France) as "en la puissance de leurs maris, et non de leurs pères" (as in Rome); and no. 57
maintaining (once progeny arrived) the two original legal categories: the rulers (husbands
who were also fathers) and the ruled (wives and children).

repetition in political maxims and a long political reign under laws correspond-ingly promulgated, the Marital Regime model defined the essence of proper government in both family and state as indisputably male. Its full articulation signalled the new contractual Marital Regime foundations laid for the early modern French monarchic state, wherein male right, secured in terms of Public Law, was concomitantly secured in terms of Civil Law.

The second rubric of the French Law Canon, Civil Law, which addressed the statutory foundations of civil society, propagated Marital Regime government through legislation that established male rule in households. In consort with kings and royal governments from the 1530s through the 1640s and beyond, legists, *parlementaires*, and other government officeholders promulgated a Marital Law Compact: ordinances, edicts, and *arrêts* (legal decisions) on mar-riage regulations, reproductive customs, marital separation arrangements, and inheritance rules.[15] As Jean de Coras deftly argued in 1557 and Jerôme Bignon and Pierre Séguier confirmed in 1633, French Law supersedes Roman Law, or Canon Law, or any other law code; and French secular cognizance over family formation determined in state courts (as opposed to Catholic church cogniz-ance in ecclesiastical courts) must be legally mandated by the state for the public good.[16] Due to the rapid development of a distinctly French venal-hereditary practice regulating government officeholding in families,[17] state building and family formation were intimately connected and placed in parallel construction.

In the first stage of office acquisition from the early 1500s to the 1600s, the practice of venal officeholding took hold whereby families purchased govern-ment offices and qualified male family members exercised them. This early venal practice harbored a serious conundrum. A long-term aim of families making costly investments in offices was to acquire nobility legally, which required that they hold and exercise ennobling charges for three generations.[18]

---

[15] For partial treatment of the Compact of Marital Civil Laws negotiated in family and state terms and some cases litigated, see Hanley, "Engendering the State," pp. 6–21, and "Family and State in Early Modern France: The Marriage Pact," chap. 1, in *Connecting Spheres: Women in the Western World, 1500 to the Present*, eds. Marilyn J. Boxer and Jean H. Quataert (New York, N.Y.: Oxford University Press, 1987); for the complete study, Hanley, *State Building in Early Modern France*.

[16] Jean de Coras, *Des mariages clandestinement, et irreveremment contractes par les enfans de famille, au deceu, ou contre le gré, vouloir, & consentement de leurs peres & meres* (Tolose, 1557), pp. 1–7; and Jerôme Bignon, letter to Pierre Séguier (17 September 1633), in Bibliothèque Nationale, Collection Thoisy, CDXVIII, fols. 242r–264r.

[17] On the growth of venality, John H. M. Salmon, *Society in Crisis: France in the Sixteenth Century* (New York: St Martin's Press, 1975), 70–79, 152–154; the rigid system in place by the late 1600s, Albert N. Hamscher, *The Parlement of Paris after the Fronde, 1653–1673* (Pittsburgh, Pa: University of Pittsburgh Press, 1976): chaps. 1 and 2; and the ennobling practice as peculiar to France, François Bluche and Pierre Durye, *L'Anoblisse-ment par charges avant 1789*, 2 volumes (Paris: Les Cahiers Nobles, 1962), 1:5, 2:23–24.

[18] The edict of 1600 confirmed the ennobling practice requiring descent from a

But succession to office ownership remained subject to the risky quasi-hereditary practice of *survivance*, which required designation of a successor to the office before decease of the incumbent. Caught in this legal limbo shadowed by death, officeholders and their families lobbied the government for hereditary rights to purchased offices. In the second stage of office acquisition from the 1600s, therefore, the government moved beyond the venal office-holding practice (legitimating purchase) and institutionalized a venal-hereditary system of officeholding (legalizing purchase and inheritance). Promulgation of the important *paulette* edict of 1604, a prime piece of inheritance legislation in the Marital Law Compact, made purchased offices fully heritable in families if the required annual fee (*droit annuel*) was paid to the government.[19] Finally, purchased offices came to be regarded legally as *propres* (lineage property) in family estates regulated by Civil Law on inheritance.[20] At this juncture, when a venal practice was transformed into a uniquely French venal-hereditary system of officeholding and when family members (men and women) routinely owned and inherited offices (or their assessed value), legists drafted into service the two axioms that defined male governance in family and state units as analogous.

In the early decades of the 1500s, the revival of the maxim, *The dead [person] seizes the living [one]* (which could have been rendered, "The husband never dies") perfectly symbolized the type of heritable succession to estate shares and particularly to government offices that officeholders (and their families) demanded. The way male dimensions were brought to family property was suggested in the 1580s. Georges Loüet argues for advantaging sons in inheritance, because daughters move family possessions into "alien" families.[21] The way male dimensions were brought to family officeholding appeared in practices of the mid and later 1600s. Regulations allow two persons to own one office (a male as incumbent and a silent partner as investor); and eventually permit

grandfather and father; François-André Isambert, et al., eds., *Recueil général des anciennes lois françaises depuis l'an 420 jusqu'à la révolution de 1789*, 29 vols. (Paris, 1821–1833), 15:234 (art. 25).

19 For the *paulette* (12 December 1604), see Antoine Fontanon, *Les edicts et ordonnances des roys de France depuis Louis VI dit le Gros, jusques à present* (Paris, 1611), 2:575. Note that by the 1590s, probably before, judges in legal decisions were treating offices as *immeubles* in family estates; see decisions of 1598 and 1607 (before and after the *paulette*); Georges Loüet, *Recueil de plusieurs arrests notables du Parlement de Paris* (ed., Paris, 1742), 2:272 (O, som. 5).

20 Paul Louis-Lucas, *Étude sur la vénalité des charges et fonctions publiques*, 2 vols. (Paris: Challamel Aîné, 1883), Vol. 1, chap. 2 (Ancien droit français) on the way legists such as Loyseau defined title to (hence exercise of) office as a male right but later allowed the transformation of offices, as property, into *propres* (as recognized by Pothier); and Giesey, "Rules of Inheritance and Strategies of Mobility in Prerevolutionary France," *The American Historical Review* 82 (1977):271–289, on familial aims.

21 Loüet, *Recueil de plusiers arrests notables* (ed., Paris, 1712), 2:816: estate shares being male property from which female dowries are removed.

officeholding *en concurrence*,[22] whereby a living male co-incumbent immediately assumes the office from the incumbent, or is "seized" by the incumbent, at the moment of his death. Likewise, the creation of a state analogue, *The king never dies*, in the 1570s symbolized male right to monarchic succession in the kingdom along the same lines. These analogous male precepts regulating officeholding in both family and state were repeatedly invoked during a time when queens ruled in Europe, queen regents were installed in France, women owned and inherited government offices, and kings regularly failed to generate progeny.[23] Surely the demonstrable frailty of male generation juxtaposed to the evident presence of female rulers, regents, and inheritors of government offices exacerbated efforts to privilege male right alone. As the decades wore on, therefore, the male right to rule in family and state was made indigenously French.

By the early 1600s the two familiar legal maxims on male right were bonded as twins. The first (on the family) was alleged to be French, and the second (on the state) was set in train. Charles Loyseau alleges that: "The first maxim of our French law [is] that *The dead [person] seizes the living [one]* . . . That is why we say in the vernacular that *The king never dies*."[24] By the mid-1600s Pierre Dupuy designated these twin maxims dictating male rule in family and state as French "fundamental law." The French, he says, "hold as a fundamental law that *The dead [person] seizes the living [one]* and that *The king does not die in France*."[25] Allied to the marital maxim, *The king is the husband of the kingdom*, these twin maxims conjured up the immortal, or perpetual, attributes of Marital Regime government based on male right in family (husband) and state (king) and exercised through Civil Law and Public Law. Furthermore, when legists and political theorists from the 1570s on pointedly referred to these political maxims as "fundamental," they stated a crucial proposition long understood: that French monarchic government legally framed along the lines of an immortal, or

[22] Louis-Lucas, *Étude sur la vénalité* (n. 20 above), outlines theory and practice. See Hamscher, *The Parlement of Paris after the Fronde*, chaps. 1 and 2; and David Parker, "Sovereignty, Absolutism, and the Function of the Law in Seventeenth-Century France," *Past and Present*, 122 (1989), 36–74, on the way familial enclaves of officeholding impeded proper judicial practice.

[23] In the 1500s only two of the five Valois kings (and queens) had marital progeny (in legal terms, "enfants de famille"): Francis I (Claude of France, later Eleanor of Spain) and Henry II (Catherine de Médicis); the others not, Francis II (Mary Stuart [later queen of Scots]); Charles IX (Elizabeth of Austria), Henry III (Louise of Lorraine). In the early 1600s the Bourbons found solutions: dissolution of marriage for Henry IV and Marguerite of Valois (1599) and remarriage to Marie de Médicis (progeny (Louis [XIII], 1601); unexpected success (after 23 years of marriage) for Louis XIII and Anne of Austria (Louis [XIV], 1638).

[24] Charles Loyseau, *Cinq livres du droit des offices. Les Oeuvres de Loyseau* (Paris, 1666), I, x, 58.

[25] Pierre Dupuy, *Traité de la majorité de nos rois et des régences du royaume* (Paris, 1655), pp. 1–13.

continuous, Marital Regime, was rooted not only in law but also in nature, the most fundamental of all grounds. In fact, it was the Natural Law foundation for the Marital Regime system that girded male right so well.

The third rubric of the French Law Canon, Natural Law, which addressed the universal celestial-terrestrial connection apprehended through human reason, gave Marital Regime governance roots in nature. From the mid-1500s through the 1600s, legists developed and then repeated throughout the 1700s biogenetic seminal propositions that fixed male rulership with the authoritative stamp of nature. In a treatise on legitimate governance, the *Political Discourses* (1574), the anonymous author (a legal humanist and most certainly a *parlementaire*) set forth a powerful case for male right without ever mentioning a Salic Law or even a salic custom.[26] To begin with, he argues that human authority in household and polity derives not from original sin but from nature. Then he locates the right to govern in males by virtue of a political theory that may be characterized as a "biogenetic seminal theory of authority."[27] According to this view, a husband through nature (i.e. seminal transmission) creates heirs who continue the family; likewise a king creates successors who perpetuate the monarchy. Although a woman reproduces, she does not seminally create; hence, a French queen through marriage and "foreign [male] seed (*semence*)" is unable to generate proper royal progeny. In his ken the rule of men in family and state is natural and legitimate; that of women unnatural and forbidden. The author then confirms male right on moral grounds: he cites the sexual and moral perversity of *woman* that makes women unfit to govern household or

---

26 *Discours politiques des diverses puissances establies de Dieu du monde, du gouvernement legitime d'icelles, & du devoir de ceux qui y sont assujettis* (anonymous, s.l. 1574), published in [Simon Goulart, ed.], *Mémoires de l'estat de France, sous Charles neufiesme* ([Geneva], 1579), III, fols. 147v–213r; analyzed by Sarah Hanley, "The French Constitution Revised: Representative Assemblies and Resistance Right in the Sixteenth Century," chap. 2, in *Society and Institutions in Renaissance and Early Modern France*, ed. Mack P. Holt (Athens, Ga: University of Georgia Press, 1991).

27 Here my term "biogenetic seminal theory" refers to this fully developed early modern political theory for male rule, as opposed to the suggestive but undeveloped medieval philosophical allusion to the "natural filiation" (actually "natural [male] filiation") of father and son made by the *avocat* Jean de Terre Rouge (fl. 1420), *Contra rebelles suorum regum* (Lyons, 1527), ed. Jacques Bonaud de Sauset; cited in Giesey, "The Juristic Basis," p. 15, n. 47, and pp. 38–39, who notes in this study (1961) the need to trace such notions in early modern times. In doing that here, it should be noted that these ideas spring from the Aristotelian idea of the male as active in generation (supplying the formative male seed); the female as passive (contributing only matter). On such ideas, see Maryanne Cline Horowitz, "The 'Science' of Embryology before the Discovery of the Ovum," in *Connecting Spheres*, chap. 4; and their transmission, Ian MacLean, *The Renaissance Notion of Woman: A Study in the Fortunes of Scholasticism and Medical Science in European Intellectual Life* (Cambridge, Eng: Cambridge University Press, 1980), chap. 3. In the 1500s, however, the Galenic alternative (making female seed active) was available but was not adopted by political writers.

state.[28] From these tenets it follows that males naturally embody and thus legitimately govern both household and political units. This autogenetic seminal theory of authority and its biogenetic consequences transformed male generative capacity into an irrefutable principle of nature necessarily mirrored in family and state properly governed.

During the 1570s and 1580s writers, readers, and observers realized that the seminal foundations of Marital Regime governance aptly conveyed the masculine nature of authority itself. Although deeply immersed in contemporary female defamation tactics, Pierre de Belloy actually confessed that "French Law" excludes women from monarchic rule (as observed in salic custom) not because of the recognized "stupidity and weakness" of women but because of the necessity to keep the Crown from falling into "foreign hands" and to assure that the kingdom is governed "only by a French male who is of the same blood and origin as his father" and therefore has a "natural interest in the welfare and conservation of the country."[29] Given the troubling fact that five reigning kings (out of seven) actually failed, or nearly failed, the political generative mission between 1515 and 1638, seminal transmission theory opportunely upheld male right by virtue of actual or potential generative capacity and female exclusion by virtue of actual generative incapacity. Finally, the monarchic government in the 1570s turned seminal theory into public policy by establishing a special category, "Princes of the Blood," which identified royal males capable of being "seized" as king should an incumbent ruler die without issue. That category officially separated royal princes not only from French peers, as has been pointed out,[30] but also from royal princesses hereby identified as lacking the seminal connection. Although eminently guarded in this manner, adherance to male right through seminal seizure elicited thorny political dilemmas.

From 1559 through 1589 three Valois kings in succession failed to generate any progeny: Francis II, Charles IX, and Henry III. Yet despite long interludes

---

[28] *Discours politiques*: argues that political power, or authority, issues from nature, fols. 147v–158r; claims that women defer to men in the family because of ". . . the honor due to the 'source' from which children originate" (i.e. semen as the source of progeny), fols. 149r–152v, also fols. 170r and 171v; refers to foreign, or alien, elements that would be introduced by a ruling queen, ". . . it is within the power of a ruling queen to constitute through marriage [and male generation of progeny] a king over the people . . . who is a foreigner," fol. 171v; cites the demise of a state headed by a female ruler, fols. 166v, 193v, and 197v; and combines misogyny tropes and female defamation, fols. 159v–172r, 182v.

[29] Pierre de Belloy, *De l'Authorité du roy, et crimes de leze majeste* (s.l. 1587), pp. 52–53. It is important to note that during this period the words "semen" and "blood" are used interchangeably. Londa Scheibinger, *The Mind Has no Sex? Women in the Origins of Modern Science* (Cambridge, Ma: Harvard University Press, 1989), 199–200, explains the way contemporary Hippocratic physiology denoted anatomical pathways of interconversion wherein semen was refined out of blood, passed from the brain through the spinal cord, kidneys, testicles, and into the penis.

[30] Richard A. Jackson, "Peers of France and Princes of the Blood," *French Historical Studies* 7:1 (1971), 27–46, on the delineation of blood princes from peers.

fraught with political problems, not one of the brothers-in-waiting (candidates for the office) was allowed to procreate ahead of the king. Even in the later 1570s and 1580s when Henry III's sexual incapacity was well known, the fiction of potential generative capacity prevailed; and his brother, the Duke of Anjou (the last Valois), eagerly awaited his marital generative turn for naught.[31] As a result of this policy, the Valois male line ended at the death of Henry III in 1589, and the successor king was a Bourbon prince of the blood, Henry IV, a protestant. Once Henry IV's succession was challenged, edicts issued in this context confirmed his seminal right to rule even before his official conversion to Catholicism. In 1591 and 1593 an edict and a royal council arrêt combine in the allegation "natural (naturel)" the territorial theme of citizenry (birth place) and the seminal theme of succession (biogenetic origins) to signify Henry IV as a "king and natural prince" ruling over "natural subjects."[32] In 1593 an arrêt of the Parlement of Paris explains such seminal reasoning. On grounds of custom and law, it declares that any attempt to confer monarchic office on a "foreign prince or princess" is a contravention of "salic law [custom] and other fundamental laws of this kingdom." In fact, the unnamed "foreign" princess who posed a threat to male right was Isabelle-Claire-Eugénie (the infanta of Spain), who was a granddaughter of Henry II and a niece of the recently deceased Henry III.[33] As defined here, therefore, Isabelle not only was foreign by domicile (civil status, the law of aubain, that could be changed) but also by generative incapacity (seminal status, fundamental Natural Law, that could not be changed).

In 1594 the Coronation rubrics for Henry IV ritually demonstrated the marital regime maxim, The king is the husband of the kingdom; and he quickly demonstrated the allied lesson that male generative capacity informs political power. Having managed in 1599 the dissolution of a first marriage of 1572 to Marguerite de Valois (17 years without progeny), Henry wed Marie de Médicis in 1600 and brought generative faculties to fruition (Louis [XIII]) in 1601.[33] Designation of male right (in tune with custom) as fundamental, identification of the successor king as a natural prince (by territory and biogenesis), exclusion of the foreigner Isabelle (presently by domicile, permanently by biogenesis) as a potential successor, and marital dissolution (unmaking a crowned queen and

---

31 Mack P. Holt, The Duke of Anjou and the Politique Struggle during the Wars of Religion (Cambridge, Eng: Cambridge University Press, 1980): chap. 6, details marriage negotiations for Anjou with queen Elizabeth I, who was beyond childbearing age; Anjou predeceased Henry III.

32 For the edict (July 1591) and arrêt (27 January 1593), see Isambert, Recueil, 15:28–31, 55–58.

33 For the Parlement arrêt (28 June 1593); Isambert, Recueil, 15:71. This important text (linking a salic custom with Public fundamental laws) was cited around 1600 by Loisel, Pasquier, ou dialogue des advocats du Parlement de Paris, ed. M. Dupin (Paris: Videcoq Père et Fils, Libraire, 1844), pp. 266–267. Henry IV made his profession of Catholic faith 25 July 1593; Isambert, Recueil, 15:72–73.

wife) to ensure generative potential fit the seminal bill. Even so, the problem of sustaining a political policy (monarchic male right), that was tied to generative capacity crucially aligned with political power continued to be problematic.

By the 1620s the dilemma posed by the relation between male generative capacity and potent political power was spelled out in no uncertain terms. Although there was enormous concern about Louis XIII's lack of progeny after a dozen years of marriage, royal advisers in 1626 vehemently opposed the marriage of his brother, Gaston d'Orléans, on the grounds that the king's generative capacity itself (potential or actual) constituted a formidable element of political authority. If the brother should produce progeny before the king, they warned, the king's political power to command would be severely curtailed.[34] Given the extinction of Valois kings who had disallowed such marriages, Louis XIII eschewed Valois policy based on fictive generative potential and opted to insure Bourbon continuity by arranging Gaston's marriage.[35] Then, confounding all in 1638, Louis XIII (with Anne of Austria) after 23 years of marriage accomplished the necessary generative task (Louis [XIV]). In these decades supportive pens widened the parameters of this biogenetic seminal purview now alleged as fundamental, or Natural Law, supporting the unique male right to rule.

Writing in the 1630s Nicolas Bergier defended male right and seminal theory by pushing generative capacity and nature to the limit. First he cites the well-known, now French, twin marital regime maxims, *The dead [person] opens the eyes of the living [one]* (an alternate for *The dead [person] seizes the living [one]*), and *The king of France never dies*. Then he explains the biogenetic principle embedded in them. A royal male is designated successor king, he says, even if he [seed or fetus] is "still in the womb of his mother and not yet born and named." Finally, he repeats the important point made earlier: that the precept of male right (entailed in seminal theory) is founded in "law and nature."[36] In fact, all along "fundamental law" referred to the fundamental Law of Nature founded in the seminal connection, which offered a biogenetic chain enabling progenitors to "seize" seminally related males in proper sequence and thus perpetuate male right over time.[37] French law, these theorists maintained, naturally followed suit.

In these times legists and *parlementaires* repeatedly argued that male right

---

[34] For the letter of 1626 (sent to Richelieu and shown immediately to the king), see Pierre Grillon, ed., *Les Papiers de Richelieu: Section politique interieure, correspondance et papiers d'Etat* (Paris: A. Pedone, 1975–1985), 1:382–385.

[35] Gaston married Marie de Bourbon-Montspensier, who died in childbirth in 1627.

[36] Nicolas Bergier [and P. de La Salle], *Le Bouquet royal ou le parterre des riches inventions qui ont servy à l'entrée du roy Louis le Juste en sa ville de Reims* (Reims, 1637), fol. 55r–v, 57r.

[37] My rendition of the political theory characterized as "biogenetic seminal theory" is not considered among the theories discussed by André Lemaire, *Les Lois fondamentales de la monarchie française d'après les théoriciens de l'ancien régime* (Paris: A. Fontemoing, 1907). Early modern monarchies should not be characterized simply as dynastic but must be

exercised in both Public Law and Civil Law was perfectly mirrored in Natural Law. In the 1570s Jean Bodin stated that proposition: "The monarchy must only descend to males, since gynecocracy [female rule] is rightly against the laws of nature . . . not only in the government of kingdoms . . . but also in the [government of the] family."[38] Fellow legists through the 1600s, both emboldened by these Natural Law seminal notions and unnerved by the past and recent presence of female regents in office claimed that the French monarchy constituted a unique form of government. Louis Turquet de Mayerne and Cardin Le Bret both explain that the French monarchic state is not only a legitimate form of government but also a superior one, because it conforms to the dictates of both "law and nature" evidenced in the inferior non-generative physiology of the female body. A state governed by a French queen, they warn, is not a monarchy but a gynecocracy: that is, a type of rule that is both unnatural and illegal.[39] As set forth in theory by these legists, it is illegal for a French queen to rule the kingdom, because Public Law prohibits female rule in France. It is unnatural, because unlike the monarchy, which is modeled on the male body and symbolized by the seminal maxim *The king never dies* designating the immortality of the state; gynecocracy, which is modeled on the female body and bound to the contrary non-seminal assumption (left unstated), "The queen dies," spells the imminent death of the state. Rigidly tied to gender contraries rendered through biogenetic notions presumed fundamental and conceptually clothed as Natural Law, this political theory of male right depended on a deliberate twist of reason that disconnected women from the generative act in reproduction and situated them as "foreigners" or "aliens" within the family and by definition within the state. When adherants avowed in poetry, statuary, medallions, and engravings that the king was a "French Phoenix" (arisen from the ashes of the progenitor) and cast him as the mediator between Natural Law and French Law,[40] the seminal implications of Marital Regime government in the French monarchic state were represented in cultural terms that supported political expression.

As a Law of Nature politicized, seminal theory legitimated male rule alone by

considered specifically as either gender inclusive or exclusive dynastic systems given the important political differences entailed.

[38] Jean Bodin, *Les Six livres de la république* (Paris, 1577), Bk. 7, chap. 5, p. 757: he warns also that the husband of a female ruler loses proper place as husband and head of the family and gives as negative examples the husbands of queen Isabella in Spain, queen Mary in England, and others from antiquity on down.

[39] Louis Turquet de Mayerne, *La Monarchie aristodemocratique* (Paris, 1611), p. 59; and Cardin Le Bret, *De la Souveraineté du roi* (Paris, 1632), p. 42. The *Commentaires sur l'ordonnance de la majorité des rois* [anonymous] (n.p., n.d.) [written c.1638], fols. 76r–77v, 81v, repeats that a female ruler might cause the French Crown to fall (through marriage and resulting progeny) into "foreign" hands.

[40] Ibid., pp. 249, 262–265, for engravings, paintings, and texts; and figure 9 on Louis XIII as phoenix.

making autogenetic male generative capacity an integral facet of the power to embody family and state units and therefore to govern them. That is why the weighty presence of queen regents posed a troubling contradiction in this era of eminent *femmes fortes*, women wielding political authority. Leaving nothing to chance, therefore, the French Law Canon also justified Marital Regime governance (male rule) by resort to Moral Law; that is, social mores (*moeurs*) or customs, by invoking early modern female defamation lessons (visual and verbal) on the dire consequences of female rule in family and state.[41] First inscribed in the French Law Canon, then prescribed by those laws and legal case precedents, French monarchic government legally framed as a Marital Regime prevailed amidst innumerable difficulties from the 1500s through around the 1650s at a time when male right, bereft of the dismissed fraudulent Salic Law, was institutionalized on indigenous French juridical grounds. As any governing system over time, however, the Marital Regime model of government in the monarchic state, once assimilated, faced persistent anomalies eventually challenged, first in social, then in political terms.

In the early modern French family, marital rule stood on grounds increasingly contested from the 1650s when some women and men, well attuned to alternatives in an era marked by queen regents, publicly condemned the system. These women repeatedly equated male rule in the family not with monarchy but with despotism and negatively characterized husbands as "masters" and wives as "slaves."[42] At times politically charged words were accompanied by legal deeds. Some wives went to court and sued for marital separation and restoration of dowry funds (*propres*), charging husbands with sexual impotence (hence male generative incapacity) and with debauchery (hence dissipation of female honor and financial assets).[43] Other wives defended themselves in court against

[41] For early modern female defamation tactics (political and legal lessons defaming women), see Hanley, *State Building in Early Modern France*, including the inordinately perverse turn to witch mania by the famous political theorist, Jean Bodin, *De la Démonomanie des sorciers* [1580] (Paris: J. du Puys, 1587; Gutenberg Reprints, 1979); and for the aggressive and successful political moves of queen regents to sit in Parlement (Catherine in 1563, Marie in 1610, Anne in 1643), see Hanley, *The Lit de Justice of the Kings of France*, chaps. 7–13.

[42] In the play of Pierre Matthieu, *Vasthi* [1589], the wife questions the tyrannical rule of husbands, as well as the marital family-state analogy that supports it; among others, Madeleine de Scudéry in her novel, *Artemène ou Le Grand Cyrus* [1649–1653], has the heroine decry marriage as a "long slavery;" Hanley, *State Building in Early Modern France*. Writers associated with salons in the mid 1600s indict forcible subjection of women as immoral and note that salon women liken marital subjection to slavery; Carolyn C. Lougee, *Le Paradis des femmes: Women, Salons, and Social Stratification in Seventeenth-Century France* (Princeton, NJ: Princeton University Press, 1976), chap. 1.

[43] Among others, the cases of *Perreau—Semitte* in Hanley, "Engendering the State," pp. 15–21; and *Aurillon–Sorny* and *Aublay–Guerou* in Hanley, *State Building in Early Modern France*. Lisa Lavoir, "Factums et mémoires d'avocats aux XVIIème et XVIIIème siècles: Une regard sur une société (environ 1620–1760)," *Histoire, Economie, et Société*, 7:2 (1988):221–42, details the appalling severity of some conflicts.

husbands' charges of adultery, a female crime that imposed on convicted women a form of civil death (loss of household space, dowry and dower funds, and children). Many women moved their cases from the courts to the streets and addressed "the public" directly.[44] Faced with such lawsuits, on the rise by the 1670s, steeply by the early 1700s, legists and husbands wrapped angry reactions in conservative legal opinion. In the 1750s Robert-Joseph-Pothier commented on the propriety of marital family rule (akin to orderly state governance) in sexualized marital-political terms. He posits the husband as the ruler of the family, the wife as subject: "It is not the place of the woman who is an inferior to inspect the conduct of her husband who is her superior; she must presume that he is faithful, and [female] jealousy is not a sufficient reason for investigating his [sexual] conduct."[45] Lawsuits challenging familial rule in closed courtrooms were serious enough, but those moved in print to the streets for public consumption proved politically volatile.[46]

In the early modern French state where the analogic relationship of husbands and kings as rulers had been readily comprehended for two centuries, public contests over male governance in the family eventually waxed political. In a state where politicians legally regulated a slave system in the colonies but legally limited access of slaves (with masters) to France because slavery at home was illegal,[47] the political equation of French husbands as despotic masters, wives as subjected slaves, opened a route, by inference, to tar kings with the same brush. In the 1700s political debates and disturbances reflected the ways the once reputable marital maxim for state governance (king as husband of kingdom, master of subjects) had come to constitute a discursive quagmire that

---

44 For example, the cases *Cardoüan (de Langey)–Saint-Simon, Pigousse–Saint Remy, Mascranni–Potier de Gesvres, Machy–Michel,* and others. The vigor with which they took lawsuits (held in closed courts) to the streets in the later 1600s and 1700s suggests that litigants intended, as they said, to address "the public;" see Hanley, *State Building in Early Modern France.* This early modern situation is the opposite of that noted by William Reddy, "Marriage, Honor, and the Public Sphere in Postrevolutionary France: *Séparations de Corps,* 1815–1848," *Journal of Modern History* 65:3 (1993), 437–472, who suggests litigants were shamed by these later procedures (held in open courts) making cases public. Perhaps in the 1800s the determining variable was the newspaper coverage rather than the type of court procedure.

45 Among others, Robert-Joseph Pothier, *Oeuvres de Pothier: Traité du contrat de mariage* (Paris, 1818): Pt. 6, chap. 2, no. 516, developed a category for commentary, "Power of the Husband."

46 Hanley, *State Building in Early Modern France,* shows the way legal cases informed local knowledge in public enclaves of discussants, 1600s through the 1700s. Sarah Maza, "Le Tribunal de la nation: les mémoires judiciares et l'opinion publique à la fin de l'ancien régime," *Annales: E.S.C.* 42:1 (1987), 73–90, treats later Parisian public opinion, 1770s and 1780s.

47 Sue Lee Peabody, *'There are no Slaves in France:' Law, Culture, and Society in Early Modern France* (Ph.D. dissertation, University of Iowa, 1993), traces the legal use of the maxim forbidding slavery, which provided grounds for slaves kept illegally in Paris to win lawsuits for freedom.

invited political recrimination. In the 1730s and 1740s Louis XV was publicly mocked (along with husbands) for debauchery and Louis XVI for the purported inability to generate progeny.[48] In the 1760s and during the severe crises of the 1770s, radical politicians and legists labeled Louis XV and Louis XVI despots and masters who wished to rule tyranically over citizens as subjected slaves.[49] In the late 1780s the author of a political rhyme commented on the impropriety of state rule (akin to disorderly family governance) in sexualized political-marital terms. The rhyme indicts Louis XVI for the ruin of the consort kingdom (represented by Lady Justice, or the Parlement of Paris), as follows:

> Have you heard what they say in Paris?
> Madame Justice [i.e. Parlement of Paris] is brokenhearted;
> The king is ensconced in her bed [i.e. *Lit de Justice*];
> [And] everyone knows he raped her.[50]

Clearly by the 1700s marital legal fictions once rhetorically fit for the parallel endeavors of state building and family formation had turned socially sour and politically risky. Caught in this vise, kings left the marital arena to husbands and sought political representation in safer spiritual terms.

Reverting to the traditional religious context of past centuries, kings were recast in the familiar universal spiritual pose as benign and loving *Father [king] of the country*, who rules over children, not subjects, just as the *Father [God] of the heavens* likewise rules with "paternal sovereignty."[51] Focused on transcendant love, this renewed spiritual axiom, which had been overshadowed for centuries by nationalistic juridical maxims, enabled kings to make a dignified royal exit from the increasingly unpopular marital-political trap shared by kings and husbands to the universal-spiritual cocoon of fatherhood shared by kings and God. In the 1700s, therefore, the signification of king as spiritually defined father (rather than legally defined husband) was related directly to this opportune royal retreat from the long-established Marital Regime model of rulership,

---

[48] Thomas E. Kaiser, "Louis the Bien-Aimé and the Rhetoric of the Royal Body," in *Constructing the Body in the Seventeenth and Eighteenth Centuries*, eds. Anne Mellor, Sara Melzer, Kathryn Norberg (Cambridge, Eng: Cambridge University Press, forthcoming); Merrick, "Sexual Politics and Public Order in Late Eighteenth-Century France: The *Mémoires secrètes* and the *Correspondance secrète;*" *The Journal of the History of Sexuality*, 1:1 (1990), 68–84; and Elizabeth Colwill, " 'Just another *citoyenne?*' Marie-Antoinette on Trial 1790–1793, *History Workshop Journal* 28 (1989), 63–87.

[49] Shanti Marie Singham, *Rehearsal for Revolution: Political Opposition in France during the Maupeou Years, 1770–1775* (in progress), details escalating charges.

[50] *Correspondence secrète, politique, et littéraire* (London, 1787–1790), 1:69.

[51] For a classic formulation from the 1680s, see Jacques Bénigne Bossuet, *Politique tirée des propres paroles de l'Écriture sainte* (Paris, 1824), pp. 141–145: the conservative idea that God the Father loved what he created (as do kings) and thus people serve kings (as fathers) just as Jesus served God in this "empire paternelle" (Book 2); and see Kaiser, "Louis the Bien-Aimé," on efforts to rehabilitate Louis XV's image.

not the result of subscription to a family model of politics that entailed paternal power.[52] In the same era, after all, derivative paternal authority (itself beholden to Marital Regime rule) was equally sullied given the numerous lawsuits filed by daughters and sons (some famous writers and *philosophes*) who took both fathers and mothers to court and challenged parental control over marriage and inheritance arrangements.[53] While the shift from the legal fiction of king as marital husband to the religious axiom of king as spiritual father signalled the demise of the Marital Regime model of government as a useful legal prototype for legitimating male rule (and female exclusion) in the French monarchic state, the move did not signal the end of male right. Although totally anachronistic toward the 1700s, the old biogenetic seminal theory of male right, now transformed into a Natural Law base for political theory, had been written into the influential French Law Canon from the 1500s and therefore defied reform even in the face of inordinately powerful critiques from men and women.[54] In the future, therefore, it was the ubiquitous Natural Law umbrella, accompanied as always by varied modes of female defamation, that

[52] See n. 14 above; Lynn Hunt, *The Family Romance of the French Revolution* (Berkeley, Ca: University of California Press, 1992), chap. 1, adopted the notion of a family model (albeit undefined) in order to link fathers and sons in a purported Freudian "family romance" of the later 1700s; and Jeffrey Merrick, "Fathers and kings: patriarchalism and absolutism in eighteenth-century French politics," *Studies on Voltaire and the Eighteenth Century*, 308 (1993), 281–303, and "Family and Festivals: Social Integration and Disintegration in Morellet's Critique of the French Revolution," *History of European Ideas* 17:5 (1993), 599–614, adopted the family model (still undefined) purportedly in place by the 1700s to explain increasing use of paternal images—king as father—later in the 1700s. Here my historical and legal definition of the Marital Regime model of government, which encompasses both family and state units undergoing the process of *parallel* legal construction (not evolutionary growth), offers an interpretation substantively different from those of Hunt and Merrick.

[53] Relevant legal cases are in Hanley, *State Building in Early Modern France*. Denis Diderot, *The Nun* [*La Religieuse*], trans. Leonard W. Tancock (London: Harmondsworth, Penguin, 1974) equates despotism (marital power) in family and state; Lyndon Shanley and Peter G. Stillman, "Political and Marital Despotism: Montesquieu's *Persian Letters*," in *The Family in Political Thought*, ed. Jean Bethke Elshtain (Amherst: University of Massachusetts Press, 1982), pp. 66–79; and Gabriel-Honoré de Riquetti, comte de Mirabeau, *Essai sur le despotisme* [third edn, Paris, 1792] (Paris: Bailleul, 1821, pp. 32–38, 320; and *Des Lettres de Cachet et des prisons d'etat* [1778] (Hambourg, 1782) on improper exercise of parental authority.

[54] For anti-Aristotelian views in science and natural philosophy, see Horowitz, "The 'Science' of Embryology," recounting arguments between the Spermaticists (following Aristotle) and the Ovists; and Scheibinger, *The Mind has no Sex?*, chaps. 6 and 7 (including Descartes' mind-body dualism); for legal critiques in case law, see Hanley, *State Building in Early Modern France*; and for literary ones, see Lougee, *Les Paradis des Femmes*, chap. 1; Erica Harth, *Cartesian Women: Versions and Subversions of Rational Discourse in the Old Regime* (Ithaca, NY: Cornell University Press, 1992), chap. 4; Ian Maclean, *Woman Triumphant: Feminism in French Literature, 1610–1652* (Oxford, Eng: Clarendon Press, 1977), viii; Paul Hoffman, *La Femme dans la pensée des lumières* (Paris: Ophyrs, 1977), pp. 45–52; Joan DeJean, *Tender Geographies* (New York, NY: Columbia University Press, 1991), chaps.

was committed to human memory and sustained male rule in social and political practice without attendant political maxims, legal grounds, scientific data, or logical explanations.

Despite the opportune crossroads for change created by the French Revolution of 1789, when monarchic government was reformed and venal-hereditary officeholding suppressed, male rule and female exclusion remained legitimate. On the social front, Pothier's influential opinions on family law were adopted (posthumously) to formulate laws for the Napoleonic Code Civil (1803).[55] The Code Civil moved far beyond its predecessor, the Marital Law Compact in the monarchic state, and invoked the "laws of nature" to promulgate inordinately severe new laws in the modern state upholding male dominance and female dependance in the family right into the 1980s.[56] On the political front, the deputies in the National Constituent Assembly wrote a new constitution in 1791 that restricted the executive power of the king, instituted a separation of powers, guarded natural and civil rights, and made marriage a civil act. At the same time, however, under the rubric of "Liberty, Equality, and Fraternity" the deputies not only preserved but also extended the male right to political rule. They decreed that "Monarchy is indivisible and is delegated hereditarily to the reigning family, from *male to male*, by order of primogeniture, to the perpetual exclusion of women and their descendants," and further decreed that in the future (unlike the past) all regents would be male.[57]

In republics and monarchies during the 1800s, commentators revived debates about an ancient Salic Law, some historians discussed female exclusion under the rubric of Salic Law just as if that disreputable ancient ordinance (interpolated and forged) had never been found fraudulent and dismissed, and still others, such as Jules Michelet, attributed state continuity, the preservation of "French identity and spirit," to the national tradition of male governance. When the death of Charles de Gaulle in 1970 occasioned the remark that "France is a widow," the provenance of that faint echo of the old marital regime metaphor legitimating male rule in the era of early state building was not difficult to ascertain.[58] In the French Republic of the 1990s, the political

---

1 and 3; and Joan Hinde Stewart, *Gynographes* (Lincoln, Ne: University of Nebraska Press, 1993), chaps. 5, 6, and 10.

[55] Pothier, *Oeuvres de Pothier* (new edn Paris: Béchet Aîné Libraire, 1824): the editor, M. Dupin, states that more than three quarters of the Code was extracted from these treatises (1:cxiv–cxv).

[56] *Code Civil* (Paris: Prat/Europa, 1987), art. 213.

[57] *Constitution of 1791*, tit. 3, chap. 2, sec. 1, art. 1 (on monarchs) [my italics]; and tit. 3, sec. 2, art. 1 and 2 (on regents). See Christine Fauré, *Les Déclarations des droits de l'homme de 1789* (Paris: Pagot, 1988), p. 116, on the National Assembly debates (July 27–28, December 22, 1789) about male rule.

[58] Arguing against the new advocates of Salic Law (male right), see M. Thomassy, *De la nécessité d'appeler au trône les filles de France: ouvrage précédé d'un examin de la loi salique* (Paris: A. Égron Libraire, 1820), pp. 52–72, holding that female exclusion is not law but custom which can be changed. For female exclusion treated under "Salic Law," see the

problem of national identity built on the male right to govern continues to vex a democratic state committed to representation in government. The newly framed political demands, therefore, address female exclusion from proper representation in the nation. The political manifesto, *To Power Women Citizens! Liberty, Equality, Parity* (1992), written by Anne Le Gall, Claude Servan-Schreiber and Françoise Gaspard; and the Parity Movement political petition (1993), signed by 289 women and 288 men (symbolizing the 577 members in the National Assembly), call for "democratic parity" to be attained through an equal division of elective offices along male and female lines.[59] This bold political solution—gender parity— directly challenges the centuries-old entrenchment of the male right to govern not just from the French Revolution of 1789, when revolutionary women made valiant bids for political inclusion in the first Republic,[60] but actually from the era of state building in the 1500s, when kings and officeholders, legists and historians, engaged in early monarchic state building legitimized monarchic government juridically along the lines of a Marital Regime that excluded women from the polity and privileged the male right to rule in household and state.

comments of Dupin (editor) in Loisel, *Pasquier, ou dialogue des advocats*, pp. 266–267, and *Institutes Coutumières*, I:xliv. See Jules Michelet, *Histoire de France* (Paris: Flammarion, 1971), 2:229, on male right embodying the state; and Georges Pompidou's marital metaphor in *Le Monde* at the death of De Gaulle, 9 November 1970.

[59] *Au Pouvoir, Citoyennes! Liberté, Égalité, Parité* (Paris: Éditions du Sevil, 1992); and for the Parité petition, see *Le Monde*, 10 November 1993. Following elections (March 1993) when only 6% of the deputies elected were women (who constituted 20% of the candidates), the banner carried in the Parity Movement demonstration read: "Non à l'Assemblée Nationale \ Oui à la Parité Hommes/Femmes." The problem addressed was the low representation of French women in the main legislative assembly (6.1%), more akin to the failures of Britain (9.1%), Italy (8.1%), and the United States (11% House, 7% Senate) than to the successes of Norway (38%), Denmark (33.5%), Sweden (32.6%), Netherlands (27.3%), Germany (21.6%), and Spain (15.7%). French women did not gain the right to vote until 1944, much later than Spain 1931, Britain 1928, United States 1920, Germany 1919, Russia 1917.

[60] For the documentary history, see Darlene Gay Levy, Harriet Branson Applewhite, Mary Durham Johnson, eds., *Women in Revolutionary Paris, 1789–1795* (Champagne, Il: University of Illinois Press, 1979); and Paule Marie Duhet, ed., *Cahiers de doléances des femmes en 1789 et autres textes* (Paris, 1989); and for the way paradoxes inherent in "natural rights" subverted attempts to discuss equal rights thereafter, see Joan Wallach Scott, "French Feminists and the 'Rights of Man': Olympe de Gouges' Declarations," *History Workshop Journal* (1989): 1–21.

8

Men of Law and the French Revolution

DONALD R. KELLEY

The French Revolution marked both the end of an old legal tradition and the beginning of a new social ideal that nevertheless invoked ancient values and terminology. "Here is how I define the Revolution," wrote Jules Michelet: "the coming of Law, the resurrection of Right, the reaction of Justice."[1] None of the generation of 1789 better understood this ideal than the lawyers who moved into public life in the spring of that year—those men of law who were left over from that carefully ranked and privileged corporation which was disappearing along with the rest of the "society of orders." Institutionally cut off from the past (their "Order" having been abolished in September 1790), the former *avocats* were nonetheless equipped professionally to deal with the future, especially in times of social turmoil and political maneuvering, at least in an ad hoc way. By education and training they were prepared to understand social and constitutional issues, and always to take the lead in argument and persuasion.[2] From what better vantage point can we assess the French Revolution as a social process which began, for many of its participants as well as many later historians, with a quest for justice, social as well as political?

---

[1] *La Révolution française*, introduction. Bibliographical and historiographical references will be limited to those bearing on this fairly specialized topic; unless otherwise noted, place of publication is always Paris.

[2] See above all Michael Fitzsimmons, *The Parisian Order of Barristers and the French Revolution* (Cambridge, Mass., 1987), and the important new collection, *La Révolution et l'ordre juridique privé: Rationalité ou scandale?* Actes du colloque d'Orléans, 11–13 septembre 1986 (1988). For background on the lawyers see also J. P. Royer, *La Société judiciaire depuis le XVIIIe siécle* (1979); Lenard Berlanstein, "Lawyers in Prerevolutionary France," in *Lawyers in Early Modern Europe*, ed. W. Prest (New York, 1980); Isser Wolloch "The Fall and Resurrection of the French Civil Bar, 1789–1820s," *French Historical Studies* 15 (1987), 241–62; Francis Delbeke, *L'Action politique et sociale des avocats au XVIIIe siécle* (Louvain, 1927); A. J. Arnaud, *Les Juristes face à la société du XIX siècle à nos jours* (1975); R. Marie, *Le Recrutement de la magistrature pendant la periode révolutionnaire* (Rennes, 1909); A. Bardoux, *Les Légistes, leur influence sur la société française* (1877); Gaudry, *Histoire du barreau de Paris* (1864); V. Jeanvrot, *La Magistrature* (1882); and J. Bourdon, *La Magistrature sous le Consulat et l'Empire* (Rodez, 1942).

Legal history has been out of fashion for at least two generations in revolutionary studies, but there are significant advantages deriving from the materials and attitudes of this old scholarly tradition.[3] In general legal sources, especially jurisprudence and discussion of judicial organization and reform, represent a compressed, if distorted version of historical experience and aspiration; and they suggest a level of social and political thinking which is at once more immediate and less fanciful, more practical and less interested, more concrete and personal, than that of conventional political philosophy or polemic, from which our interpretations of revolutionary ideology and experience are largely derived.

My main concern here is with the long-term impact of revolutionary efforts (from the 1780s to the 1830s), with the continuities rather than with the ups, downs, and reversals of politics and war; and so I attend not to the great movers and shakers, not to the mass of the moved and the shaken, but rather to an intermediate range of social and intellectual agents. This middle-range activity is well represented by the professional (and para-professional) group defined, in the democratic fashion of the 1790s, as "men of law"—there were of course no women—who were involved in the everyday operations of judicial and social institutions, or the devising of new ones, under whatever political structures happened to prevail at the moment in the tumultuous last decade of the eighteenth century.

What the Revolution offered these *hommes de loi* was an extraordinary laboratory for political and social experiment—experiment based in part on Enlightenment theories but was carried out in a social ferment which had ostensibly wiped away the institutional heritage of many centuries. More than the great orators of the revolutionary assemblies or the famous statesmen who rose and fell across the political spectrum of that age, the lawyers were the real experts of the systematic approach to the understanding and regulation of collective human behavior. If they had suffered a decline as political theorists (as William Church argued),[4] they enjoyed a remarkable rise to prominence in the context of what they themselves were first to call "la science sociale," and this is the main subject of this inquiry.

---

[3] On French legal history in general, Jacques Godechot, *Les Institutions de la Révolution et l'Empire* (1968; 2nd ed.); Philippe Sagnac, *La Législation de la révolution française (1789–1792), Essai d'histoire sociale* (1898); P. P. Viard, *Histoire générale du droit privé français (1789–1830,* (1931); E. Seligman, *La Justice en France pendant la révolution (1789–1792)* (1901); A. Mater, *L'Histoire juridique de la révolution* (Besançon, 1919); Hiver, *Histoire critique des institutions judiciares de la France de 1789 à 1848* (1848); Louis La Ferrière, *Histoire des principes, des institutions et des lois pendant la révolution française* (1851–52); and C. A. L. Rasenack, *Gesetz und Verordnung in Frankreich seit 1789* (Berlin, 1967).

[4] "The Decline of French Jurists as Political Theorists, 1660–1789," *French Historical Studies* 5 (1967), 1–40.

The fundamental dilemma of political and social thought has never been better expressed than by one of the most distinguished of these men of law, Citizen (later Count) Portalis, one of the reactors of the Civil Code of 1804:

> How can we control the action of time? How resist the course of events or the imperceptible force of custom? How know and calculate in advance what experience alone can reveal to us? Can foresight ever be extended to objects which thought itself cannot yet grasp?[5]

Portalis's even more distinguished colleague Cambacérès (playing Second to Napoleon's First Consul) certainly thought so, and said as much in the civil legislation on which he had been working since the first years of the Revolution. His hope not only to "reform everything" but also to "foresee everything" defined a basic issue dividing lawyers over three centuries of attempts at legal reform and unification.

After 1789 the spirits of Montesquieu and Rousseau—the "spirit of the law" and the voice of the "social"—contended with one another in the debates of the men of law in the revolutionary assemblies. On the one hand was the principle of the "division of powers," in which the judiciary guarded against legislative tyranny; on the other hand the insistence on the "general will" exercised by political virtuosi (and of course most conspicuously by Napoleon). Such were the terms in which lawyers began to construct what Cambacérès himself designated "social science."[6] On the level not only of high politics but also of social behavior, then, it was the lawyers above all who gave theoretical and practical expression to the experience of revolution.

At the beginning of 1789 the legal profession, replica and guarantor of the old society of orders, was full of inertia—full of itself, that is to say, and of its traditions and privileges. In December of the previous year the President of the Parlement of Paris complained of the literary and social "effervescence" and "ideas of innovation" threatening his "sovereign court" as well as the crown itself.[7] Jurists on the heights of their career ladders, both lawyers and magistrates, tended to be suspicious of change. The proud Order of Advocates luxuriated in an antiquity and a pedigree almost as impressive as its mother institution, the Parlement of Paris, which, with its provincial extensions, formed a "mystical body" devoted to royal justice and an intellectual and a

---

5 F. A. Fenet, *Recueil complet des travaux préparatoires du Code Civil* (1827), I, 469; and see L. Schimséwitsch, *Portalis et son temps* (1936).

6 *Discours sur la science social* (1789), and cf. Jussieu, *Discours* (to Corps Législatif and Conseil des Cinq-cents [An 7 1799]; BN Le433606). See also Georges Gusdorf, *Les Sciences humaines*, VIII (1978), 401; Sergio Moravia, *Il Pensiero degli idéologues: scienza e filosofia in Francia (1780–1815)* (Florence, 1974), 746; and B. W. Head, *Ideology and Social Science: Destutt de Tracy and French Liberalism* (The Hague, 1985), 109.

7 Flammermont, *Remonstrances du Parlement de Paris au XVIIIe siècle* (1898), III, 795. Legal Pamphlets in Bibliothèque Nationale, shelf-mark "Lb39".

professional elite based on a monopoly of "legal science" as taught in the faculties of law and as practiced in the royal, municipal, and seigneurial courts. Professors of civil law quarrelled with the more recently licensed professors of French customary law, but never about the preeminence of their common profession.[8] Along with a powerful *esprit de corps* and a sense of tradition going back, at least mythologically, to classical antiquity as well as to the "lawyers of the last Capetians", these jurists had accumulated privileges which made them, no less traditionally, the target of intense social criticism, satire, and abuse. "Duplicity," venality, and corruption were only a few of the charges which spoiled the lawyers' self-image as caretakers of the Constitution and "priests of the law." The *cahiers de doléance* of 1789 were filled with such complaints about the old judicial order.[9]

Yet—two-faced as usual—the legal profession had always been in the forefront of social change, playing a central role in the formulation of these cahiers and in a sense beginning the revolutionary process, through the so-called "judicial uprising" (*émeute judiciaire*) of 1788, when the Parlement defied the king and was sent, in the official phrase, "on permanent vacation."[10] This was the last political gasp of the Parlement, as the king's act of suppression was carried out by the last *lit de justice* of the French monarchy. To Tocqueville this affair demonstrated "how the Parlement with the aid of its precedents overturned the monarchy." In any case the parlementaire mentality persisted into the revolution, especially in the form of concern for "liberties" and the "French constitution," and it would make an even more prominent come-back under Napoleon and the Restoration.

In some ways the Estates General offered a more attractive forum for ambitious lawyers than either the *barreau* or the Parlement; for with the transformation of the Estates into a "National Constituent Assembly," they had the chance to become legislators as well as judges and advocates. They flourished in the last years of the monarchy. Over half of the deputies to the Estates were "advocates" by education if not occupation, and 70 of them were officially inscribed in the Order of Advocates for 1789.[11] That their ideological

---

8   Christian Chêne, *L'Enseignement du droit de français en pays de droit écrit (1679–1789)* (Geneva, 1982).

9   [Bergasse], *Cahiers du tiers-état* (1 Jan. 1789); *Extraits des Cahiers de Etats Generaux. Sur la Réformation de la Justice* (n.d.; BN Lf2351), citing the cahiers of 1560 and later; see also R. Aubin, *L'Organisation judiciaire d'après les cahiers de 1789* (1928), E. Champion, *Le France d'après les cahiers de 1789* (1897), Guy Chassinand-Nogaret, *The French Nobility in the Eighteenth Century*, tr. W. Doyle (Cambridge, Eng., 1987), on the cahiers of the nobility, and Phillip Dawson, "The Bourgeoisie de Robe in 1789," *French Historical Studies* 4 (1965), 1–21; also D. R. Kelley, "Lord Deliver Us from Justice," *Yale Journal of Law and the Humanities* 5 (1993), 159–68.

10   Flammermont, III, 735; cf. Tocqueville, *L'Ancien régime et la révolution*, ed. A. Jardin (1953), II, 53 (from unfinished fragments), and Jacqueline Lafon, "La Fin du Parlement de Paris," *Etudes d'histoire du droit parisien* (1970), 229–46.

11   See *Almanach national* (1789).

importance far outweighed their impressive numbers is shown by the flood of "brochures" and journals, official and unofficial. "Discourses," "Reports," and, endlessly, "Opinions" (a legal genre democratized in the context of revolutionary journalism and polemic) competed for the attention of literate and engaged Parisians and the provincials swept into politics from the spring of '89; and the tide continued to rise over the next decades. There was a pandemonium of professional (and para-professional) ideas about how to build a new social system and attain liberty and equality, if not fraternity, and to fulfill the ideal of nationality.

The members of what used to be regarded as the "fourth estate" ranged from the most radical, beginning with Robespierre, to the most conservative, such as Nicolas Bergasse, who resigned in protest from the National Assembly and lived to defend the interests of his fellow emigres and royalists a generation later. Three were victims of the Terror (Le Chapelier and, on the same day, Thouret and Epremesnil); but most had extensive life spans; and many of them, together with colleagues who rose to prominence in the 1790s, continued to maneuver and to opinionate over several decades—and, with Talleyrand, to "survive."[12]

What enhanced the position of lawyers at the end of the old regime was the emergence of a new political culture, which is most clearly defined in transformations of vocabulary and forms of discourse, perhaps even more than in the substantive issues being debated.[13] Revolutionaries acquired their own code and keywords, inflating some and devaluing others in their pursuit of particular causes. "Innovation" was the order of the day: "Do you want good laws?" Voltaire had asked; "then burn yours and make new ones"; and this is just what the men of law on the left proposed to do. "Destruction" was thus often a more favorable term than "reformation," "prediction" more than "prudence." "Antiquity," "honor," "custom," and "tempered" government were regarded as almost dirty words, such as the term "advocate" itself, which suggested champions of particular "interests" of the old regime and which would be officially banned. Everybody spoke of "liberty," "property," the "social," the "constitution," and especially "revolution" but more often than not—as Edmund

12 The major guide is A. Martin and G. Walter, *Catalogue de l'histoire de la révolution française*, 5 vols. (1941–50), listing over 50,000 items and some 2000 *hommes de loi*. For activities of the licensed *avocats* Fitzsimmon's *The Parisian Order of Barristers* is invaluable, but it does not cover all the writing and teaching of "men of law."

13 Keith Baker, *Inventing the French Revolution* (Cambridge, 1990); cf. Janis Langins, "Words and Institutions during the French Revolution: the case of Revolutionary Scientific and Technical Education," in *The Social History of Language*, ed. Peter Burke and Roy Porter (Cambridge, 1987), 136–60, and Jacques Guilhaumou, "Qu est-ce fair parler la loi?" in *La Révolution et l'ordre juridique*, I, 127; William Sewell, *Work and Revolution in France* (Cambridge, 1980); and the old study of Jean Belin, *La Logique d'une idée-force: l'idée d'utilité sociale et la révolution française (1789–1792)*, and his supplementary thesis, *Les Démarches de la pensée sociale* (1939).

Burke showed in his *Reflections on the Revolution in France*—in opposed senses. Thus Bergasse agreed that there should be an "absolute revolution" (*révolution absolue*) but he meant this in a gradual, a planetary rather than a political sense.[14] So the "carnival of words" continued, and with it the social and political influence of the men of law.

Behind this logomachy was not only a grim reality but also an unprecedented opportunity, for lawyers, to construct a "new judicial order." From late August 1789 to late August 1790 members of the Committee for the Constitution (including Talleyrand as well as working members like Sieyès, Duport, Le Chapelier, and Thouret) confronted the question crucial to the principles of the Declaration of the Rights of Man and the New Constitution, just off the press, concerning "the organization of judicial power," and in this context the most basic questions of judicial control and national goals. Some lawyers succombed to what Mona Ozouf has called the "don-Quichottisme du Comité de la Constitution," but they were always drawn back to practical questions by their more conservative colleagues. In these debates, in any case, began one of the seminal ages of social science (as the lawyers believed and began to proclaim) and indeed of social engineering (as we may infer), which culminated in 1804 with the publication of the "Civil Code of the French People," soon to be called the Code Napoléon.

The opening statement on judicial reorganization was made by Nicolas Bergasse on 17 August 1789. "Judicial power" (*pouvoir judiciaire*) was superior to all other public powers, he declared, recalling the terrible *lettres de cachet*.[15] In his youth Bergasse had admired Turgot and had enjoyed an afternoon's conversation with the elderly Rousseau—who avoided discussing Bergasse's work but who predicted the political storms to come. Bergasse had also written and

14 *Archives parlementaires*, VIII, 440ff. For convenience I refer to this collection (which is fuller than the contemporary *Moniteur*), although most of the research was done in the original pamphlets, mostly listed in Marin and Walter under the author or title (in case of anonymous publications) with the BN shelf mark. See also F. A. Aulard, *Les Orateurs de L'Assemblée Constituante* (1882), and G. Guatherot, *L'Assemblée Constituante, Le Philosophisme en action* (1914), as well as A. Lameth, *Histoire de l'Assemblée Constituante* (1828–29), and individual biographies. Bernardi published an "Essai sur les révolutions du droit français" in 1785; see also J. M. Goulemot, "Le Mot Révolution et la formation du concept de Révolution politique (fin XVII siècle)," *Annales historiques de la révolution française* 39 (1967), 417–44.

15 *Discours sur les crimes et les tribunaux de Haute traison* (1790; BN Le29138–75A); see also Etienne Lamy, *Un défenseur des principes traditionels sous la Révolution, Nicolas Bergasse* (1920), and Jean Egret, *La Révolution des notables, Mounier et les monarchiens 1789* (1959). Bergasse's position was by no means as conservative as that of others, some of whom wanted no changes at all and who rejected ever Bergasse's modest proposals; e.g. Louis-René Chauveau, *Sur l'organisation du pouvoir judiciaire* (Dec. 1789). In a "tragi-politi-comique" drama published in 1790 (*La Journée des dupes*) Bergasse complained of "ces avocats, dont la horde obscurcit l'assemblée [nationale], se croyant autant de potentats."

dedicated to Voltaire an idealistic work on "the humanity of the judge," in which he attacked all forms of social and political "prejudice"; and he carried some of this idealism over into the Committee on the Constitution. He hoped that justice would express the "national will" and be free and non-venal, and he supported the notion that the people should have a say in the selection of their judges. However, he also praised the old magistracy, argued for royal control over judicial appointments, and reproached what he called "dissociability" and the contempt for experience associated with Rousseau. Bergasse's plan for reform, following the English model recommended by Montesquieu, was "loudly applauded," according to the *Archives parlementaires*, and commended in the *Moniteur* and *Mercure*. Yet the Assembly rejected his proposal. "The moment was not favorable to moderation," Bergasse admitted ruefully, and along with his colleague Mounier he soon resigned.

Over the next seven months other plans were submitted and discussed. The "code" assembled by Sieyès, no jurist, was also discarded. That of Thouret, which kept faith with the *cahiers* by emphasizing both the "rights of man" and the "separation of powers," was looked on more favorably. Most radical of all was the proposal of Adrien Duport, whose searching if somewhat utopian views helped to define the terms of the debates over "judicial power" in the new social order. In his enthusiasm Duport went so far as to suggest that revolutionary justice might dispense altogether with the legal profession which he had himself served so faithfully. "No more judges!" he cried. "No more courts!"[16] Duport made the beau geste of bestowing the income of his parlementary office on the state; and he argued that achieving justice was a purely logical process, a syllogism in which the facts formed the minor premise, the pertinent law the major, and the judgment the conclusion. In a democratic regime laws were not professional secrets understood only by privileged experts, not mysteries of the "priests of the laws," but "social conventions" that could be understood or applied by any fellow citizen (*concitoyen*).[17]

Duport's ideas went too far, of course—even Robespierre put in a kind word for the lawyers—but they were in keeping with one of the most extraordinary acts of 1790, the suppression of the Order of Advocates. After September of that year there were no longer *juges, avocats, procureurs*, and other kinds of *gens de robe*—nor indeed would there be any more of the "accursed robes," as Duport's friend Chabroud called them.[18] There would be only defrocked *hommes de loi* who would speak for the judicial aspect of the "general will."

16 *Archives parlementaires*, XII, 570: "Point de juges! Point de tribunaux!"; and see G. Michin, *Essai sur l'histoire du parti feuillant, Adrien Duport* (1924).

17 *Principes et plan sur l'etablissement de l'ordre judiciaire* (1790; BN Le^{29}.536); *Archives parlementaires*, XII, 570); cf. the "Opinion" (30 March 1790) by Charles Chabroud; also G. Michin, *Essai sur l'histoire du parti feuillant, Adrien Duport* (1924), and Fournel, *Histoire du barreau*, 79.

18 *Archives parlementaires*, esp. XII, 574, 408ff; and see Fitzsimmons, *The Parisian Order of Barristers*, 33ff.

Protests had been made by lawyers against the suppression of the Parlement—by Cazalès, for example, by the Parlement of Toulouse, and (secretly) by the Parlement of Paris—but threats of treason charges (*lèse nation*) ended such protests, as the elections produced replacements for the old magistracy.

As J. P. Fournel lamented, the degradation of the Order took place in the presence of its most distinguished members, including the *bâtonnier* Tronchet and probably Fournel himself, who added bitterly, "Ma carrière est terminée."[19] It is a curious and never satisfactorily explained circumstance that none of the over one hundred men of law in the Assembly objected publicly to the abolition of their corporation. One reason was that the parlementary spirit—the esprit de corps repeatedly denounced by critics of the old regime—lived on; and the "former advocates" (*ci-devant avocats* being the official phrase) did not expect to have, and in fact did not generally have, much trouble in finding a place in the "new judicial order."

What was the place of this order in the brave new world of the Constitutional Monarchy? In a discourse of 24 May 1790 J. G. Thouret praised judicial power as having unparalleled "influence on the happiness of individuals, the progress of public spirit, and on the stability of the new constitution." Yet questions remained; and in the first journal of the new men of law, the *Gazette de nouveaux tribunaux*, featuring Thouret's discourse as its editorial statement, a qualification was registered.[20] No doubt it was essential "to obey the general will," he wrote, "but patriotism has its doubts, and the Committee on the Constitution will consider these in the following articles." The major questions were reduced to ten and submitted by Bertrand Barère to the Assembly for deliberation:[21] should there be juries *à l'Anglais* for civil and criminal justice? Should the courts be sedentary or ambulatory? Should there be degrees of jurisdiction, i.e., courts of appeal and revisions of judgment? Should judges have life tenure? Should they be chosen by the people or by the king? And should a committee be appointed to discuss these and other questions?

Under the influence of *Anglomanie*, a fashion since Voltaire's day, the *jurés* and the *juges de paix* would form the lowest level of the new order.[22] Invoking the name of Burke, Duport defended this as a healthy "restitution" of Frankish

---

[19] *Histoire des avocats au parlement* (1813), II, 544.

[20] *Gazette des nouveaux tribunaux*, I (1791), reprinting as its editorial statement Therout's discourse (24 May 1790): "Le pouvoir judiciaire est celui des pouvoirs public, dont l'exercice habituel aura le plus d'influence sur le bonheur des particuliers, sur les progrès de l'sprit, sur le maintien de par l'ordre politique, et sur la stabilité de la constitution."

[21] *Archives parlementaires*, XII, 489; and cf. Barère, *Montesquieu peint d'après ses ouvrages* (Suisse, an V [1797]).

[22] *Histoire du barreau de Paris dans le cours de la révolution* (1816), 104; and see Richard M. Andrews, "The Justices of the Peace of Revolutionary Paris," in Douglas Johnson (ed.), *French Society and the Revolution* (Cambridge, Eng., 1976), 167–216.

custom and other "liberties" of Germanic provenance. More conservative jurists were contemptuous of this importation. Fournel later scoffed that in the countryside this office had been familiar for centuries under feudal terminology (*châtelains, syndics, procureurs, fiscaux*, etc.). This most unrepentant of former advocates recognized "three kinds of revolutionaries: the tricksters, the tricked, and the trumpeters" (*les trompeurs, les trompés et les trompettes*), and by 1790 the latter seemed to prevail. Anyway, the office of justice of the peace, open to any male citizen over 30, expressed the committee's desire for popular justice, and it was adopted by the Assembly.

On a higher level the democratic character of the new judiciary was encouraged by the provision for popular election. One immediate endorsement came from Jeremy Bentham, who saw "unpopularity" as the only alternative.[23] Related to this was the age-old question of life-tenure (*l'inamovabilté*) of judges. A reading of Rousseau suggested that magistrates should be directly responsible to, hence dismissible by, the General Will, while students of Montesquieu argued that "irremovability" was needed as a protections against legislative or executive tyranny. The men of law were bound to root out the private interests of the old magistracy; yet many had fond memories of its accomplishments as a counterbalance to monarchy. In the end they decided on a tenure of six years as a symbol, but the movement for complete *inamovabilité* was never abandoned.

As for the possibility of legal appeal and revision of judgment, some men of law objected because it implied imperfection in revolution legislation. If law was identified with reason, how could one anticipate disagreements among reasonable men? The answer, according to one lawyer, was that appeal signified merely review and so reinforced the rationality of the judicial process. The crucial step was taken of establishing higher courts called *tribunaux de cassation*, each possessing six judges and an alternate, to give final expression to "judicial power" in the new order.[24] All male citizens over 30 were eligible, but not surprisingly lawyers predominated in the elections. In Paris all 42 of the judges elected were *hommes de loi*, 29 of them "former advocates" and 4 judges, not counting those with judicial experience in the provinces—now organized as "departments."

It would be difficult and not especially rewarding to follow all the twistings and turnings of the *droit intermédiaire* through the upheavals of the First French Republic, especially in times of Jacobin extremism. The self-righteous

23 *Archives parlementaires*, XV, 370; and cf. Bentham, *Draught of a new plan for the organisation of the Judicial establishment in France* (n.p., 21 Dec. 1789).

24 From 1796 this court issued its own *Bulletin*; see J. Crépon, *Cour de Cassation, origines, organisation, attributions* (1892).

radicalism of the Jacobin view of law is captured (if caricatured) well in a verse quoted by a lawyer who had lived through the period:[25]

> When God to the lawless Hebrews spake,
> When He His wisest laws did make,
> He spoke His words not from the Plain
> But from, on high, the great Mountain,
> [refrain:] The great Mountain.

This was legislative hubris with a vengeance, but it was a not an attitude which many practicing lawyers could share, at least until the advent of Napoleon as law-maker.

During the period of "intermediary law," the "new judicial order" was subjected to further reforms and innovations (as well as disruptions by the extraordinary jurisdictions of the Terror), although professional journals such as the *Gazette des nouveaux tribunaux* tried to collect a settled and settling jurisprudence out of revolutionary practice.[26] Few members of the Order of Advocates participated in the "revolutionary justice" of 1794 (just 5 of 54 elected judges), though many resumed their careers in 1795 and later. Some men of law moved into retreat (e.g., Fournel and Tronchet) or into exile (Bergasse and Duport), while others were (as Fournel put it) "tués révolutionnairement" (Thouret and Le Chapelier as well as Robespierre and Barnave); but many more stayed, survived, and even rose to high office (Cambacérès and, after a time in exile, Portalis). Throughout this period the legal profession was accommodated if not wholly recognized, but its role was severely reduced by the innovations of civil (citizens') and political justice. Lawyerly skills were obviated on the one hand by the encouragement of voluntary and forced arbitration (*arbitrage*) and the untrained justices of the peace, and on the other hand by the fetish of legislative remedy and suspicion of uncontrolled, interpretive "jurisprudence."

Yet the break was not complete, and some elements of legal continuity can be seen. A certain level of professionalism was ensured by the preservation, in the Constitutions of 1793, 1795, and 1797, of the Tribunal of Cassation; by 1804 this (renamed) *Cour de Cassation* and other "courts of the first instance" restored much of the old undemocratic hierarchy of jurisdictions, in which

[25] Berriat-Saint-Prix, *La Justice révolutionnaire* (1870), 70:
> Quand Dieu fit entendre sa voix,
> A l'Hebreu rebelle et volage;
> Quand l'Eternelle dicta des lois,
> Qui devait le rendre plus sage;
> Pour prononcer de tels arrets,
> Il ne s'est par mis en campagne,
> Mais il a donné ses decrets
> Du Haut de la Montagne (bis).

[26] Fitzsimmons, *The Parisian Order of Barristers*, 61, n. 72, 70, n. 11, and 277–78.

judicial expertise was again required and rewarded. Despite the dissolution of the law faculties in 1795, the teaching of law, too, was continued on at least an elementary level in the *écoles centrales* established the next year—e.g., by J. P. Proudhon in Besançon, by Henrion de Pansey in the Haute-Garonne, by Berthelot in Garde, and by Perreau in the central school of the Panthéon. Under the Consulate the founding of the *Académie de Législation* (in which Bernardi taught) and the *Université de Jurisprudence* reflected still more serious efforts to encourage the professional and even historical and theoretical study of law, though to be sure in post-revolutionary terms.[27]

Jurisprudence, although it was suspect in the wake of revolutionary legislation, could never be completely neglected. At first it was limited largely to interpretation of laws made since 1790 and attended to by old-fashioned jurists. A prime example is the royalist Auguste-Charles Guichard, who assembled a series of codes on practical aspects of the *droit intermédiaire*, especially property, confiscation, succession, justices of the peace, and the Tribunal of Cassation.[28] This author of *Le Code des juges de paix* (1795), according to the editorial blurb, "is a man who since the beginning of the revolution has never stopped preaching the observation of law, the respect for property and individual liberty . . . , who is the openly declared enemy of the destroyers [*disorganisateurs*], intriguers, and rascals, and has not escaped the rule of these monsters [of the Terror] who have usurped supreme power."[29] Fortunately, this statement goes on, "the miraculous fall of these tyrants" has encouraged "the return to order and justice." For Guichard justice meant jurisprudence, and three years later his "code and memorial" of the Tribunal of Cassation was advertized as a collection of judicial "decisions, whose authority is as great as that of the laws themselves."

The problem for the jurists of that generation, however, was that "the laws themselves" were still unstable, unsystematic, and subject to shifts in the political climate—*lois de circonstance*—and the "general will" required a more formal and comprehensive expression of its socio-juridical base. Henrion de Pansey, an old regime legal scholar who became a baron of the Empire and who would end

---

27 Jean Imbert, "L'Enseignement du droit dans les ècoles centrales sous la révolution," *La Révolution et l'ordre judiciaire*, 248–65; and Hugues Richard, *Bénigne Poncet, le professeur de législation a l'école central de la Cote d'Or* (Dijon, 1977); cf. H. B. Gibault, *De l'Enseignement dans ses rapports avec l'ordre politique* (n.d.).

28 *Code des Juges de Paix* (An II "avis de l'éditeur," and *Code et mémorial du Tribunal de Cassation* (An VI [1798]); also *Code des confiscations et sequestres* (An III [1795]), denouncing "populicide"; and cf. *Journal typographique et bibliographique*, ed. P. Roux (An VI [1797–98]). From 1798 there was a category of "jurisprudence" as well as "législation" in the *Journal général de la littérature de France* (an VI).

29 A few years later Guichard defended Joseph Arena, a conspirator in a plot to assassinate Napoleon.

his life as a Restoration judge, put it this way: "It is not enough to constitute a government; it is equally necessary to organize society."[30]

This was the condition underlying that question so fundamental to the "new judicial order—namely, codification. Since the late middle ages the ideal of legal unification had been discussed; but not until the feudal regime had been "entirely abolished" and the old laws had been in effect and in a few cases actually (in Voltaire's image) "burned" could this goal be realized. As Merlin de Douai observed in his collection of "intermediary jurisprudence" of 1801, the voice of France had been calling out for a "new edifice" of law for over a decade.[31] "There will be made a code of civil laws common to the whole kingdom," declared the Assembly in September 1791; and two years later Cambacérès presented the first "project" for codification. It was a time of Jacobin euphoria and an apparent awakening of the national will, expressed just two weeks before in the famous levée en masse. "The age so devoutly wished for has finally arrived to fix forever the empire of liberty and the destinies of France," proclaimed Cambacérès.[32] He dedicated two further projects to this "grand edifice of legislation," and Jacqueminot a fourth, before a government commission came up with the plan which evolved into the Civil Code of 1804.

The Civil Code was created in an imperial rather than a revolutionary spirit. In the wake of the excesses of Jacobinism, legislative virtuosity, and especially the Terror, the esprit philosophique was increasingly overshadowed by the esprit juridique, as Sagnac remarked;[33] and this renewed appreciation for legal science encouraged the delicate work of codification which Napoleon, as First Consul, inaugurated in 1800. On the committee of four jurists assigned to the task of "civil legislation" were Portalis, recently returned from exile in Germany and appointed to the Conseil d'Etat the next year; Tronchet, former advocate (and in 1789 bâtonnier) of the Order, counsel for Louis XVI at his trial, and first president of the Court of Cassation; Bigot de Préaumeneu, also a former member of the Order, a judge in 1790, and a prisoner under the Convention before reemerging to enjoy Bonapartist favor; and Jacques Maleville, another member of the monarchist party (with Portalis and Tronchet), judge on the Tribunal of Cassation in 1791, and secretary of the committee.[34] To these names might be

---

30 Oeuvres juridiques, ed. Rozet (1834), 191; and see J. H. M. Salmon, "Constitutions, Old and New: Henrion de Pansey before and after the Revolution" (forthcoming) Historical Journal.

31 Recueil alphabétique des questions de droit (an IX [1801]), "avertissement."

32 F. Papillard, Cambacérès (1961). See Fenet, I, 1; also I, 11, "En détruisant les lois et les coutumes existants, il fallait leur substituer une législation parfaite, qui ne laissât plus de doutes à resoudre, ni difficultés à craindre." According to Gaudry (Histoire du barreau, II, 494), Cambacérès agreed with Napoleon to "couper la langue de tout avocat qui lui aurait déplu."

33 La Législation civile, 396.

34 Lydie Schimséwitsch, Portalis et son temps. See Portalis, De l'usage et de l'Abus de l'Esprit philosophique durant le dix-huitième siecle (1827); Fenet, I, 467, etc.; François Villaret, Le bâtonnier Tronchet et la naissance d'un droit nouveau (extr. La Vie judiciaire); and Jean

added those of J. M. Locré, another former advocate and from 1800 secretary to the Conseil d'Etat, whose *procès verbaux* were the basis of important works on the "spirit" of the new French codes, and Merlin de Douai, former member of the Committee on Feudalism *procureur-général* of the Tribunal of Cassation, member of the Conseil d'Etat, and compiler of collections of revolutionary (and pre-revolutionary) jurisprudence, who did not attend the meetings of the committee on codification but who, as Napoleon remarked, was certainly there "in spirit."[35]

The process of codification (begun 11 August 1800, published 21 March 1804) was another "carnival of words," but in this case more legalistic than ideological. Over the previous decade the "men of law" had created many new laws, and abolished old ones, but now they enjoyed the unique opportunity of legislating on a large scale. In general the procedure was for the committee members to present arguments for the respective titles and then for select respondents—the Tribunal of Cassation, "tribunes" from the twenty-eight appeal courts, and finally spokesmen for the Conseil d'Etat, itself composed mainly of lawyers—to present positions pro or con. In this way the texts of the Code were worried over and hammered out. The First Consul himself (who had once dreamed of a society without lawyers) attended over half—57 of 100—of the sessions, supplying blunt, practical, self-serving, and transparently imperialistic comments.[36]

In official rhetoric and public imagination the Civil Code was represented as a derivation of pure reason and "natural law." For *Le Peuple*, for example, "the truth is one and indivisible, and so should be its law." In fact it was not a statement of theory but rather, as Sagnac put it, a work of transaction. What is more, the mentality of the men of law acted to preserve and to renew the force of legal tradition; for the doctrinal origins of the Code can be traced back not only to old regime jurisprudence, notably to the work of Jean Domat and R.-J. Pothier (accounting for over half the 2281 articles), but also to Roman law, which had furnished Napoleon's primary model, especially in matters of property and the partriarchal family. "The Revolution has made possible a new creation," wrote the earliest commentator, Riffé, in 1803; and the Code was indeed surrounded by the official rhetoric of rationalism and natural law. Yet, in view both of the form and ideological intent of Napoleon's legislative work, it is

Latour, *Jacques de Maleville (1741–1824) l'homme politique et le jurisconsulte* (Bordeaux, 1929).

[35] Louis Gruffy, *La Vie et oeuvre juridique de Merlin de Douai* (1934).

[36] Fenet, III-VI; *CODE CIVIL des François, Avec les Discours qui ont été prononcés par les Orateurs du Gouvernement, nommé par le PREMIER CONSUL pour exposer, devant le Corps Législatif, le motif les Lois dont le Code est Composé (an XIII)* (1804); J. Maleville, *Analyse raisonnée de la discussion du Code Civil* (1805); Locré, *Esprit du Code Napoléon, tiré de la discussion* (1805); and see also A. J. Arnaud, *Les Origines doctrinales du code civil français* (1969); R. Batiza, *Domat, Pothier and the Code* (n. p., 1973); and *Le Code Civil, 1804–1904, Livre du Centenaire*, 2 vols. (1904).

hard to disagree with Riffé's further acknowledgement, that "This code is founded mainly on Roman law."[37]

After the coup of 18 Brumaire the Roman analogy was increasingly plain, for the next day Napoleon inaugurated his legislative designs, and a month later a *senatusconsultum* established both a "senate" and a "tribunate" as well as his own "consular" office. In these early months of ostentatious republicanism Napoleon fumed at an anonymous pamphlet entitled "Caesar, Cromwell, Napoléon"; but an adviser remarked that there was nothing to criticize except the timing. A better parallel however, was the imperial author of the *Corpus Civilis*; for Napoleon truly fancied himself to be the new Justinian, with his "citizen-redactors" recapitulating the roles of Tribonian and his colleagues who assembled the texts of Romano-Byzantine law. The story is told that during the first months of Revolution, while confined to his quarters in Auxonne, Napoleon had spent twenty-four hours in a room with only Justinian's Digest for company, and his recollection of the work had amazed his colleagues during debates.[38] Justinian, too, had achieved mighty conquests, abolished the republican constitution of the Consulate (as Napoleon would soon do), and claimed a popular mandate—the Rousseauist General Will being the counterpart of the legendary *lex regia* by which the Roman *princeps* claimed his authority. The imperialist formula "What pleases the prince has the force of law" was cited regularly by Bonapartist as well as Byzantine jurists.[39]

Like Justinian, too, Napoleon provided for a pedagogical and professional foundation for his legislative creation—to produce Bonapartist jurists like the "Justinian's freshmen" (*novi Justiniani*, as the Byzantine law students were called). Neither the *Académie de Législation* (first called the "Institute of Jurisprudence and Political Economy") nor the *Université de Jurisprudence*, founded respectively in 1800 and 1801, really accomplished this, although various associated publications began to collect materials for a new jurisprudence and to represent it as a "science" no less essential than legislation—"the first of all the sciences . . . because it linked man at once to heaven and to earth."[40] To replace these institutions of the *droit intermédiaire* the law school of Paris finally opened in 1806 and began a distinguished tradition of academic jurisprudence, including C. E. Delvincourt, a former advocate installed as first professor of the "Code Napoléon," and J. F. Berthelot, professor of Roman law (as he had been before the Revolution).[41] In 1806 there were some 2000 students enrolled in the

---

[37] Riffé-Caubray, *Les Pandectes françaises* (1803); and on property, *Code civil*, arts. 544–45.

[38] Louis Madelin, *Histoire du Consulat et de l'Empire*, VI (1939), 186ff.

[39] *Digest* I.4.1: "Quod principi placuit legis habet vigorem."

[40] *Journal de Jurisprudence* (publié par l'Académie de Législation, n.d.), 5f; cf. *Procès-verbal de la séance d'ouverture de l'école de droit de Paris, le Mardi 5 Frimaire au 2me année de L'Empire et du règne du NAPOLEON* (n. d.), 14, and Rondonneau, *Napoléon le grand, considéré comme législateur* (1808).

[41] Delvincourt, *Institutes du droit civil français* (1808), and Berthelot, *Apologie du droit*

twelve new French law schools, the first of a new generation of professional jurists who, encouraged by the restoration of the Order of Advocates in 1810, would begin applying the Code to a modernizing society.

Another striking parallel between the French and Byzantine emperors was the determination that their codifications should, in Justinian's words, "be valid for all times." Yet it was precisely the creations of the systems of legal education that created the "vain discord of posterity" dreaded by Justinian and witnessed by Napoleon. What one historian has called the "renaissance of legal studies under the Consulate" acted not only to do but also to undo the Emperor's will.[42] What came out of the pandora's box opened up by Napoleon's new lawyers, practical as well as academic jurists, was that most fearful of all juridical concepts—"interpretation." Justinian had explicitly banned the practice; and common juridical wisdom, repeated by Robespierre among others, was that the interpretation of the law belonged exclusively to the power that had originally made it. Thus A. S. G. Coffinières, in his collection of Napoleonic jurisprudence (based on decisions of the Conseil d'Etat and the Court of Cassation) repeated the old Romanist adage that the power of interpretation was the power of legislation (*ejus est legem interpretari, cujus est legem condere*)—adding that today (1809) such power belonged exclusively to *Sa Majesté*.[43]

During the deliberations over the Code, Bonapartist jurists had professed shock at even hearing the term mentioned during discussions of article 5 of the Code. Through the loophole of "interpretation" all the abuses of the old regime would return, worried one magistrate, and "the empire of [feudal] custom would be reborn."[44] This warning was prophetic, for in the wake of codification neo-feudal constructions indeed resurfaced both through judicial decisions (publicized in the collections of jurisprudence of Merlin and others) and through those academic commentaries which, as Baron Locré lamented, "kill the law".[45]

In the long run neither the Emperor's will nor the legal fundamentalism of Jacobins and Bonapartists could withstand the encroachments of social reality or the process of legal interpretation required to accommodate the law to the shifting contours of that reality. And without such license to interpret, asked

---

romain ou de la raison écrite (n.d.), responding to criticism by Garat; cf. Perreau's course of 1799, in *Elémens de législation naturelle* (1834, 2nd ed.).

[42] H. Hayem, "La Renaissance des études juridiques en France sous le Consulat," *Nouvelle revue historique du droit français et étranger*, 29 (1905), a volume containing other useful studies.

[43] *Le Code Napoléon expliqué par les décisions suprèmes de la cour de cassation et du conseil d'état* (1809).

[44] Fenet, VI, 169 (Maillir-Garat); and in general see J. Bonnecase, *La Pensée juridique française* (Bordeaux, 1933), and E. Gaudemet, *L'interprétation du Code Civil en France depuis 1804* (Geneva, 1935), 13.

[45] Locré, *Esprit*, 1: "On a dit, avec raison, de ces commentateurs qu'ils tuent la loi."

readers of Montesquieu, how could there be "judicial power" comparable to the legislative power of the state? "There were judges before there were laws," argued one defender of interpretation—and, implicitly, of the old magistrature which had so effectively preserved this principle.

In 1810 Henrion de Pansey published a defense of "judicial authority" (including *inamovabilité*), associating it with the old legal tradition, (which he had celebrated in his first book forty years before on the legendary sixteenth-century jurist Charles Dumoulin, hero of the codification movement) and the "fundamental laws" of the old "tempered monarchy," and citing the sixteenth-century Chancellor de l'Hôpital that "the prince should never meddle with the exercise of judicial authority."[46]

Notions of judicial discretion were reinforced by more theoretical liberties taken by academic jurists with the text of the law. Succeeding the "cult of 1804" was a series of schools of interpretation which (virtually recapitulating the history of Roman law in its European afterlife) moved still further from the intention of the original legislator in the effort to accommodate the law to the social and economic conditions of the nineteenth century. Such interpretations, academic and judicial, entailed, at least surreptitiously, a return to the old legal traditions and old regime attitudes and practices, especially with regard to ideas about the role of the judiciary, about the stabilizing function of the family, and about that fundamental and problematic expression of the human condition, "absolute" (but not absolute) private property. In various ways there was, as Sagnac put it, "a return to custom."[47]

In the wake of revolution and empire, in other words, feudalism and corporatism raised their heads, or at least lurked beneath the surface of the jurisprudence generated by the Code; and the justification was still that time-honored formula preserved in Justinian's Digest, that "Custom is the best interpreter of the law."[48] Moreover, Napoleon's magistracy was a continuation of the judicial establishment of the old regime, not only through preservation of the old esprit which haunted the corridors of the Palais (home of the Court of Cassation as it had been of the Parlement, and adorned with portraits of old regime jurists) but also through the careers of particular lawyers, judicial Talleyrands who also "survived" and carried over into the Restoration many elements of the old legal mentality.

They had survived, of course, by serving, in lawyerly fashion, many masters and clients—and many values. In the 1790s the *hommes de loi* had learned the language of Jacobinism, and a decade later they adopted as easily the new

46 *De l'authorité judiciaire*, in *Oeuvres juridiques*, and cf. Fenet, VI, 151.

47 *La Législation civile*, 187, and see Valette, *De la Durée persistante de l'ensemble du droit civil pendant et depuis la révolution* (1872).

48 *Digest*, I, 3, 37: "Consuetudo optima legum interpres"; and see my "The Idea of Custom in European Law, Society, and Culture," *The Transmission of Culture in Early Modern Europe*, ed. A. Grafton and A. Blair (Philadelphia, 1990), 131–72.

imperial style. Prudently, the faculty of law cheered as loudly for Napoleon on his return in 1814 as they had, and would, for Louis XVIII on his first, and second, restorations.[49] After such formalities, of course, men of law went about their business, which had to do above all with property and succession questions in the wake of political disruption, and so, in a legalistic way, with reshaping the new post-revolutionary world, or in some cases to restore the old pre-revolutionary one—all, needless to say, in the language of Restoration society.

The "men of law" who survived (and sometimes even profitted from) the Revolution helped to carry on or to create several conduits of old regime learning, attitudes, habits, and values, which went beyond the historical curiosity of scholars like Augustin Thierry or resentment of victims like Fournel. As one advocate wrote in 1814, "The glory of the bar is like a beautiful tree whose branches seem from a distance to touch the ground."[50] In academic and professional terms the old legal tradition, with roots in the old regime and contacts with the people, was given renewed vitality, and its members tried not only to reestablish their position as legal experts and arbiters but also to represent their discipline as the essential "social science" of the Restoration period. In 1810 Cotelle, professor of French law under Napoleon, took up the baton of the old Order of Advocates dropped by Tronchet in 1789 and, along with this symbol, some of the projects of the order. In 1822 Cotelle's successor Billecocq revived the "conferences" held in the Library of the Advocates (also restored, although the books had been dispersed during the Revolution) as a way of reinforcing the old esprit de corps—both by instructing young advocates and by strengthening ties between lawyers and judges.[51]

Upon the restoration of the Bourbon dynasty—"in the nineteenth year of the reign of Louis XVIII"—the lawyers were ready to adapt to the new Charter and the language of neo-royalism and constitutional monarchy. A.-A.-P. Dupin (the very first graduate of Napoleon's law school) addressed his colleagues (25 June 1814) to remind them that the purpose of this document was "to seek [its] principles in the French character and in the venerable monuments of the past." "Why has the ancient judiciary been so highly regarded and the tribunals of the Revolution so little?" Dupin went on to ask.[52] The answer was that the

---

[49] G. Colmet Daage, L'École de droit de Paris en 1814, 1815 et 1816 (1887); cf. A. J. Tonneau, Un jurisconsulte de transition, Charles Toullier (Rennes, 1962), 171; and see especially Werner Giesselman, Die brumairische Elite: Kontinuität und Wandel der französischen Führungsschicht zwischen Ancien Regime und Julimonarchie (Stuttgart, 1976).

[50] Gibault, Guide de l'avocat (1814).

[51] Billecocq, Discours prononcé pour la réprise des conférences de la Bibliothèque des avocats (mardi 12 nov. 1822), invoking "nos sages dévanciers."

[52] Dupin, Les Magistrats d'autrefois de la révolution (25 juin 1814); and cf. Mémoires (1855). There is still no adequate biography of this juridical Guizot; and the same goes for many of these jurists—Bernardi, Gin, Bergasse, Guichard, and others.

old jurists had judged according to conscience, and he himself spent much of his later scholarly efforts (over almost sixty years) championing and publishing the work of his predecessors going back especially to the golden age of French legal science in the sixteenth century, represented especially by Antoine Loisel's *Pasquier, ou dialogue des avocats* (1602), which was a landmark and a centerpiece in the canon of the French legal profession and in the defense of "judicial power."[53]

From the standpoint of intellectual history the story of the men of law in France from old regime to Restoration can be seen as a grand struggle for the control of words. After 1789 they had to learn, in political terms, first the new language of natural rights and "general will," then that of republican and imperial government, and finally that of constitutional monarchy.[54] The dissolution of the old Order of Advocates was accompanied by efforts to expunge its symbols and language. In order to erase the memory of the past an emperor of China had tried to burn all books, wrote J. E. D. Bernardi; the Revolution went one better by rendering the old books of authority not only obsolete but unintelligible.[55]

Yet the men of law kept much of the old lingo, and Portalis and his colleagues in particular spoke the same language as Dumoulin and Pothier. Discussing the rights of ownership, Henrion de Pansey apologized for using the word *seigneur*, adding that he had no desire to revive the old "feudal idiom";[56] but in fact, like Toullier and other conservative colleagues, Henrion did continue to exploit old feudal "opinions" and customary practices; and of course Dupin's scholarly labors were intended to resurrect the language and life of his colleagues across several centuries of professional activity (and across the caesura created by the Revolution) and to reconcile them with the legacy of revolution.

Like the Bourbons, then, the men of law of the older generation seemed to have forgotten nothing, but unlike that unlucky family, they had learned a great deal. Had they, however, learned enough? In the Restoration the legal profession found new life and a new relationship with politics and the new propertied, ruling elite, with whom the "fortunes" (favorite word of magistrates and bourgeois) of the lawyers was closely bound up. Over a generation of noisy

53 Reprinted in Dupin's famous handbook for lawyers, *Profession d'avocat*, 2 vols. (1832), first edition (by Camus) 1770; and cf. Henri Bordier, *Le Archives de la France* (1855), 2–15; also D. R. Kelley, "Ancient Verses on New Ideas: Legal Tradition and the French Historical School," *History and Theory* 3 (1987), 319–38.

54 P. L. C. Gin, for one, had taken up the old theme of linguistic virtuosity in *De l'Eloquence du Barreau* (1803; lst ed. 1767), remarking (3) that "le nouveau barreau s'élève sur les ruines de l'ancien."

55 *De l'Origine et des progrés de la législation française* (1816), introduction, remarking that "le fil de nos traditions nationales sera totalement rompu"; and (iii) on "property."

56 *Oeuvres judiciaires*, 327: "On ne suppose pas l'intention de faire revivre l'idiome féodale."

political experience lawyers had learned the uses of the word, and concept, "revolution"; and they would put it to good use in the constitutional transformation of 1830, sometimes referred to, because of its aftermath as well as inception, as the "revolution of the advocates."

Dupin, in the discourse he gave in 1829 when he became *bâtonnier* of the Order of Advocates, celebrated the old legal tradition, quoting Montesquieu's famous aphorism, to "illuminate the laws by history and history by the laws".[57] Read Bodin, he advised his younger colleagues, read Coquille, Loyseau, and especially Dumoulin; and you will "march with the power of five centuries of precedents." Dupin cited again the final words of Loisel's *Pasquier*, demanding that they "conserve for our Order the rank and honor which our ancestors have acquired by their merits and works in order to pass them on to our successors." This was the basis of Dupin's idea of "revolution," and the premises he maintained as an active supporter of the Orleanist party and participant in the "three glorious" July days the following summer. Less than a month later he dedicated the new edition of his *Profession d'Avocat* (1830) to Louis-Philippe (on whose *Conseil privé* he had served "for many years") and thanked him for receiving the deputation from the Order of Advocates after the July Revolution and for giving his support.[58] Like Loisel, Dupin addressed his book to the advocates of his time as a "as a work of family, of community," which brought the wisdom and the prejudices of the centuries to the July Monarchy.

No more than the July Monarchy itself, however, were jurists like Dupin, for all their learning, able to come to terms with new economic and social realities, especially the class divisions and other dislocations of an industrializing society in which Labor was coming to count as much as Property. The new forms of "social science"—political economy and then sociology—attacked such questions directly, while the old jurisprudence was still burdened with its ancient heritage, forms, and values, and of course its commitment to prevailing political structures. In retrospect the Revolution of 1848 transformed the legal tradition more fundamentally than the Revolution of 1789 had done, and the contending ideologies of liberalism and socialism made old-fashioned jurisprudence increasingly irrelevant to—or rather rendered it powerless before—a politics preoccupied by the Social Question and the specter of Revolution.[59]

After 1848, then, the old legal tradition was apparently dead, and its claims to be a science of society were largely discredited. With the experience, the process, and the historical interpretation of Revolution, however, its connections were profound and immediate; and historians of the revolutionary period and its various aftermaths cannot afford to neglect the insights offered by the

---

[57] *Profession d'avocat*, 5.

[58] *Profession d'avocat*, 2 vols. (1832), iii, 721.

[59] See, e.g., Gaston Morin, *La Révolte des faits contre le Code* (1920) and *La Révolte du droit contre le Code* (1945).

"men of law" in their struggles to grasp and to exercise control over history. We may pretend, with the help of modern social sciences, to achieve on a grand scale that old hermeneutical dream, to know the past better than it knew itself; but this will not exhaust the processes of historical understanding and the many layers of historical experience; and in these terms the Revolution remains—and changes—with us.

PART THREE

Historiography and Political Theory

9

Jacques Almain on *Dominium*: A Neglected Text

J. H. BURNS

The Gallican ecclesiology that was so prominent a feature of the intellectual landscape in the period of French history to which John Salmon has made magisterial contributions was closely linked to the conciliarism which had prevailed in the university of Paris since the turn of the fourteenth and fifteenth centuries. If the tie between the two was not quite an indissoluble marriage, it was at least a stable and enduring relationship. Its persistence was manifested in a number of ways, among which not the least important, for the history of ideas, was the printing and reprinting of critically important conciliarist texts. The outstanding, though not the only, illustrations of this are the two major editions, separated by exactly a hundred years, of the works of Jean Gerson, each including important supplementary material by other writers.[1] One of these was Jacques Almain (c.1480–1515), three of whose works were to be reprinted both in the 1606 and in the 1706 edition.[2] Thirty years ago, Francis Oakley wrote of Almain that he had 'attracted less attention that he deserves and his name is well-nigh forgotten.'[3] To the extent that this was the case, Oakley himself did much to set matters right; and within a few years other scholars had also devoted considerable attention to Almain.[4] This was in part

---

[1]   The first of these (4 vols.: Paris, 1606), was edited by Edmond Richer (1559–1631), Syndic of the Sorbonne 1608–15, himself of course an important figure in the Gallican tradition. The second (5 vols.: Antwerp, 1706; 2nd edn, The Hague, 1728) was the work of Louis Ellies du Pin.

[2]   See n. 6 below. For Almain's career see esp. J. K. Farge, *Biographical Dictionary of Paris Doctors of Theology, 1500–1536* (Toronto, 1980), 15–19.

[3]   F. Oakley, *The Political Thought of Pierre d'Ailly: The Voluntarist Tradition* (New Haven and London, 1964), 203 n. 22.

[4]   F. Oakley, "Almain and Major: Conciliar Theory on the Eve of the Reformation," *American Historical Review* 70 (1964–5), 673–90; id., "Conciliarism in the Sixteenth Century: Jacques Almain Again," *Archiv für Reformationsgeschichte* 68 (1977), 111–32. (Both these articles are reprinted in id., *Natural Law, Conciliarism and Consent: Studies in Ecclesiastical and Intellectual History* (London, 1984), chaps X and XII.) A year after

the result of that surge of interest in the conciliar theory which was precipitated by the Second Vatican Council, though it is fair to add that important foundations had been laid by the earlier work of such scholars as Yves Congar, Hubert Jedin, and Brian Tierney.[5]

In such a context it was natural that scholars considering Almain should concentrate, as they did, on those of his writings which bore most directly upon the ecclesiological issues that divided conciliarists from papalists and upon the related aspects of political theory. And those works were also, for the bibliographical reasons stated above, the most accessible: the *Libellus de auctoritate Ecclesiae* and the *Expositio circa decisiones . . . M. Guillermi Ockam*. There was, somewhat surprisingly, less reference to the equally accessible *Quaestio resumptiva . . . de dominio naturali, civili, & ecclesiastico*.[6] The concept of *dominium* was plainly central in Almain's thinking: yet his most sustained discussion of it has received very little scholarly attention. In the 1512 *Quaestio*, written at the very outset of his brief career as a fully qualified master in the Paris theology faculty, the general treatment of the theme, though important, is comparatively brief, much of the work being given over to the ecclesiastical aspect of 'lordship'. Two years or so later Almain was able to return to the subject more expansively in a work which, though twice printed within a dozen years of his death, was not to achieve the wider circulation afforded by the seventeenth- and eighteenth-century editions already described.[7]

Oakley's book on d'Ailly appeared, Olivier de la Brosse, in *Le Pape et le Concile: la comparaison de leurs pouvoirs à la veille de la Réforme* (Paris, 1965) undertook a close analysis of the ecclesiological debate between Almain and Tommaso de Vio (Cajetan): see esp. pt. III, 183–315. On a smaller scale but with a wider perspective, Friedrich Merzbacher dealt with "Die Kirchenn- une Staatsgewalt bei J. Almain" in *Speculum iuris et ecclesiarum: Festschrift für W. M. Plöchl* (Vienna, 1967), 211ff (reprinted Merzbacher, *Recht – Staat – Kirche: Ausgewählte Aufsätze* (Vienna, Cologne, Graz, 1989), 369–84. See also the references to Almain by Remigius Bäumer, *Nachwirkung des konziliaren Gedankens in der Theologie und Kanonistik des frühen 16. Jahrhunderts* (Münster, 1971). In justice to earlier scholarship, it should be noted that A. J. Carlyle gave significant attention to Almain: *A History of Mediaeval Political Theory in the West*, vol. VI (Edinburgh and London, 1936), 241–6.

[5] From Congar's wide-ranging work see esp. the items collected in *Sainte Eglise: Etudes et approches ecclésiologiques* (Paris, 1963); Jedin, *Geschichte des Konzils von Trient*, vol. I (Freiburg, 1947) [translated by E. Graf as *A History of the Council of Trent*, vol. I (London, 1957)]; Tierney, *Foundations of the Conciliar Theory: The Contribution of the Medieval Canonists from Gratian to the Great Schism* (Cambridge, England, 1955).

[6] Gerson, *Opera Omnia*, 1706, vol. II, cols. 961–1120 (following 1606 edn, vol I, cols. 687–876). The *Expositio* was also reprinted, under the title *Expositio, De Suprema Potestate Ecclesiastica et Laica*, by M. Goldast, *Monarchia S. Romani Imperii*, [vol. I] (Hanover, 1611), fos. 588–647. An English translation of the *Quaestio* (under its original title, *Questio in vesperiis habita*), by A. S. McGrade, will be published in J. Kraye (ed.) *Cambridge Translations of Renaissance Philosophical Texts: Moral and Political Philosophy* (New York and Cambridge, forthcoming). Of Almain's theological works other than the *Libellus* and the *Expositio*, Merzbacher (*Recht – Staat – Kirche*, 370) says that they "scheiden . . . für unsere Fragestellung aus."

[7] References below are to the text included by Vincent Doesmier and Olivier de Lyon

The context now was Almain's exposition and analysis of the treatment by Duns Scotus of certain questions in the fourth book of Peter Lombard's *Sentences* – still, in the early sixteenth century, a standard medium of teaching in the Paris faculty.[8] Though his course of lectures was, we are told, cut short by other commitments, Almain did cover a substantial part of sacramental theology, with specific reference to penance, holy orders, and marriage.[9] Of these, however, it was penance that occupied by far the greater part of his attention; and this enabled him to deal at some length and in some detail with the nature and varieties of *dominium*. It is not surprising, therefore, that one of the few references to this text in recent scholarship occurs when Richard Tuck enlists Almain in support of his interesting, if debatable, thesis regarding a "Gersonian theory of rights".[10] That, however, is no more than a passing reference to something which, this paper is concerned to argue, merits fuller consideration and analysis.

Because penance involved, in all appropriate cases, an insistence on restitution as part of the penitent's "satisfaction" for sin, the discussion of that sacrament became, for scholastic theologians, a *locus classicus* for issues regarding rights. In particular, though not exclusively, they were concerned with what we should call property rights—for them, essentially, the rights associated with *dominium* or lordship in its various forms. Rights—*iura*—were at the same time inextricably connected with law (*ius* or *lex*), again in its various forms; and it may be useful to begin the analysis of Almain's exposition with a point he makes briefly about law near the beginning of the text. In his discussion of the fourteenth "distinction," Almain deals with the difference between divine and human law. Each is made by a *legislator*; but in the case of human, positive law the end or goal of lawmaking is not the good of the lawgiver but the common good of those who are to be governed by the law. In the case of divine law, since the lawgiver is himself the supreme good, his law can have no purpose other than to embody and manifest that good. From this difference, Almain remarks,

---

in their edition of Almain's *Aurea . . . opuscula* (Paris, 1518, with separate foliation. On the title-page it is listed as *De penitentia siue in quartum lectura*; but the full title (fo. 1) was used when the work was printed on its own as M. *Iacobi Almain . . . a decimaquarta distinctione questiones Scoti profitentis perutilis admodum lectura* (Paris, 1526). J. F. von Schulte, *Die Geschichte der Quellen und Literatur des Canonisches Rechts von Gratian bis auf die Gegenwart*, II (Stuttgart, 1877), 375, refers to edtions published at Cologne in 1514 and at Paris in 1516 under the title *De poenitentia & matrimonio*, but no copies of these have been found.

8 Almain himself wrote substantial commentaries on Book III and, in *Dictata super sententias Holcot*, on other parts of Book IV.

9 The phrase *a decimaquarta distinctione* simply indicates the starting-point of Almain's lectures: he continued his commentary from there down to dist. 37. The colophon (fol. 204r) refers to the demands of his other commitments.

10 R. Tuck, *Natural Rights Theories: Their Origin and Development* (Cambridge, 1979), 28–9 & n. 58. Oakley, in his 1977 article (n. 4 above) refers briefly to the *De penitentia* (119 nn. 31, 33).

it would be possible to develop an argument to prove that the weight of punishment should be proportionate, not to the effect of the offence on the good of the commonwealth (*bonum reipublice*), but to its intrinsic moral gravity. The argument, however, is not developed at this point; and what matters for present purposes is Almain's firm emphasis on the principle that human law is intended for the benefit of its subjects and not for the selfish advantage of those who enact it.[11]

The theme of the fifteenth 'distinction', like that of the fourteenth, is satisfaction for sin; but whereas dist. 14 dealt with the topic in the context of the sinner's relationship with God, dist. 15 examines rather his relationship with other human beings—with his 'neighbor' in the gospel sense of the term. The elucidation of such relationships requires an understanding of what rightfully pertains to an individual and of the basis of that rightful claim; and a large part of the answer has to do with a person's status as a *dominus*, with the *dominium* he enjoys or can legitimately assert. To a considerable extent, but by no means exclusively, this is a matter of 'civil dominion' (*dominium civile*); for an essential feature of this kind of 'lordship' is that it pertains to one person rather than another. Now, Almain argues, the allocation of such exclusive *dominium* was not effected either by divine law or by purely natural law. Taking the common ground shared by scholastic and patristic thinkers, he holds that neither survival nor 'peaceable intercourse' (*pacificam conuersationem*) among human beings would, in the 'state of innocence', have required individual appropriation; for no one in that state would have had motive or inclination to take what he did not need or what was needed by someone else.

There are, it is true, two modifications to be noted. First, according to Almain, we must differentiate between what is required for individual sustenance and what is necessary for the survival of the species, of the human race. For the latter, he maintains, there would from the first have had to be individual marital rights. Even if life had continued in Eden, 'Adam would have been Eve's husband and no one else would have had lordship over her body'. The other modification is perhaps of greater significance here. It consists in Almain's acknowledging that private appropriation *could* have been introduced, even in the state of innocence, 'by common consent' (*ex communi consensu*). This would not have been necessary and might not have seemed expedient; but its possibility enables us to recognize from this early stage the creative potential of consent in Almain's theory—a theory, it may be added, revealing here especially the Scotist element in its inspiration.[12]

The Scotist theme continues when Almain considers various ways of interpreting the natural-law element in the case. Scotus, he points out, argues that different rules may be prescribed by, or compatible with, the law of nature

---

[11] *De penitentia*, fo. 8r. (For ease of reference the running title *De penitentia*, which covers all relevant parts of the text, will be used when necessary in subsequent notes).

[12] Ibid., fos. 26r–27r.

according to varying conditions or situations. In the 'fallen' state of man, when sin has perverted nature, the law of nature itself may demand the institution of private property. This does not mean, however, that the specific allocation of property to individual owners was or could have been the work of natural law. Drawing an interesting political analogy, Almain points out that while it is in accordance with natural law that coercive authority should exist among sinful human beings, the location of that authority is a matter, not for natural, but for positive law.[13]

The specific needs of human life as we know it, then, can be met only by the establishment and maintenance of 'civil dominion'. This, however, is only one species of the genus *dominium*; and Almain is concerned to analyse more closely both the generic and the specific nature of the concept. This leads him into the complex area where *dominium* is related to *ius*, 'lordship' to 'right'. His language here is pervasively and avowedly Gersonian:

> *Dominium* of every kind is nothing but a right [*ius*] of using something in accordance with right reason; and *ius* (as Gerson says) is nothing but an immediate [*propinqua*] power or faculty belonging to a certain individual in accordance with the dictate of right reason . . . *Dominium* in general, then, is that faculty or power by virtue of which someone has the immediate use of something, whether by leasing it, or selling it, or consuming it . . . Such a person may be said to have right and lordship [*ius & dominium*] over the object in question.[14]

Thus *dominium* is a kind of *ius*; and on this basis Almain proceeds to make three points and to draw a conclusion from them. First, everyone is obliged by natural right to preserve himself (*iure naturali quilibet tenetur se conseruare in esse*). Crucially, this underlines the duality (which would not have been seen as an ambiguity) in the concept of *ius*: self-preservation is not—or not only—a subjective *right*; it is an objective *duty*. The second point is that positive right or law cannot derogate from natural right. Thirdly, private property (*appropriatio*) is based on positive law. it follows, Almain argues, that anyone who needs something for the preservation and prolongation of his life has 'natural lordship' (*dominium naturale*) over it, even if by positive law it is someone else's property. This is not to say that positive law can never entrench upon the domain of natural law: where the latter is merely permissive, human law may make its own provisions; but a mandatory law of nature, such as that enjoining self-preservation, is in all circumstances paramount. *Dominium naturale*, again, is, according to Genesis, chapter 1, God's gift to his rational creatures: God is 'the supreme lord of all', and it is only by his free gift (*ex pura & liberali*

---

[13] Ibid., fo. 27r–v.
[14] Ibid., fo. 27v.

donatione) that anyone can enjoy *dominium*. Nor can natural *dominium* be renounced, either wholly, or in regard to any particular kind of food or drink.[15]

Two 'difficulties' arise at this point. First, can a human judge deprive someone of *dominium naturale* (as he can, of course, deprive an offender of his *dominium civile*—specifically, of his property)? Almain's answer, citing and agreeing with Aquinas, is that no judge can do this. On the other hand—this is the second 'difficulty'—God, who has conferred *dominium naturale*, can, if he so chooses, deprive someone of it.[16]

Dominium naturale is fundamental; but *dominium civile* is, so to speak, the stuff of everyday human life, and its basis is human law. It is therefore important for Almain to consider the characteristics of positive law. Being indeed positive, that law presupposes a lawgiver (*legislator*): what are the qualities required by that office? Wisdom (*prudentia*), Almain answers, and authority (*auctoritas*). In regard to the first of these qualities Almain at once makes an interesting and important qualification: 'wisdom is required in a lawgiver, but this is to be understood as referring either to the lawgiver himself or to the counsellors whose advice he takes in the task of legislation.'[17] This was of course an essential element in the theory of government, and especially of monarchical government, as it developed in the late medieval period; and its significance for the theory of kingship in Almain's native France was to survive for two centuries and more after his death.[18] Authority, the other required ingredient, presented more complex problems.

Without appropriate authority, law would lack its essential *binding* force: Almain adopts the then prevalent, if dubious, derivation of *lex* from *ligare*. There are, for him, two basic forms of authority. There is paternal authority, based on natural, not positive, right; and this, Almain says, extends to all the father's progeny, even if they happen to be members of different political societies (*de diversis politiis*). Political authority, on the other hand, rests on positive, not natural, right: "No one," Almain remarks a little further on, "is born a king by nature" (*Nullus . . . naturaliter nascitur rex*). Kingship, in any case, is only one of several equally legitimate forms of political organization. Authority may be vested in a number of people: if their number is small, the system is aristocratic; if large, it is "timocratic". It is worth noting that Almain seems nowhere to use the term "democratic" to designate a legitimate political system. He does, however, have interesting points to make about non-monarchical systems; and this is indeed one of the notable aspects of his thinking, at a time when so much discussion of the theory and practice of

---

[15] Ibid., fos. 27v–28r. On *dominium naturale* cf. *Questio in vesperiis habita*, fo. 62r–v. (The *Questio* is foliated with the *Libellus de auctoritate ecclesie* in the 1518 collection).

[16] *De penitentia*, fos. 28v–29r.

[17] Ibid., fo. 29r–v.

[18] See, e.g., Bossuet, *Politique tirée des propres paroles de l'Ecriture Sainte*, V.ii: P. Riley (ed.), *Politics Drawn from Holy Scripture* (Cambridge, England, 1990), esp. 135–40.

government was dominated by the concerns and problems of monarchy. Almain carefully underlines the point that, in an aristocracy or 'timocracy', no individual on his own (*seorsum*) has any authority. It is only when the relevant individuals act together (*simul cuncti*) that effective political power can be exercised. An individual citizen can take political action only by virtue of a 'commission' from his fellow-citizens in their corporate capacity (*ex commissione aliorum*). Almain illustrates his analysis by invoking two analogous cases—the members of the Parlement (*domini de parlamento*) or of a cathedral chapter: in the ordinary course of procedure (*ordinarie*), neither group can take action except as a body, collectively.[19] At a later stage in his exposition, Almain comments on a point made by Ockham and illustrated from periods in the history of the Roman Empire when more than one emperor held office at the same time. In such a situation it was possible that authority in its entirety (*insolidum*) might be held by each of the incumbents. Is a system of this kind to be regarded as monarchical or aristocratic? Ockham's answer is that it is essentially regal; for—as we have just seen Almain arguing—under aristocracy or 'timocracy', authority can only be exercised jointly by those who share it, whereas 'any sovereign power belonging to a single person is called regal' (*omnis potestas primaria competens vni soli vocatur regalis*).[20]

Whichever political system may obtain, its authority is always introduced and sustained 'by human law (or right)' (*iure humano*). This means—Almain is again following a characteristic lead from Duns Scotus here—that the authority of the ruler or rulers comes 'from the free consent of the people' (*a libero consensu populi*). To be sure, Almain would not deny the divine ordination or rulers and magistrates; and he acknowledges that God could intervene directly—as he had done by installing Saul and David as kings of Israel. This, however, was and is not 'regularly' the case (*hoc tamen non fit regulariter*). And indeed, Almain adds, even if God had not conferred royal power in those exceptional cases, Saul and David would still have been kings by consent of the people, who gave them authority and submitted freely to its exercise.[21]

The definition of *dominium civile* now has to be considered. Almain rehearses various formulations—by Richard FitzRalph, by Gerson, and by Ockham—before proposing his own succinct statement that 'civil dominion is nothing but a human power of dealing with something in accordance with civil law' (*Dominium civile nihil aliud est quam potestas humana aliquam rem lege ciuili pertractandi*).[22] The reference to civil (or positive) law is to be found in all the definitions Almain considers (implicitly in Ockham, explicitly in FitzRalph and Gerson); and this leads him to further consideration of the different kinds of authority by which that law may be established. In what is at least an interesting slip of the pen (or tongue), and may be an even more interesting deliberate choice of words, Almain now refers to two kinds of 'polity' in which

---

19 *De penitentia*, fo. 29v.
20 Ibid., fo. 31r.

21 Ibid., fo. 29v.
22 Ibid., fos. 30r–31r.

positive law may be enacted. Thus in a household not, or not yet, forming part of a village or city (*in domo perfecta*), we have a paternal authority which is not despotic but, rather, similar to royal power (*magis assimilatur dominio regali*). The father, that is to say, has the same coercive power over his children as a king has in his kingdom. Adam had this power when he and his sons formed the only society in being; and so did Noah after the Flood. It was an authority which, according to Ockham (Almain notes), extended even to the power of life and death.[23]

Turning briefly to the intermediate stage of village society, Almain again follows Ockham, arguing that a village not forming part of a larger and genuinely political society might be governed in one or other of two ways. If the households constituting it were all descendants of the same family, then someone of that lineage should rule with paternal authority (*paterno dominio*). Otherwise, a ruler should be chosen by common consent; but in view of the small number of his subjects he should not have the title of 'king'.[24] Only in the 'perfect society' of the city or state can there be genuinely political authority; and kingship, properly so called, is a form of that authority.

The question of whether *dominium civile* is to be established by a *paterfamilias* or by political authority in the strict sense is thus a matter of scale. What Noah could have done patriarchally in regard to his sons could, in a more numerous society, have been done only by consent. This in turn could, and perhaps normally would, involve the appointment of a ruler, or a group of rulers, to make the necessary distribution. Yet it could also, according to Almain, have been achieved simply by the common consent of the members of the society in question acting for and among themselves.[25] What is not envisaged is a Lockean process whereby the individual makes something his own, acquires property in it, by the mere mixing of his labor with it.

The above analysis is all contained in the first of the two 'articles' into which Almain divides his discussion of question 1 of the fifteenth 'distinction'. In the second article he turns to the transfer of *dominium*. This, he says, can be effected either by the authority of law or by the authority of the private individual (*auctoritate priuate persone*). The first of these procedures plainly involves a 'public person', who—acting as king or as judge—decrees or ordains the relevant transfer. As an illustration Almain refers to the legal process used *in vsucapionibus & prescriptionibus*; and the authorities he cites at this point include the eminent jurist Johannes Andreae, as well as the theologians Henry of Ghent and James of Viterbo. Of the latter he says that James 'deals with this

23 Ibid., fo. 31r.
24 Ibid., fo. 31r, where there is an explicit reference to the majority principle: 'ex consensu omnium, vel maioris partis'.
25 Ibid., fo. 31v: 'est possibile quod ex consensu ipsorummet (antequam aliquem superiorem eligerent) diuiserint terras, & simul conuenerint, ego vtar ista re, & tu illa . . .'. Almain is explicitly following Scotus in this passage.

subject admirably and theologically'; but he is clearly aware that the issues at stake call for juristic as well as theological skill.[26] Almain's own concern is to re-emphasize a point he had previously made in his *Expositio* on Ockham: the 'public person' issuing such a decree, determining that a piece of property belongs to one claimant rather than another, acts only as *tutor & defensor* of the property in question. he cannot dispose of it at will (*pro libito suo*)—by selling it, for instance, or by giving it away. He does have *dominium* over it, but this is only *dominium iurisdictionis*, not *dominium proprietatis*. To be sure, there are circumstances in which the ruler (or a judge acting on the ruler's behalf) can claim, in effect, the full rights of ownership implied by *dominium proprietatis*. These circumstances, however, are wholly exceptional: where, for example, the defense of the state requires it, the public authorities may (as we should say) commandeer private property. In the ordinary way there is no such right. There is, however (Almain adds) another mode in which the right to transfer property may be vested in someone who has only *dominium iurisdictionis*: for an offence committed by the owner (*pro culpa primi possessoris*) property may be declared forfeit or handed over to someone else by the authority of a judge or ruler.[27]

Public powers are therefore of considerable importance in Almain's theory of *dominium*. Yet at the same time he is aware of the possibility that such powers may be abused. The kind of issue he considers here is not, as in his better-known writings, the problem posed by tyranny or misrule on, so to speak, the grand scale. He envisages here a situation in which power is certainly being tyrannically exercised—specifically by inordinate exactions levied on a community. This is not, it seems, the political community at large, but, rather, a corporate or local 'commune'. Almain postulates a decision by the rulers of this community (*rectores communitatis*) to accede to the tyrant's demands—to 'buy him off', as it were, by paying an agreed sum—and to apportion payment among its members. Suppose an individual member refuses to contribute his share: is he acting unjustly by violating a legitimate obligation? Almain's answer is in the affirmative: the recalcitrant member is morally bound to pay. This is because the agreement entered into by the *rectores* was just and reason-

[26] Ibid., fos. 31v–33r.

[27] Ibid., fo. 33r. Cf. *Expositio . . . circa decisiones* M. Guillermi Ockam, cap. 3, in *Aurea . . . opuscula*, fo. 30r–v.

[28] *De penitentia*, dist. 15, q. 2, fo. 55r. Another aspect of the problem of tyranny is discussed by Almain in his commentary on Book III of the *Sentences*, when he considers the question whether it is permissible to desire the death of a tyrant who is ruining the entire commonwealth: his answer, again following Scotus, is negative: 'Sed si esset aliquis tyrannus qui destrueret totam rempub[licam] vtrum liceret ei optare mortem simpliciter. Respondetur quod non . . .' In the *Expositio* (fo. 35r) Almain insists that a private citizen, holding no public office any kind, may not kill a wrongdoer, no matter how harmful his wrongdoing may be to the community.

able, on the grounds that it was better to suffer the limited injustice of the tyrant's exactions than to fall completely into his power.[28]

Later in the discussion (much of the detail in which need not be considered here), we are again reminded sharply of the weight carried in Almain's thinking by the paramount interest of the community as a whole. Discussing capital punishment in the fourth question of distinction 15, he refers, as he does elsewhere, to the arguments by which Aquinas, for one, draws out the implications of *membership* in an essentially organic community.[29] In another connection the same basic point is again vigorously made. The case here is that in which an individual has suffered a wrongful accusation (*crimen falsum*) by a ruler whose authority in general is none the less of great benefit to the community. For the ruler to make a public retraction of the charge would lower, or even destroy, the esteem in which he is held; and his fall from grace and perhaps from power would gravely injure the community (*si pereat sequitur magnum incommodum reipublice*). In such circumstances, Almain argues, the ruler is *not* bound to make a public withdrawal of the charge. Rather, the wronged citizen should be ready to suffer the penalty of disgrace rather than purchase the restoration of his good name at the cost of undermining that of the ruler, with the consequent damage to the commonwealth: *commune enim bonum est preferendum bono particulari*.[30]

It cannot be claimed that the text examined here radically alters our understanding of Jacques Almain's political thought. What can be claimed is that the discussion of penance in these lectures clearly identifies the two poles between which we can locate the axis of his thinking. One pole is provided here by the point made in regard to law in dist. 14. Human, positive law has only one proper end: the common good of those who are to live under its authority. To pervert the course of law in the selfish or sectional interest of the lawgiver or legislative body is to defeat its only legitimate purpose. The other pole is defined by Almain's emphasis on the collective, corporate element in the good which law and government exist to promote. No doubt his account of *dominium naturale* gives rise to what we may regard as inalienable natural rights, so that there would, in the last resort, be a kind of radical individualism here. Even so, it is noteworthy that self-preservation is, for Almain, a matter more of obligation than of subjective right. And within the ordinary framework of an established civil society his emphasis is decisively upon the need to subordinate individual interests to the overriding claims of the body politic. Neither ruler nor citizen may legitimately disregard those claims. Whatever ambiguities there may have been in Almain's late-scholastic legacy to early-modern political thought, that point at least seems unequivocal.

---

[29] *De penitentia*, dist. 15, q. 3, fol. 56r–v. Cf., e.g., *Questio in vesperiis habita*, fo. 62v.
[30] *De penitentia*, dist. 15, q. 4, fos. 57v–58r.

10

Revising the Revisionists:
Louis-Pierre Anquetil and the
Saint Bartholomew's Day Massacre

BARBARA WHITEHEAD

The Massacre of Saint Bartholomew, the 1572 slaughter of Huguenots by Parisian Catholics, has been the mainstay of French historians for over 400 years, causing, according to one writer, almost as much ink as blood to flow.[1] The massacre periodically resurfaces as a topic of interest as each new generation of historians rediscovers the complexities and mysteries of this tale of deception, destruction, and murder and announces yet another resolution of its secrets. Discovering anew historical objectivity and decrying the subjectivity of its predecessors, each generation proudly proclaims, as the historian Capefigue did in 1834, that "we are now entering into a new era of ... impartiality."[2] And each generation in turn is unconsciously influenced by the preoccupations of its own day.

One of the most persistent riddles of the Saint Bartholomew's Day massacre down through the centuries has been the question of its premeditation. Did Catherine de Medici, Charles IX, the duc de Guise (each one singly or in some conspiratorial combination) plan the 1572 slaughter of Huguenots? This question still troubles historians, as evident in the recent flurry of papers and books on the causes of the French Religious Wars and the circumstances leading up to the crime of Saint Bartholomew's Day. With the latest wave of research comes a "new" historiographical theory: the massacre as popular insurrection. Followers of this theory maintain that the French Romantic novelist, Prosper Mérimée, in the preface to his *Chronique du règne de Charles IX* (1829) first popularized

---

[1] Henri Hauser, *Les sources de l'histoire de France XVIe siècle* (Paris, 1912), III, 233.
[2] Capefigue, *Histoire de la réforme, de la ligue, et du règne de Henri IV* (Paris: Duféy, 1834), I, vi.

the idea of a non-premeditated massacre by the common people.[3] Jean-Louis Bourgeon, in particular, has gone to great lengths to bring to light Mérimée's supposed breakthrough which was that the massacre was "a popular, improvised insurrection which could not have been prevented."[4] While there is no denying that Mérimée forcefully supported the interpretation of an unpremeditated massacre, it must be pointed out that that position was first claimed and popularized nearly three-quarters of a century earlier by the now long-forgotten French historian Louis-Pierre Anquetil. Anquetil's contribution to this debate has been largely and wrongfully ignored for over 150 years.[5]

It is important to establish the correct genealogy of this event not only for the sake of finally setting to rights the historiography of an event which occurred over 400 years ago, but because a larger issue is at stake. It is a truism that contemporary events affect how history is written. The more important problem which is rarely discussed is the question of what events and influences determine which histories and historical theories are *remembered*. This point is of the utmost importance as most new, supposedly "revisionist" histories of the Saint Bartholomew's Day massacre are really only restatements of Anquetil's original position.[6] The aim of this paper is then threefold: to establish that Louis-Pierre Anquetil was the first to popularize the theory of a non-

3   See Raymond Lebègue, "La Saint-Barthélemy et la 'Chronique du règne de Charles IX'," *Revue d'histoire littéraire de la France* 73 (1973), pp. 876–881; Claude Duchet, "La Saint-Barthélemy: de la "scène historique" au drame romantique," *Revue d'histoire littéraire de la France* 73 (1973), pp. 845–851; Barbara Diefendorf, "Prologue to a Massacre: Popular Unrest in Paris 1557–1572," *American Historical Review* 90 (1985), pp. 1067–1092; Jean-Louis Bourgeon, "Les Légendes ont la vie dure: à propos de la Saint-Barthélemy et de quelques livres récents," *Revue d'histoire moderne et contemporaine* 34 (1987), pp. 102–116; Jean-Louis Bourgeon, "Pour une histoire, enfin, de la Saint-Barthélemy," *Revue historique* 282 (1989), pp. 83–142. In fact, so much has been written on the history and historiography of the massacre of late that the *Revue d'histoire moderne et contemporaine* has officially declared that it will no longer publish on this issue. "Dans plusieurs articles, dont deux ont été publiés par la R.H.M.C., Jean-Louis Bourgeon a remis en cause l'historiographie 'classique' de la Saint-Barthélemy. Le présent article soutient une position contraire. A travers les arguments opposés, chacun pourra établir sa propre opinion sur ce point d'histoire. La R.H.M.C., pour sa part, ferme ce dossier." See the first editorial footnote in Marc Venard, "Arrêtez le massacre!" *Revue d'histoire moderne et contemporaine* 39 (1992), p. 645.

4   Prosper Mérimée, *Chronique de règne de Charles IX* (Paris: Charpentier et Cie., 1873 [1829]), p. 9.

5   Two important exceptions have been the historiographies written by Herbert Butterfield, "Lord Acton and the Massacre of St. Bartholomew," in *Man on his Past* (Cambridge: Cambridge University Press, 1955), pp. 171–201, and Henri Dubief, "L'Historiographie de la Saint-Barthélemy," *Actes du colloque l'Amiral de Coligny et son temps* (Paris: Société de l'histoire du Protestantisme français, 1974), pp. 351–365. Both historians admire Anquetil for his "objective" approach to history and his careful source work.

6   Most recently, Jean-Louis Bourgeon, in the *Revue historique* 171 (1989), 83–142, put forward what has been called a "radical revision of the standard interpretation" of the Saint Bartholomew's Day Massacre. This "radical revision" is essentially that the massacre was a

premeditated massacre; to suggest that Anquetil more than likely was an important source for Mérimée; and to come to some understanding as to why Anquetil has been ignored by most historiographers of the French religious wars.

The strong and favorable impact of Anquetil's *L'Esprit de la ligue, ou histoire politique des troubles de France pendant les XVIe & XVIIe siècles* (1767) rested on the care with which Anquetil pursued the facts of the French Wars of Religion without apparently favoring any one side in the conflict over another. Contemporary reviews lauded his "love of the truth and [his] spirit of impartiality. . . ."[7] Nineteenth-century critics called the book "the first French history which reproduced the sixteenth century without adulterating it. . . ."[8] More recently Anquetil has been singled out as the first "objective" historian of the massacre.[9] Such praise is well-deserved as Anquetil exhibits in this work a care for the use and critical analysis of sources unusual for the eighteenth century. Not only did Anquetil base *L'Esprit de la ligue* on a wealth of primary and secondary sources, he analyzed the value of each one in a lengthy annotated bibliography found in the book's preface. "I show the readers my opinion of the authors," he explained, "so that they can decide whether my judgment in each case was good or bad."[10] Anquetil's objective approach becomes apparent when his assessments are compared with the more modern ones of Henri Hauser in his well-respected and authoritative study, *Les sources de l'histoire de France, XVIe siècle* (1912). In many cases, Anquetil's evaluations of the primary sources anticipate Hauser's.[11]

---

popular riot encouraged by the ultra-Catholic leader, Henri de Guise. As will be shown, the heart of this position bears some resemblance to Anquetil's position.

7   *Le Journal des sçavans*, Octobre, 1767, p. 719.

8   Augustin Thierry, *Lettres sur l'histoire de France* (Paris: Sautelet & Cie., 1829), p. 55.

9   Dubief, p. 356.

10   Louis-Pierre Anquetil, *L'Esprit de la ligue ou histoire politique des troubles de France pendant les XVIe et XVIIe siècles*, 2nd edn (Paris: De la Lain, 1771), I, xxv. Although Anquetil says he relies primarily on primary sources, "le témoignage . . . [des] auteurs contemporains" [Anquetil, I, xix–xx], he qualifies his use of them, noting that they are not always "une autorité déterminante." [Anquetil, I, xx]. What follows, his preface to the annotated bibliography, is an insightful and detailed analysis by Anquetil of the various influences on contemporary writers which could cause them to alter, consciously or unconsciously, the facts of some event, among such influences being "des préjugés d'enfance, de famille et de parti; les liaisons d'intérêt; l'amitié et la haine, l'admiration et le mépris; le caractère même de l'auteur. Le doux tolère et excuse; le vif outre et exagère; le politique voit des rafinemens où l'homme naif ne voit qu'une marche naturelle et sans dessein. L'un attribue toutes les actions à l'amour de la religion, au zèle patriotique: l'autre leur donne pour principe l'ambition, la haine, le libertinage, le dépit, la vengeance; et souvent les imputations ne sont pas les mêmes d'une année à l'autre, parce que les intérêts de l'écrivain ont changé." Anquetil, I, xx–xxi.

11   Compare, for example, the similarity of the estimations of Hauser and Anquetil on De Thou, Davila, Pasquier, and Capilupi. Anquetil, volume I, lxxv–lxxvi, liii–liv, xxxvii–xxxviii, and Hauser, volume III, 13, 133, 244, and volume II, 71.

Such close source work led Anquetil to two radically new conclusions about the Saint Bartholomew's Day massacre, unique conclusions for the mid-eighteenth century. According to Anquetil, it was only after the failed assassination of Coligny that Charles IX decided in favor of the murder of the Huguenot leaders.[12] Anquetil supports such conclusions by using his analysis of the primary sources to cast doubt on the accuracy of those sources which indicted Charles in premeditating Coligny's murder and to emphasize those which spared the monarchy. Anquetil also laid the groundwork, from the first pages of his history onward, for the theory that Catholic crowds were violent and uncontrollable; later in the book this theme resurfaces as an explanation for the general 1572 massacre of the Huguenots.

Anquetil's careful source analysis enabled him to support his theory of an unpremeditated general massacre by successfully discrediting those books crucial to the case for premeditation. Significantly, Anquetil challenges the veracity of the Italian author, Capilupi, whose book, *Le Stratagême ou la ruse de Charles IX, roi de France, contre les Huguenots rebelles à Dieu et à lui* (1574), was one of the most important sources for the premeditation theory. *Le Stratagême* was one of the earliest Catholic histories written expressly to prove the existence of, and praise the monarchy for, the premeditated massacre of the Huguenots. Capilupi's "evidence" for a premeditated massacre was an alleged conversation between Charles IX and the Pope's legate to France where Charles supposedly insisted that his reconciliation with the Huguenots was more apparent than real and hinted of the existence of a plan to exterminate the Huguenots.[13] The assumption that these words were actually spoken by Charles led historians prior to Anquetil to believe in the complicity of the young king against the Huguenots. Catholic historians liked the supposed speech because it portrayed Charles as culpable rather than Catholicism; later, Enlightenment historians chose to believe in the existence of the speech because it confirmed their prejudices about the dangers of organized religion. In the eighteenth century it was Anquetil alone who was able to approach these lines with a healthy dose of scepticism.[14] Only Anquetil questions this incident carefully. "If Charles IX had held this conversation," wrote Anquetil, "he was certainly involved in the premeditation of the massacre of Saint Bartholomew; but de Thou warns us against the Italian historians from whom this story is taken. Most of them, abused by the Guise . . . or lied to by zealous Catholics . . .

[12] Anquetil, II, 15.

[13] Anquetil, II, 13–14. Historians prior to and up through the eighteenth century, men such as Mézeray, Daniel, and Voltaire, used these lines without questioning them. Previous to Anquetil, only De Thou had questioned the veracity of Capilupi, now considered a notoriously biased source.

[14] Lacretelle in the early nineteenth century once again uses the evidence of the Italian authors, especially Capilupi, to prove the complicity of Charles IX in a premeditated massacre. See Charles Lacretelle, *Histoire de France pendant les guerres de religion* (Paris: Delaunay, 1814), pp. 298–299.

have enveloped the entire court in the conspiracy, and name the king as the chief conspirator."[15]

In opposition to the standard eighteenth-century view, Anquetil maintains that Charles agreed to an attack on the Huguenot leaders only after the attempted assassination of Coligny; his agreement came as a response to an overt challenge to his authority to rule.[16] Having a change of heart at the last minute, Charles attempted to stop the massacre, according to Anquetil. Unfortunately, the wheels had already been put into motion. The vengeful duc de Guise had not only begun the attack on the Huguenot leaders by murdering Coligny, but was inciting the Parisian crowds to a more general massacre against all Huguenots.[17] It is Guise, not the royal family, who takes responsibility for the start of the massacre in Anquetil's interpretation.[18]

After having successfully refuted the idea of a long-term, premeditated royal plot against the Protestants, Anquetil supplies an alternative explanation for the rapacious violence and destruction of the 1572 massacre. By carefully developing the theme of religious mob violence from the first pages of his history of the Wars of Religion, Anquetil is able to make a convincing argument that once sparked by Guise, the Parisian mobs flame out of control. The people of Paris ultimately must shoulder the blame for the violence of St. Bartholomew's Day.

Anquetil's emphasis on the importance of historical causation leads him to begin his analysis of the French Wars of Religion with a brief history of the development of Protestantism, first in Europe as a whole, and then in France.[19]

---

15 Anquetil, II, 14.

16 Anquetil, II, 32–33. "À la moindre apparence de collusion de la part de Charles avec les Religionnaires, les Catholiques étoient determinés à élire un Capitaine Général et à faire une ligue offensive et défensive contre les Huguenots; qu'ainsi il se trouveroit entre les deux partis, sans puissance ni autorité dans son Royaume." Anquetil, II, 34.

17 "Ils envoyèrent en diligence un Gentilhomme dire au Duc de Guise de ne rien entreprendre contre l'Amiral, ce qui auroit suspendu tout le reste; mais il étoit déjà trop tard. Le vindicatif Guise avoit à peine attendu le signal pour se rendre chez l'Amiral." Anquetil, II, 40–41. Bourgeon's "radical" new theory of the Saint Bartholomew's Day Massacre follows this summary of Anquetil's position.

18 Anquetil, in a rare lapse in his usually careful source analysis, bases this version of the events leading up to the massacre on the faulty *Discours du Roi Henri III à un Personnage d'honneur* by the doctor of Henri III, Miron. It was not until Henri-Leonard Bordier in 1877, however, that the *Discours* was proven false. Anquetil, like his contemporaries, was unaware that the tract was a fake. Anquetil may still be criticized for not attempting to apply the standards of scepticism to this source that he applied to other works in his bibliography. The only other notable lapse in Anquetil's source analysis is his acceptance of the memoirs of Marguerite de Valois as genuine.

19 "Nous avons plusieurs histoires de nos troubles, tant anciennes que modernes, tant générales que particulières; mais il m'a paru qu'il nous en manquoit encore une qui s'attachât plus aux causes qu'aux effets, et qui, écartant tout ce qui n'a pas une relation directe à nos guerres civiles, réunit sous un même point de vue, comme dans un seul tableau, le commencement, les progrès, et la fin de nos malheurs. J'ai travaillé d'après cette idée. . . ." Anquetil, I, xvii.

This unique introduction to the French Wars of Religion allows Anquetil to bring out not only the long French history of Catholic mobs murdering Protestants prior to 1572, but also enables him to make the point that it was not unusual for Catholic crowds to escalate the level of violence far beyond what their leaders could have possibly ordered.[20] Supporting the modern view that the Catholics were more violent than the Protestants in their early clashes,[21] Anquetil establishes early on the pattern of violence which he uses for the St. Bartholomew's Day massacre—the Catholic crowds are encouraged to violence initially by their leaders and then quickly exceed their orders.

Anquetil uses the 1545 Massacre of the Vaudois to establish these themes. For Anquetil, the 1545 massacre began as a royal act and ended by being a popular riot. He writes in great detail of the bloody slaughter of innocent men, women, and children in this attack, and then ends his account by asserting that "historians agree that on this occasion the orders of Francis I were exceeded and that one of his last acts was to charge his son to punish severely the guilty parties."[22] 1545 marks an important year in Anquetil's analysis of the French Wars of Religion, for in this year the crown and the crowd join hands to suppress members of "the pretended reformed religion," and in this year it becomes evident that the crowd is uncontrollable. The crowd, in its lust for violence, would exceed, both in 1545 and later in 1572, the measures approved by the Court to be used against the Protestants. In spite of the fact that the circumstances of the 1545 and 1572 massacres were quite different, Anquetil uses the earlier event in order to plant the idea that the crown is not responsible in 1572 for the violent excesses of the rioters, who, blinded by their religious fanaticism, quickly rage out of control. Anquetil is successful in establishing the point that although authority figures—priests, faction leaders,

[20] These conclusions confirm the objective tone of Anquetil's history, for even though he personally disliked the Protestants and what he called "le poison de leur mauvaise doctrine" (Anquetil, I, 20), he did not slant his history of Protestant/Catholic clashes to favor the Catholics. Sharing the Enlightenment horror of fanaticism, Anquetil denounces all religious "enthousiastes." (Anquetil, I, 3, 48, 159).

[21] For Anquetil, it was the priests who, through their strong tirades against Calvinism and encouragement of violent methods used by the crowds, were raising the levels of violence in the 1550s and 1560s. Anquetil emphasizes the early role played by men of the cloth in stirring the populace to revolt as such examples illustrate how easy it was to foment violence in sixteenth-century Catholic crowds. (Anquetil, I, 164). Natalie Davis, in "The Rites of Violence: Religious Riot in Sixteenth-Century France," agrees with Anquetil in pointing out that it was the Catholic crowds who were the more violent of the two religious crowds. "In bloodshed, the Catholics are the champions . . . the Protestants' targets were primarily priests, monks, and friars. . . . The Catholic crowds were, of course, happy to catch a pastor when they could, but the death of any heretic would help in the cause of cleansing France of these perfidious sowers of disorder and disunion." Natalie Davis, "The Rites of Violence: Religious Riot in Sixteenth-Century France," in *Society and Culture in Early Modern France* (Stanford: Stanford University Press, 1975), p. 174.

[22] Anquetil, I, 16.

kings—used the violence of the Catholic crowds to pursue their own objectives against the Protestants, those same leaders did not have control over the crowds once they began rioting.

Anquetil would not disagree that the conflicts among the great men of the sixteenth century—the Guises, Montmorencys, and Bourbons—were much more important than the popular religious riots in causing the Wars of Religion. He emphasized repeatedly that "religion was the pretext more than the motif of the civil wars of the sixteenth century."[23] His inclusion of the existing unrest among the lower orders is important in that it explains how these faction leaders were able to enroll the people in what was primarily a political power struggle. By appropriating an issue for which the unprivileged had already proven themselves willing to fight, it would be easier to involve them in the power-clash between the Guises and their Protestant rivals.

Anquetil does not claim that the religious justifications given to the wars were primarily (or even merely) a means to gain popular support by the warring leaders of the rival factions. His inclusion of the religious strife among the people in the 1560s adds to our understanding of their part in a war which was primarily a confrontation between rival political factions. It is Anquetil alone in the eighteenth century who sees the St. Bartholomew's Day Massacre as the culmination of years of religious strife marked by innumerable spontaneous popular uprisings and riots.[24]

Having set the stage for an alternative explanation of the St. Bartholomew's Day massacre, Anquetil is free to decry what he calls this "bloody catastrophe" without resorting to premeditation theories.[25] Anquetil's version of the massacre, making use, as it does, of the people as active participants, allows for a spontaneous event and mitigates the king's role in this tragedy. It was the people out of control who were, in the end, responsible for the extreme violence. Guise and other ultramontane faction leaders purposefully stirred up the Catholic Parisians, yet once enraged, the people acted on

[23] Anquetil, I, 1.
[24] Anquetil, I, 158–164. Anquetil explicitly writes of the growing violence of both Catholic and Protestant crowds leading up to the outbreak of open warfare. He recounts in detail the horrors committed by both sides in the name of religion as a way of showing the evils which arise from religious fanaticism and a lack of mutual toleration. "Catholiques ou calvinistes, il est difficile de décider lesquels se permirent des barbaries plus atroces. . . . Les annales des villes, les fastes des familles ont transmis jusqu'à nous des exemples d'inhumanité, dont la variété surprend autant que la cruauté inspire d'horreur. Des tortures adroitement ménagées pour suspendre la mort et la rendre plus douloureuse; des pères, des maris poignardés entre les bras de leurs filles et de leurs épouses outragées sous leurs yeux; des femmes, des enfants traités avec des excès de brutalité inconnus chez les peuples les plus barbares; enfin des provinces entières dévastées; le meurtre comblé par l'incendie; des magistrats vénérables devenus les victimes de la fureur d'une populace effrénée, qui, poussant la rage au-delà de leur mort, traînoit dans les rues leurs entrailles encore palpitantes, et se repaissoit de leur chair." Anquetil, I, 161–162.
[25] Anquetil, II, 4.

their own.[26] Anquetil condemns the people, not the king, for the extent of the violence, which he records at length.[27]

Anquetil in 1767, fifty-two years before Mérimée, proposed and attempted to prove as objectively as he could that the Massacre of St Bartholomew was not premeditated and that the responsibility for the excessive bloodshed lay with Guise and the crowd, not with the crown. To prove that Anquetil was the first to popularize the theory of a general non-premeditated massacre, however, it is not enough to establish that he predates Mérimée in support of this view. What must next be determined is the extent of his influence. Was he recognized by later historians as promoting a new interpretation of the massacre?

Certainly *L'Esprit de la ligue* remained popular throughout the eighteenth century and into the nineteenth. Nearly a quarter of a century after it was first written, the *Journal de Paris* called it "one of the most esteemed historical works that this century [the eighteenth] has produced."[28] In the early years of the nineteenth century, *L'Esprit de la ligue* was credited with immediately establishing for Anquetil a meritorious reputation.[29] Anquetil's theory of a non-premeditated massacre in particular appears to have been well-known and considered important as later historians felt compelled to respond to his novel position. Nineteenth-century writers continually singled out Anquetil as the eighteenth-century historian necessary to cite when discussing the massacre. Whether they agreed with him or not, the fact that all felt the need to mention Anquetil when writing of the massacre stands as a strong testament to the importance of his work and its notoriety. Charles Lacretelle, returning to the premeditation theory, refers to Anquetil several times throughout his *Histoire de France pendant les guerres de Religion* (1814) in order to combat his theories.[30] Lacretelle rebukes Anquetil by name, linking him with Père Daniel as historians who were attempting to spare the king from the awful burden of responsibility for the massacre.[31] In equating Anquetil with Daniel, Lacretelle places Anquetil, in his eyes a misguided historian, among the ranks of the greatest historians of France. He recognizes Anquetil as the most significant eighteenth-century writer of the massacre, and therefore as the one most important to correct.

P. L. Rœderer, writing at the same time as Mérimée, refers to Anquetil repeatedly and with great approval in his *Ébauche historique des premières guerres*

---

[26] Anquetil, II, 48.

[27] "Tout ce qui s'y trouve, sans distinction d'âge ni de sexe, est massacré; l'air rétentit des cris aigus des assassins, et des plaintes douloureuses des mourants: le jour vient éclairer la scène affreuse de cette sanglante tragédie. . . . Enfin, il n'y eut genre de cruauté qui ne fut commise; des enfants de dix ans tuèrent des enfants au maillot . . ." Anquetil, II, 43 and 49.

[28] *Journal de Paris*, 147 (Mai, 1780), p. 601.

[29] "Rapport historique sur les Progrès de l'histoire et de la littérature ancienne depuis 1789 et sur leur état actuel," 1 (Paris: Institut de France, 1810), p. 155.

[30] Lacretelle, pp. 200–202, 365–367.

[31] Lacretelle, p. 368.

de cour ou guerre des grands, improprement nommées guerres de religion (1830) and follows Anquetil's theory in his dramatization of the massacre in "La Proscription de la Saint-Barthélemy."[32] Rœderer's writings on the massacre, essentially restatements of Anquetil's argument, served to   popularize Anquetil's most important conclusions. Four years later, Jean-Baptiste Honoré Raymond Capefigue, in his *Histoire de la réforme, de la ligue, et du règne de Henri IV* (1834) prefaces his history with attacks on the errors of eighteenth-century historians who incorrectly interpreted the massacre. Capefigue selects Anquetil alongside Voltaire as historians in need of correction. Dismissing Voltaire's errors in a couple of lines, he spends two pages gently explaining the problems of Anquetil.[33] Capefigue's position again is similar to that staked out by Anquetil; his primary complaint is that the earlier historian did not give to the people an even greater role in the massacre. For Capefigue, "[Anquetil] forgot the people."[34]

Some of the most influential writers from the first half of the nineteenth century apparently were familiar with the ideas of Anquetil as well. Thierry praised *L'Esprit de la ligue*.[35] Prudhomme reproached Anquetil for diminishing the king's responsibility for the bloodshed.[36] Michelet, while not quoting Anquetil by name, seems to have some familiarity with the earlier historian. Michelet and Anquetil both describe the massacre in the same terms, come to the same conclusions as to why it went out of control, and blame the same people as instigators. They even make use of the same examples to make their points. Such similarities do not lead inevitably to the conclusion that Anquetil's *L'Esprit de la ligue* was well known to Michelet, but they circumstantially attest to the spreading and popularising of Anquetil's theory.

Given the evident association of Anquetil's name with the theory of a non-premeditated massacre by both those who supported and those who denied that interpretation, the argument can be made that Louis-Pierre Anquetil, not Prosper Mérimée, first popularized the notion of a non-premeditated massacre. Herbert Butterfield's claim in "Lord Acton and the Massacre of St Bartholomew" that Mérimée elaborated and popularized the theories of Jean-Marie-Vincent Audin is not as defensible.[37] Anquetil is a more likely source not only for the reasons explained above, but also for the simple reason that Mérimée's explanation of the massacre is closer to Anquetil's than to Audin's. Audin theorizes that the massacre had been planned by Catherine de Medici

32 P. L. Rœderer, "Ébauche historique des premières guerres de cour ou guerre des grands, improprement nommées guerres de religion," in *Œuvres* (Paris: Firmin Didot frères, 1853), I, 106–109, 121–126, 129, 133, 135.
33 Capefigue, xxii.
34 Capefigue, I, xxv.
35 See above p. 161.
36 Dubief, p. 357.
37 Butterfield, p. 175.

for years, that "she alone planned it and accomplished it . . .."[38] In this way Audin exculpated the Catholic Church. Following the 1570 peace, according to Audin, Catherine tells Charles of her plans for a massacre of the Huguenots.[39] In spite of this long-held desire to be rid of the Protestants shared by Charles and Catherine, in the final analysis Audin denies that Charles knew in advance about the first attempt on Coligny's life.[40] This convoluted history of the massacre bears little resemblance to Mérimée's retelling of the event. Mérimée states his position without reservation. "For me," wrote Mérimée, "I am firmly convinced that the massacre was not premeditated, and I can only conceive that the contrary opinion had been adopted by authors who present Catherine at one and the same time as a very wicked woman and as one of the most profoundly political heads of her century."[41] Moreover, Audin scoffs at the notion that Guise and the Catholic Church were involved, while Mérimée says that Guise stirred up the people for a massacre.[42] Mérimée also clearly denies any premeditation in the massacre while Audin emphasizes the premeditation of Catherine.[43]

Having established Anquetil as the first popularizer of the theory of a non-premeditated massacre, one question remains to be answered. Why has Anquetil's contribution to this history been forgotten? Why are his theories attributed to other authors? This question, the most important of the three, is also the most difficult to answer. There is no one reason for Anquetil's descent into oblivion. A number of factors worked against him. One possible explanation for his historical demise is that the even, objective tone of L'Esprit de la ligue made it difficult for biased writers either for or against the massacre to use or attack his theory, leading extremists of all stripes to ignore the book. In addition to this problem, his later, very successful universal and French histories were written in a style no longer in tune with the historiographical advances of the late eighteenth, early nineteenth centuries. In a phrase, Anquetil published and perished.

Anquetil's moderate, non-polemical interpretation of the massacre remained a minority position among French historians until the end of the nineteenth century. In the eighteenth century, extremists on the political right and left worked in odd harmony to continue the premeditation theory. Protestants

---

[38] Jean-Marie-Vincent Audin, *Histoire de la Saint-Barthélemy* (Liége: J.-G. Lardinois, 1852 [1826]), p. 54.

[39] "Nous plaçons à cette époque la manifestations des secrets de Catherine à Charles IX, que d'autres historiens ont fait remonter quelques années auparavant." Audin, p. 73.

[40] "Il n'est donc pas vraisemblable que le roi ait connu le projet de l'assassinat de l'amiral. C'est un crime dont il n'a pas dû répondre devant le tribunal de Dieu. L'histoire ne doit pas l'en charger: il aurait peut-être embrassé la main du meurtrier si sa mère la lui avait présentée; mais il ne mit pas le fer dans cette main." Audin, p. 134.

[41] Mérimée, p. 6.

[42] Audin, p. 229, Mérimée, p. 10.

[43] Mérimée, p. 6.

maintained this position as proof of a Catholic/Valois conspiracy against them. Philosophic historians took up the premeditation theory as a way to attack both religious fanaticism and tyranny. Voltaire, chief among the philosophes in his attacks on religion, returned to the Saint Bartholomew's Day massacre repeatedly in order to hammer home his point that the massacre was the result of religious fanaticism.[44] Agreeing with Mézeray, Voltaire blamed Catherine de Medici and Charles IX for having planned the general massacre for two years.[45] His chief works on the subject systematically blacken the role of the Church in the massacre and whitewash the role of the protestants.[46]

Writing in opposition to Voltaire, the Abbé Novi de Caveirac proposed an equally extremist *non-premeditated* interpretation of the massacre which attempted to show that the Church had no role in the massacre and that the crown was justified in its acts due to the on-going rebellion of the Huguenots.[47] Anquetil was alone among the historians of his day in taking a moderate stance. Although Novi de Caveirac shared his belief in an unpremeditated general massacre, he did so expressly to exonerate the Catholic church and condemn the Protestants just as Voltaire's interpretation was based upon his desire to prove the evils of organized religion. Only Anquetil refused to use the massacre as a way of promoting a private agenda. Unlike both Caveirac and Voltaire, Anquetil avoided the passions that this topic aroused and kept as strictly as possible to what he perceived as the facts of the event. For this reason, extremists of the right and left ignored him as Anquetil's painstaking development of his thesis did not lend itself to an easy attack.

The plausibility of this conclusion is evidenced by Voltaire's differing reactions to Anquetil's and Caveirac's writings, both of which dispute Voltaire's position that the massacre was planned for two years. Compelled to respond to the overt Catholic bias in Caveirac's work, Voltaire wrote strongly against Caveirac in numerous pieces, including, *Les éclaircissements historiques* (1763), *Desconspirations contre les peuples* (1776), *Les réflexions philosophiques sur le procès de Mlle Camp* (1772), *Fragment sur l'histoire générale* (1773), and numerous letters.[48] In contrast, Voltaire mentioned Anquetil's *L'Esprit de la ligue* only

---

44 "The most detestable example of fanaticism was that of the burghers of Paris who on St Bartholomew's Night went about assassinating and butchering all their fellow citizens who did not go to mass, throwing them out of windows, cutting them in pieces," he wrote in the entry for fanaticism in his *Philosophical Dictionary*. Voltaire, *Philosophical Dictionary*, trans. and ed. by Peter Gay (New York: Harcourt, Brace & World, 1962), pp. 267–268.

45 O. R. Taylor, "Voltaire et la Saint-Barthélemy," *Revue d'histoire littéraire de la France* 73 (1973), p. 836.

46 Taylor, p. 837.

47 Jean Novi de Caveirac, *Apologie de Louis XIV et de son Conseil, sur la Révocation de l'Edit de Nantes. Pour servir de réponse à la lettre d'un patriote sur la tolérance civile des Protestants de France. Avec une dissertation sur la journée de la Saint-Barthélemy* (New Haven: Yale University Microfilming, 1988 [1758]).

48 See Janine Estebe, *Tocsin pour un massacre* (Paris: Editions du Centurion, 1968), p. 39, Jacques Bailbé, "La Saint-Barthélemy dans la littérature française," *Revue d'histoire*

once, his request to be sent a copy of the work. Since Voltaire never again wrote of Anquetil or his book, we cannot know his specific opinion of it. The case can be argued, however, that Voltaire, unable to dissect Anquetil's carefully crafted theory, chose instead to pursue the easier target of Caveirac's inflammatory prose.

Throughout the eighteenth century, this response to Anquetil's theory prevailed among those historians who were using an extreme interpretation of the massacre to forward a particular religious or political position. Although *L'Esprit de la ligue* was recognized in its day as an important history and was influential among early nineteenth-century writers, it was never mentioned by eighteenth-century polemicists for or against the massacre. Incapable of refuting Anquetil, this group ignored him. Just as Caveirac's name lives on because his one-sided interpretation of the massacre made it highly controversial and easy to attack, Anquetil's name has faded away in part because those writers seeking simplistic, biased targets ignored his *L'Esprit de la ligue*.

In France until the end of the nineteenth century, the theory of a premeditated massacre prevailed among those historians with an axe to grind. The years immediately following publication of *L'Esprit de la ligue* saw a return to the theory of royal premeditation. Such works as Henri Griffet's *Traité des différentes sortes de Preuves qui servent à établir la vérité de l'histoire* (1769), and Gabriel Brizard's *Du Massacre de la Saint-Barthélemi, et de l'influence des étrangers en France durant la Ligue* (1790), insist on a theory of long-term premeditation. The motivations behind such conspiracy theories, however, had changed by this time. During and after the French Revolution, the polemic turned towards more fully indicting the monarchy in the crime of the massacre, as in the enormously popular play about the massacre by Marie Chénier.[49] Under the First Empire, this trend continued with more emphasis on the role of Catherine.[50] Even constitutional royalists followed this line.[51] It was not until Mérimée and Rœderer in the late 1820s early 1830s that Anquetil's moderate theory of an unpremeditated massacre was corroborated by other French writers.

---

littéraire de la France 73 (1973), p. 775, Taylor, p. 838. Voltaire matched enflamed rhetoric word-for-word with Caveirac, calling his book an "ouvrage abominable . . . [où] les faits sont déguisez, les raisonements faux, le stile déclamatoire, et les principes affreux." In later writings he shifted his criticisms from the "horrible et détestable" book and resorted to ad hominen attacks on the author, calling Caveirac ". . . [un] homme fort méprisé et qui cherche à faire fortune à quelque prix que ce soit," and more simply, referring to him as "ce monstre." Voltaire, letters to Nicolas Claude Thieriot, 24 December, 1758 and 25 January 1759, and letter to Jacob Vernes, February 1759, in *The Complete Works of Voltaire*, ed. Theodore Besterman and others (Geneva: Institut et Musée Voltaire, 1968), CIII, 298, 299, 358, 403.

[49] Marie-Joseph Chénier, *Charles IX; ou l'école des rois, tragédie* (Paris, 1790).

[50] Dubief, p. 357.

[51] Dubief, p. 358.

By the late 1860s, however, the premeditation theory was again going strong, this time as a result of the efforts of Lord Acton, who saw the Court planning as early as February 1572 for the massacre.[52] His work was followed by that of Henri Bordier, who in 1879 renewed the controversy in *La St Barthélemy et la critique moderne* as he forcefully reasserted the case for premeditation.[53] The premeditation theory held primacy of place among French historians for the next few years until the publication of primary materials, the letters of Catherine de Medici in particular, helped to put this theory to rest.

Through the course of the controversy, Anquetil was slowly forgotten. Lord Acton, first involved in the Saint Bartholomew's Day massacre when writing a historiography of the event, inexplicably left Anquetil's name out of his survey of historians who had written on the topic. Why? One reason could be that Acton was trying to promote anew the theory of a premeditated massacre and so chose not to address Anquetil's work which denied such premeditation. That conclusion would not speak well of Acton as an historian and is not supported by what is known of Acton's careful research methods. Another reason could be that Acton did not include Anquetil in his historiography because he either was unaware of Anquetil's existence due to the earlier silence surrounding Anquetil's work by the very prolific polemicists of the eighteenth century, or because Anquetil was no longer considered an important or reputable historian. It is this second conjecture that now needs examination.

L'Esprit de la ligue and its sequel, *L'Intrigue du cabinet* (1780), established Anquetil's reputation as one of the premier historians in eighteenth-century France. His later writings destroyed that reputation. Whereas his early works, with their emphasis on primary research, close analysis and an attempt at objectivity, were ahead of the prevailing standards of historical scholarship in the mid-eighteenth century, his later works saw a return to a humanist style of writing associated with such seventeenth-century historians as Mézeray and Daniel. Contemporaries were sharply critical of these later historical efforts. Jean-François de La Harpe called Anquetil's *Histoire Universelle* (1799) "weak and feeble;"[54] Dacier, perpetual secretary of the Class of History and Ancient Literature at the Institute of France, in his 1808 eulogy of Anquetil, avoided direct criticism by politely stating that "out of respect for [Anquetil's] memory, we will say nothing about the voluminous works of his old age."[55] Anquetil himself was more direct. He acknowledged the change in his scholarship when

---

[52] Butterfield, p. 185.

[53] Butterfield, p. 191.

[54] Jean-François d La Harpe, *Cours de Littérature ancienne et moderne* (Paris: Firmin Didot Frères, 1840 [1799–1805]), p. 517.

[55] M. Dacier, *Rapport historique sur les progrès de l'histoire et de la littérature ancienne depuis 1789 et sur leur état actuel* (Paris: 1810), I, 156.

he wrote in the preface of *Louis XIV, sa cour, et le régent* (1789), "as for this book, I would not hazard to call it a history . . . it is inferior to that name."[56]

There are a variety of reasons for the change in Anquetil's research methods and writing styles ranging from a lack of time to a lack of access to libraries, from a change in his politics to his personal experiences in the French Revolution. What is known about the genesis of what is clearly Anquetil's worst, and unfortunately for him, his most popular history, *L'Histoire de France* (1805), is that Napoleon, familiar with the earlier histories of Anquetil,[57] specifically asked him to write a history of France along the lines of such seventeenth-century historians as Mézéray and Daniel.[58] Anquetil obliged his new master and published in the year XIII (1804–05) his *L'Histoire de France* as a humanist history. It turned out to be a wildly popular book, the most popular history of his long career. *L'Histoire de France* has over eighty-nine printings, the last in 1880, and thirty-one different continuators.[59]

With this book, both the capstone and the worst history of his career, Anquetil betrayed the historical standards he had established for himself in his earlier histories. His exacting scholarly methods—his emphasis on primary sources, the careful evaluation of the potential biases in sources—all are gone. *L'Histoire de France* marked the end of what had been, in its earliest days, an important historical career. Instead of being the pinnacle of that career as Anquetil had hoped, this last book was the nadir.

This history, rightfully called "the weakest of his works" by a nineteenth-century critic, was also acknowledged to be Anquetil's most popular book and the one upon which his reputation came to be established.[60] At the end of the nineteenth century, the popularity of this work was still raging on. "In spite of its mediocrity," mused one historian in 1877, "*L'Histoire de France* has a vogue

---

56 Louis-Pierre Anquetil, *Louis XIV, sa cour, et le régent* (Paris: Coutard, 1789), I, xi.

57 Napoleon, pleased with Anquetil's work, awarded Anquetil "la Croix d'honneur [et] une pension digne à la fois du premier Monarque de l'Europe, et du Nestor de la Littérature." "Notice sur M. Anquetil, chanoine régulier de Sainte-Geneviève et membre de l'Institut national de France," Bibliothèque de Sainte-Geneviève, ms 1174, *Registre des Cérémonies extraordinaires de l'abbaye de Ste.-Geneviève commencé dans 1764 jusqu'en 1795*, p. 258.

58 "S.M. l'Empereur [Anquetil écrit dans la préface de l'*Histoire de France*], étant premier consul, me fit l'honneur, il y a quatre ans, de m'inviter à Malmaison: là, s'entretenant avec moi des historiens de France, après les avoir passés légèrement en revue, il me dit qu'il serait à souhaiter qu'on s'occupât d'une histoire dégagée des détails et des accessoires qui rendent celle de France si volumineuse, et qui ne contînt que les faits absolument particuliers à la nation." Anquetil, *Histoire de France depuis les Gaulois jusqu'à la mort de Louis XVI* (Paris: Garnery, 1805), I, ii.

59 Continuators were writers who added on to or "continued" previously published books. In the early nineteenth century it was legal in France for a continuator to copyright someone else's book under his own name if at least 25% of the final text were the continuator's additions. With their rights protected, continuators found it lucrative to take a popular history, add chapters at the end to make the history current, and republish it.

60 *Grand Dictionnaire universel du XIXe siècle* (Paris: Larousse, 1869), I, 418.

which continues to our day."[61] Because of the popularity of a book so out of step with their historical methods, the nineteenth-century French Romantics waged a bitter campaign against L'Histoire de France and Anquetil. Anquetil became for them the symbol of the type of history and historian who must be purged from the discipline. Thierry singled out Anquetil by name as one of two historians representing an old style of history "which, old and worn out, must make room for a new science."[62] Ignoring his earlier histories, they forever linked Anquetil's name with his worst effort. Time has proven the Romantics successful in this campaign. By the end of the nineteenth century, those historians who remembered Anquetil at all remembered him with derision for L'Histoire de France. The Romantics effectively destroyed Anquetil's reputation by the mid-nineteenth century; by the end of the nineteenth century, what was left of his battered reputation had been forgotten.

Anquetil's pioneering work on the St. Bartholomew's Day massacre was lost along with his name. Nearly two hundred years have passed since his death, and only now are his theories unwittingly resurfacing in others' works as "new" revisionist interpretations of the massacre. Most prolifically, Jean-Louis Bourgeon in several recent articles parallels Anquetil when he writes that Charles IX agreed to the massacre under pressure and only after the attempt on Coligny when his rule was overtly challenged.[63] The shifting of responsibility from the royal family to Guise is again Anquetil's, not Bourgeon's, innovation. Denis Crouzet's and Natalie Davis's emphasis on the role of priests and ministers in promoting the violence of the people again is a modern restatement of a position staked out earlier by Anquetil.[64] Unfortunately for Louis-Pierre Anquetil, his closing words in the preface to the Histoire de France were truer than he would have hoped. This history, in more ways than one, was truly "his farewell to France."[65]

---

[61] Ludovic La Lanne, Dictionnaire historique de la France (Paris: Libraire Hachette, 1877), I, 85.

[62] The other historian named was Velly. Augustin Thierry, Dix ans d'études historiques (Paris: Jouvet et Cie., [1835] 1884), p. 13.

[63] See footnote number three.

[64] Denis Crouzet, Les guerriers de Dieu: La violence au temps des troubles de religion (vers 1525–1610), two volumes (Seyssel: Champ Vallon, 1990) and Natalie Davis, "The Rites of Violence: Religious Riot in Sixteenth-Century France," in Society and Culture in Early Modern France (Stanford: Stanford University Press, 1975), p. 174.

[65] Anquetil, Histoire de France, I, ix–x.

11

Locke on the Dissolution of Society

JULIAN H. FRANKLIN

At the beginning of chapter XIX of his *Second Treatise of Government*, Locke distinguishes between the dissolution of society and the dissolution of government. His explanation of the first of these concepts is confined to a single paragraph (sec.211). And since his language not only in this paragraph but throughout chapter XIX is sometimes misleading, there is much uncertainty as to his meaning in the secondary literature. Nevertheless, the dissolution of society raises questions that go to the very core of Locke's political doctrine. And so I shall try, in this article, to clarify his usage of the concept and to offer some critical reflections on its theoretical adequacy.[1] It seems best to begin with a brief explanation of the underlying problem.

The idea that society may be dissolved follows from the very logic of Locke's social contract. When free individuals no longer accept the inconveniences for the state of nature, they enter into an agreement to act collectively in order to form a government. This, in short, is the social contract. And the agreement thus entered into creates a corporate body, which acts by the vote of the majority of those who were parties to the contract. This is the body that Locke refers to sometimes as the "society" and at other times as the "community", "people", "political society", or "commonwealth." It is the locus of what we would call "constituent authority", or what some of Locke's most theoretically sophisticated contemporaries called "real majesty" to describe the ultimate owner of sovereignty as distinguished from the holders of "personal majesty", who have been merely authorized to exercise it. In Locke's terminology, the corporate "society" or "community" is the body that makes the decision as to what the government is to be and endows it with authority. It is also the body to which authority normally reverts when, as a result of abuses, a government forfeits its legitimacy and is thereby legally dissolved. When government

[1] I wish to thank Ms. Karen Ballentine and Professor David Johnston of Columbia University for their helpful comments on this manuscript at various stages of its preparation.

becomes tyrannical, in other words, it is the right of the people to alter or abolish it. In Locke's words, when the legitimacy of government lapses, ". . . the People have a Right to act as Supreme, and continue the Legislative in themselves, or erect a new Form, or under the old form place it in new hands, as they think good." (sec.243)

Since the "community" or "society" that does all this is not, at least in principle, a fact of nature but the outcome of a voluntary contract among free individuals, the obligation of the members to support it cannot be other than conditional. The "society", "community", or "people" must, in other words, itself be liable to dissolution if it fails to perform its function. The ultimate purpose for which society is formed is to protect the individual. It achieves this end by creating and sustaining a decent government. If it becomes unable to do that, the obligation to support it is dissolved, and the individual is free to seek protection elsewhere.

But this conclusion is at odds with common sense. Most of us do not believe that a political community simply disappears when its freedoms are suppressed or even when it has been deprived of the power to defend itself. We may admit that particular individuals, faced with dire threats to their existence, may exercise the right of emigration. But we normally assume that those who remain have some sort of continuing obligation.

An extreme example may serve to clarify the point. Let us suppose a political society that has been subjected to brutal and protracted tyranny either from within or by foreign conquest. Let us suppose, further, that this tyranny is suddenly removed. The issue, then, is whether the individual residents of that territory, who were formerly members of the political community, have been and now remain in a state of nature in consequence of the tyranny, or whether there is still a community which they have a moral obligation to acknowledge. The first alternative follows from a strict interpretation of Locke's criterion. The second is what I would call the common moral view. The latter, furthermore, would not require that, once liberated, the surviving members of the restored society would be morally required to reconstitute the old arrangements as to government. The old government is assumed to be dissolved and the people are completely free either to retain it or to change its form. The critical point for theory is that no new agreement is needed to keep the community in being. Thus in the aftermath of World War II no one doubted that the peoples of (West) Germany, France, the Netherlands, and other subjugated communities continued as political entities. And no one doubted either that individuals within any one of these communities were bound by any reasonable constitution of government to which its people might freely consent.

Where the subjugated entity was a multinational federation, the consequence of freedom may be a dissolution of the union into its component ethnic parts, as in the Soviet Union, Yugoslavia, and Czechoslovakia. But this is not to be taken as reversion to a state of nature. The standard claim in such dissolutions is that the federal union had always been or had become oppressive, on which account the subjugated people is entitled to be free and sovereign. But there is no suggestion that the right of that community to act must be established by a new agreement among independent individuals.

Hence the common sense approach to the dissolution of society is that a community is not dissolved unless the conditions of its suppression are extreme. But this is at odds with Locke's basic conception of the social contract since it implies that individuals may have an obligation to support their community long after it has ceased to protect them and at potentially great cost to their well-being and security.

Given Locke's individualist version of the social contract, therefore, the dissolution of society posed a profound dilemma, which, understandably enough, he never deliberately confronted, or attempted to resolve. My own reading of the *Second Treatise*, however, is that Locke opted, instinctively but firmly, for a loose version of the common sense solution. For that is the natural construction of his language in sec.211:

> He that will with any clearness speak of the *Dissolution of Government*, ought, in the first place to distinguish between the *Dissolution of Society* and the *Dissolution of Government*. That which makes the Community, and brings men out of the loose State of Nature into *one Politick Society*, is the Agreement every one has with the rest to incorporate, and act as one Body, and so be one distinct Commonwealth. The usual, and almost only way whereby *this Union is dissolved*, is the Inroad of Foreign Force making a Conquest upon them. For in that Case, (not being able to maintain and support themselves, as *one intire* and *independent Body*) the Union belonging to that Body which consisted therein, must necessarily cease, and so every one return to the state he was in before, with a liberty to shift for himself, and provide for his own Safety as he thinks fit in some other Society. Whenever the *Society is dissolved*, 'tis certain the Government of that Society cannot remain. Thus Conquerours swords often cut up Governments by the Roots, and mangle Societies to pieces, separating the subdued or scattered Multitude from the Protection of, and Dependence on that Society which ought to have preserved them from violence. The World is too well instructed, and too forward to allow of this way of dissolving Governments to need any more to be said of it: and there wants not much Argument to prove that where the *Society is dissolved*, the Government cannot remain; that being as impossible, as for the Frame of an House to subsist when the Materials of it are scattered, and dissipated by a Whirlwind, or jumbled into a confused heap by an Earthquake. (sec. 211)[2]

Despite certain hesitations in this paragraph, the natural reading of it is reasonably clear. A society is dissolved only when a people has been utterly fragmented, when it has been "mangled to pieces" by a ruthless force and its members turned into a "scattered multitude". Foreign conquest is "almost [the]

2   All Locke quotations are from John Locke, *Two Treatises of Government*, Peter Laslett, ed. (Cambridge, 1988).

only way" such dismemberment is brought about. But foreign conquests do not always work such a dissolution, and domestic tyrannies do so only very rarely if at all. The dissolution of society follows only upon systematic repression savagely executed by an invading force or its equivalent. And the test of dissolution, accordingly, is the incapacity or unwillingness of its members to act together for their mutual protection. But the mere dissolution of legitimate government, either by foreign conquest or domestic tyranny, would not of itself bring about that outcome.

But this interpretation of sec.211 is to be offset by certain implications to the contrary elsewhere in chapter XIX. The rest of Locke's discussion is devoted to the various ways in which government can be dissolved from within. In taking up the more usual and familiar forms of domestic tyranny, Locke says nothing expressly about the dissolution of society. But his language often suggests a reversion to the state of nature whenever a tyranny succeeds. And reversion to a state of nature seems to imply the dissolution of society even though no violent fragmentation has occurred.

Thus according to sec.212, the dissolution of government occurs whenever the legislative is altered from that which the people have established. Locke observes that the legislative ". . . *is the Soul that gives Form, Life and Unity to the Commonwealth*", and when it is altered "Dissolution and Death follows". And at the end of this very long paragraph the seeming dissolution of society is put in yet another way. "Every one," says Locke, "is at the disposure of his own Will, when those who had by the delegation of the Society, the declaring of the Public Will, are excluded from it, and others usurp the place who had no such Authority or Delegation".

A circumstance in which everyone is "at the disposure of his own Will" sounds very much like the juridical definition of a state of nature, which would supervene, of course, only if society had been dissolved. The same implication seems also to arise in Sec. 219 and so strongly, indeed, that the main part of the paragraph should be quoted in full:

> There is one way more such a Government [i.e. one like England's] can be dissolved, and that is, when he who has the Supreme Executive Power, neglects and abandons that charge, so that the Laws already made can no longer be put in execution. This is demonstrably to reduce all to Anarchy, and so effectually to *dissolve the Government*. For Laws not being made for themselves, but to be by their execution the Bonds of Society, to keep every part of the Body Politick in its due place and function, when that totally ceases, the *Government* visibly *ceases*, and the People become a confused Multitude, without Order or Connexion.

The reference to anarchy in this passage is already suggestive of a state of nature. But the image of "a confused Multitude, without Order or Connexion" is especially arresting. It calls to mind the "scattered multitude" described in sec.211 as one of the direst marks of a society dissolved.

Yet another seeming association of the state of nature with dissolution of government appears, albeit briefly, in sec.205 of Chapter XVII, "Of Tyranny". Locke is here commenting on the rule of English law that opposition may be made to illegal acts of the king's officers. This need not provoke a crisis unless the prince will ". . . by actually putting himself into a State of War with his people, dissolve the Government, and leave them to that defence, which belongs to everyone in the State of Nature."

In all these passages, as well as others less dramatic, the dissolution of society seems to follow directly upon the dissolution of government. But now a puzzling inconsistency appears. For they are all counterbalanced, as it were, by the assertion, oft repeated in the *Second Treatise*, that the normal consequence of tyranny is reversion of power to the society, people, or community. But if this be so, and the people is still entitled to act as a corporate entity, there is no reversion to a state of nature, and no dissolution of society!

This apparent inconsistency in Locke has become a point of considerable controversy in the secondary literature. At one time most commentators on Locke's political thought said nothing or very little about the dissolution of society. And many of those who noticed it, did not fully grasp the issue of consistency because they did not attend to Locke's idea of real majesty, or constituent authority, in the community as distinct from the power of the government.[3] These tended, therefore, to equate Locke's term "society" with non-political associations like the family, which only deepens the confusion.

But there have been some notable exceptions. Peter Laslett has suggested that the line between the loose association of the state of nature and an actual formed community is imprecise enough in Locke for reversion to the state of nature and reversion to the community to blend into each other.[4] But the juridical gap between a loose association and an incorporated community cannot be elided that easily, in my opinion, and especially not since Locke often (but not exclusively[5]) speaks as though the incorporated community comes into possession of all the powers of its members and could act as a full-fledged democracy the moment it was formed. John Dunn, on the other hand, has made an heroic and almost persuasive attempt to show that the state of nature suggested in the sections of the *Second Treatise* just mentioned refer not to the relations among individuals, and so to a dissolution of society, but only to the

---

[3] For the state of commentary on these questions at the end of the 1960s see Martin Seliger, *The Liberal Politics of John Locke* (London, 1968), esp. ch. iv. For the newer view of Locke's theory of sovereignty, see Julian H. Franklin, *John Locke and the Theory of Sovereignty* (Cambridge, 1978).

[4] *Two Treatises of Government* (Cambridge, 1988) Introduction, p. 116. For a point of view somewhat similar to Laslett's and worked out more elaborately see Richard Ashcraft, *Locke's Two Treatises of Government* (London, 1987), pp. 114–117 and especially pp. 216–220. Ashcraft, however, is less concerned with trying to resolve theoretical conflicts in Locke than with attempting to relate Locke's statements to his political objectives.

[5] On the variations here, see the careful discussion, *Ibid.*

relation between the ruler and the society, and so to a dissolution only of the government.[6] But there are at least some passages among those I have cited that simply seem not to yield to that.

Within the last fifteen years, however, a full-scale solution has been offered that I find ingenious even though I am finally unable to agree with it. In an audacious article of 1981, Nathan Tarcov rightly notes that Locke offers not one but two main ways in which government may be dissolved.[7] The first is where the legislature has been illegally altered; the second is where the prince or the legislative act, or conspire to act, in violation of their trust. But all, or virtually all, of Locke's remarks on reversion to a state of nature come with respect to the first of these situations, Tarcov argues. And that is because the alteration of the legislative works a dissolution of society as well as a dissolution of the government. For where the legislative is suppressed or perverted, the people are denied their means of protest and redress and can no longer act as a corporate entity. Locke does no doubt speak of a reversion of power to society where the government has been dissolved. But this, holds Tarcov, refers only to the second situation. Where the subversion of the constitution is still an endeavor rather than accomplished fact, the community is still in possession of the means to act and is not as yet dissolved.

For all its ingenuity this interpretation seems not to remove Locke's inconsistency.[8] Were it really true that upon any of these seeming reversions to a state of nature, the community was stopped from acting in a corporate capacity, some bizarre results would follow. It would mean that the English, about whom Locke is mostly speaking here, would cease to exist as a people, and that they could be reconstituted as a political society only by the unanimous consent of the former members to recreate their own community! Locke could hardly have had *that* in mind even when he was speaking of the alteration of the legislature and the "dissolution and death" of the commonwealth. And it becomes even more unlikely for the event he has in mind in sec.219, which is James II's alleged withdrawal from the kingdom. Here supposedly the executive had "abandoned" its charge and Locke, rising to the heights of melodrama, speaks of "a confused Multitude, without Order or Connexion". But could Locke really have meant by this that upon James II's alleged abandonment of the kingdom English society was juridically dissolved, that its various subdivisions down to each and every individual were now completely free to remain independent or to form new sovereignties?

6   John Dunn, *The Political Thought of John Locke* (Cambridge, 1969), p. 181, n. 2.
7   Nathan Tarcov, "The Best Fence Against Rebellion," *The Review of Politics,* 43:2 (1982), 198–217.
8   Many of the difficulties in Tarcov's argument are taken up in a masterful seminar paper by Ms. Karen Ballentine of Columbia University which I hope she will revise for publication. My initial comment on Tarcov's thesis appears in a review of Ruth W. Grant, *John Locke's Liberalism* (Chicago, 1987) in *Political Theory* (1989), 157–60. Grant takes over Tarcov's views on this question although not without some subtle refinements of her own.

That Locke did not think so seems clear enough to me from the language of sec.220 which concludes his account of the "first way" in which government may be dissolved. From sec. 212 to 219 Locke has mentioned as instances of dissolution from within: alteration of the legislative, hindering meeting of the legislative, changing the rules of election contrary to the people's interest, delivery of the people into subjection to a Foreign power, and the executive's abandonment of its charge. And he now sums up as to the remedy:

> In these and the like Cases, *when the Government is dissolved*, the People are at liberty to provide for themselves, by erecting a new Legislative, differing from the other, by the change of Persons, or Form, or both as they shall find it most for their safety and good. For the Society can never, by the fault of another, lose the Native and Original Right it has to preserve it self, which can only be done by a settled Legislative, and a fair and impartial execution of the Laws made by it. But the state of Mankind is not so miserable that they are not capable of using this Remedy, till it be too late to look for any. To tell *People they may provide for themselves*, by erecting a new Legislative, when by Oppression, Artifice, or being delivered over to a Foreign Power, their old one is gone, is only to tell them they may expect Relief, when it is too late, and the evil is past Cure. This is in effect no more than to bid them first be Slaves; and when their Chains are on, tell them, they may act like Freemen. This, if barely so, is rather Mockery than Relief; and Men can never be secure from Tyranny, if there be no means to escape it till they are perfectly under it: And therefore it is, that they have not only a Right to get out of it, but to prevent it.

Tarcov would take this as confirming his interpretation. The society dissolves as a corporate entity as soon as it no longer has its proper legislative, i.e. as soon as the tyranny is carried out. And that explains why all of Locke's references to collective action, either to resist the tyranny or to reconstitute a government once it has been overthrown, come in his account of the "second way" in which the tyranny is still an "endeavor" not yet completely carried out.[9]

But this reading, I believe, is forced. Locke is not at all denying that the community is entitled to resist collectively in the "first way" of tyranny from within and indeed he expressly adverts, at the end of the paragraph, to "their Right to get out of it". The point of the paragraph, rather, is merely that the right of resistance can be invoked even sooner, that the people do not have to wait. Sec.222 now undertakes to show that mere endeavor to establish tyranny is enough to work a dissolution of the government. But that does not affect the rights of the people as a corporate body to act at any time they are ready and have an opportunity. If from this point to the end of the Chapter, Locke most

---

[9] Tarcov, loc. cit., p. 209. I might also add my belief that Tarcov also misreads the remark "which can only be done by a settled Legislative". That refers to what society hopes to bring about by resistance. It is not, as Tarcov suggests (p. 209) a test as to whether society has already been dissolved.

often uses the imagery of prevention, it is because that is the policy he wishes to urge upon the English at the time his book was written. The shift that begins with sec.222 is of emphasis and not of theory.

But if Locke did not hold that an executed tyranny automatically dissolves society, why, in the passages quoted, does he use language so suggestive of a state of nature? The answer, I believe, has to do with a certain ambiguity in Locke's usage of the phrase "state of nature". The ambiguity goes back to his account of the transition from the state of nature to civil society. In certain passages (esp. secs.87, 89) the state of nature ends only when protection is actually provided to those individuals who have joined together in the social contract, and so only when a government is formed. Where there is no government, there cannot be a standing statutory law, recognized judges, or a legally constituted executive force. It is like a state of nature even though a society exists. But in other passages (esp. secs.95–99, 149) the state of nature ends as soon as individuals become incorporated. By agreeing to form a government, they become bound to the community, even before a government is formed.

Locke, then, uses the phrase "state of nature" in two different senses. In the first, and looser, sense it does not deny that a society exists.[10] But in the second, and stricter, sense it excludes the existence of society. Locke's meaning for this phrase may thus depend upon the context. And when context is attended to in the "state of nature" passages in chapter XIX, his apparent inconsistency evaporates. They are all examples of the looser usage where reversion to a state of nature is used for rhetorical effect. It serves to portray the tyrannical misdeeds of the later Stuarts as enormities. By dissolving the government, they have left the English without any valid statutory law, or legitimately established judges, or legally constituted executive force. In the absence of a lawful government, individuals have been temporarily thrown back upon their own resources, as in a state of nature. But Locke does not deny the physical or moral capacity of the English to act as a collective body in order to reconstitute a legitimate authority.

I conclude, therefore, that Locke does not go back on the thrust of sec.211 and that his view on the dissolution of society tends to what I have called the

---

[10] In sec. 136, Locke's language almost, although not quite fully, seems to imply the ideas of a "quasi state of nature". He is making the point that the legislative instituted by society is not entitled to overstep the bounds imposed upon it. Among other things, trespass of limits would undermine the right of property. Locke then goes on to a concluding observation:

> To this end [of securing their properties] it is that men give up all their Natural Power to the Society which they enter into, and the Community put the Legislative Power into such hands as they think fit, with this trust, that they shall be govern'd by *declared Laws*, or else their Peace, Quiet, and Property will still be at the same uncertainty, it was in the State of Nature.

Locke seems here to be assuming that a society can exist along with great uncertainty as to rights as in a state of nature.

common-sense position. But Locke does not embrace that conception fully nor does he explore its implications. He could not have done so within the framework of an individualist social contract. His test for dissolution implies, as we have said, an enduring commitment to community that goes well beyond the protection of individual rights.

A doctrine of community more consistent with that test can, however, be found in the work of George Lawson writing in the Interregnum of the English civil war. Lawson's theory of sovereignty is very similar to Locke's who, as I have elsewhere tried to show, was heavily indebted to it.[11] For both writers the power of making and unmaking governments belongs to the community, or political society, which retains its constituent authority even after a government is instituted. Their ideas on the dissolution of government are thus substantially the same. Lawson's account of the community, however, is informed by a kind of Christian Aristotelianism. It does not begin with an agreement of isolated individuals. It is rooted rather in the affective association of families and neighborhoods brought together by "vicinity of place". This informal community becomes a full political society, or *civitas*, by agreement of its members. But their aim in forming it is not so much to provide security for individuals as to promote a more perfect common life in accordance with the will of God.

The duty of individuals to remain loyal to the political community in which they live is therefore understood as overriding.[12] This, for Lawson, was the very meaning of his literary enterprise. Writing in the Interregnum, when the English nation seemed all but hopelessly divided, he wished to show that a people still existed to which the individual owed ultimate allegiance. In one very powerful passage he asserts that a people, or community, is virtually indestructible. The sole exception is the all but complete extermination of its members, as with the Biblical Amalekites and Canaanites or the inhabitants of Sodom and Gomorrah:

> Sometimes it falls out, and is so ordered by Providence, that a People who have continued for a certain time under a form of Government, return unto their first liberty; yet even then, when God doth offer them an opportunity to establish the best form and constitution they are fearfully divided. Some are for the former Government, others idolize some new idea framed in their own brains. Others in the meantime get the sword into their hands, and once

---

[11] *John Locke and the Theory of Sovereignty* (Cambridge, 1978). The connection between Locke and Lawson was originally shown by A. H. Maclean both in his unpublished doctoral dissertation, "The Origins of the Political Opinions of John Locke," Cambridge University, 1947 and in "George Lawson and John Locke," *Cambridge Historical Journal* 9:1 (1947), 68–77.

[12] His main work on politics is *Political Sacra et Civilis*, originally published, London, 1660 and now republished as George Lawson, *Political Sacra et Civilis*, Conal Condren, ed. (Cambridge, 1992).

possessed of Power, are unwilling to part with it. Yet these sometimes are dispossessed again; in the meantime the People like so many waves of the Sea, are tossed this way and that way, by contrary winds, like as in *Daniel's* vision, when he saw the four winds strive upon the great Sea, out of which arose the great Empires of the world, *Dan.*7.2,3, etc. And all this comes to pass through the just judgment of God, and the willful folly of men, who are enemies to their own Peace. Lastly, in these many alterations of Governors and forms of Government, the Community abides the same, except it be cut off by the sword, as the *Amalekites* and *Canaanites* were, or destroyed by some extraordinary Judgment, as *Sodom* and *Gomorra* with fire and brimstone from heaven.[13]

Notwithstanding his religious imagery, Lawson's view of dissolution is broadly similar to Locke's. For him, too, there had been a dissolution of government (going back to 1642), which left the English people free to reconstitute a more effective system. Like Locke also, but most explicitly, he does not admit a reversion to the state of nature. Throughout all the divisions and usurpations of the Interregnum, "the community abides the same". It continues to exist unless its members are annihilated or dispersed. Lawson's Biblical images are more powerful and drastic than Locke's. Yet there is perhaps an echo of Lawson in the reference to conquerors who "mangle Societies to pieces" and leave its members as though "dissipated by a Whirl-wind, or jumbled into a confused heap by an Earthquake."

The really significant difference between Locke and Lawson has to do with the foundation of their views. Locke's, as we have said, is inconsistent with his version of the social contract. If the end of society is merely to protect individual rights and interests, the obligation to support it ought to terminate as soon as that protection fails. Lawson, on the other hand, is consistent in concluding that there is a duty of faithfulness to one's community until such time as it is all but literally destroyed. He comes to that result because he holds that the purpose of association is not only to obtain conveniences and to assure one's safety but to realize a common bond. "This consent [to form a community]", says Lawson, "whether tacit or express is grounded upon love and good affection with an intention to do good and just things one for another, according to the word of the eternal law written in their hearts."[14]

---

[13] *An Examination of the Political Part of Mr. Hobbs his Leviathan* (London, 1657), p. 6.
[14] *Political Sacra et Civilis* (1992), p. 28.

The Contributors

Adrianna E. Bakos, assistant professor of history at the University of Rochester, has published articles on French constitutionalism in *The Sixteenth Century Journal* and the *Journal of the History of Ideas*. She is currently completing a book entitled *Tangled Webs: Louis XI and Images of Kingship in Early Modern France.*

Frederic J. Baumgartner, professor of history at Virginia Polytechnic and State University, is the author of several books, including *Radical Reactionaries: The Political Thought of the French Catholic League* and *Henry II, King of France 1547–1559.* He has just completed a biography of Louis XII.

James H. Burns, Professor Emeritus, University College London, has written prolifically on varied aspects of early modern political thought. His books include *The Cambridge History of Medieval Political Thought c. 350 – c. 1450* and, most recently, *Kingship, Lordship and Empire: The Idea of Monarchy 1400–1525.*

Sir Geoffrey Elton, Fellow, Clare College, Cambridge University, has been pre-eminent in the field of Tudor-Stuart England for over thirty years. He was Regius Professor of Modern History at Cambridge University, 1983–1988. Among his many books are *The Tudor Revolution in Government, Studies in Tudor and Stuart Politics* and his most recent work, *The English.*

Julian H. Franklin, professor of political science at Columbia University is the author of several books on sixteenth- and seventeenth-century political thought including *Jean Bodin and the Rise of Absolutist Theory* and *John Locke and the Theory of Sovereignty.*

Richard M. Golden, professor of history and chair of the department of history at the University of North Texas, is currently writing a book entitled *The Witch Hunters.* He has edited a number of books, including *Church, State and Society under the Bourbon Kings of France* and is the author of *The Godly Rebellion: Parisian Curés and the Religious Fronde, 1652–1662.*

Mark Greengrass, senior lecturer of history at the University of Sheffield, is the author of *The French Reformation* and *France in the Age of Henri IV: the Struggle for Stability.*

Sarah Hanley, professor of history at the University of Iowa, is the author of *The Lit de Justice of the Kings of France: Constitutional Ideology in Legend, Ritual and Discourse.* Her forthcoming book is entitled, *State Building in Early Modern France: Law, Litigation, and Local Knowledge.*

Donald R. Kelley, James Westfall Thompson Professor of History at Rutgers University, is the editor of the *Journal of the History of Ideas* and has written a number of books on early modern European law and politics, among them *The Beginnings of Ideology* and, most recently, *Renaissance Humanism.*

Lisa Ferraro Parmelee, adjunct professor at Villanova University, writes on the Tudor-Stuart period and has recently published an article on French propaganda in Elizabethan England in *The Sixteenth Century Journal*.

Orest Ranum, professor of history at Johns Hopkins University, is the author of *Artisans of Glory: Writers and Historical Thought in Seventeeth-Century France*. With Robert Forster, he has edited several collections of essays addressing issues in the social and cultural history of early modern Europe. He has recently published a book entitled *The Fronde*.

Barbara Whitehead, assistant professor of history at DePauw University, writes on French historiography. She is currently working on a monograph on the eighteenth-century French historian, Louis-Pierre Anquetil.

Tabula Gratulatoria

Subscribers

Deborah Abbott
Bernard Barbiche
William Beik
Philip Benedict
Charles M. Brand
Elizabeth A. R. Brown
Lawrence M. Bryant
William J. Connell
Barbara B. Davis
Natalie Z. Davis
William P. Davisson
Margaret G. Dean
Barbara Diefendorf
Brian R. Dunn
Amanda Ehrich
Josephine Ford
Albert N. Hamscher
John M. Headley
Margaret Hoag
Mack P. Holt
Robert M. Kingdon
Ruth Kleinman
Mark Konnert
Alan Charles Kors
Marybeth T. Lavrakas

Harriet Lightman
Andrew Lossky
Maryam n'ha Margo
Sheilah J. McKenna
Angelo Thomas Montante
A. Lloyd Moote
Kathleen Parrow
Joanne D'Elia Payson
Jon D. Rudd
John C. Rule
John T. Ryan, S. J.
Zachary S. Schiffman
Eileen O'Donnell Schlichting
Alexander Sedgwick
Lynne C. Shigley
Scott Silverman
A. J. Slavin
Jay M. Smith
Brian Strayer
Betty T. Uzman
Jennifer Westhoven
Michael Wolfe
D. R. Woolf
Jenny Wormald
Glen Zeitzer